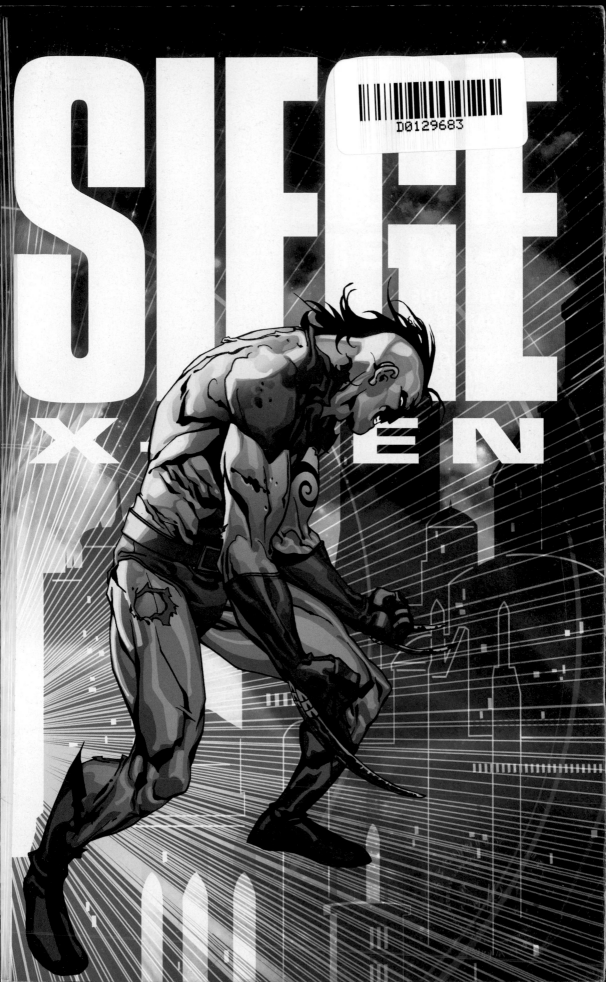

D0129683

SIEGE
X-MEN

DARK WOLVERINE #82-84
WRITERS: **DANIEL WAY** & **MARJORIE LIU**
PENCILER: **GIUSEPPE CAMUNCOLI**
INKER: **ONOFRIO CATACCHIO**
COLORISTS: **MARTE GRACIA** WITH **ANTONIO FABELA**
LETTERER: **VC'S CORY PETIT**
COVER ART: **SALVADOR LARROCA** WITH **FRANK D'ARMATA**
LETTERER: **VC'S CORY PETIT**
ASSISTANT EDITOR: **JODY LEHEUP**
EDITOR: **JEANINE SCHAEFER**
EXECUTIVE EDITOR: **AXEL ALONSO**

NEW MUTANTS #11
WRITER: **KIERON GILLEN**
ART: **NIKO HENRICHON**
LETTERER: **VC'S JOE CARAMAGNA**
COVER ART: **TERRY DODSON** & **RACHEL DODSON**
ASSOCIATE EDITOR: **DANIEL KETCHUM**
EDITOR: **NICK LOWE**

SIEGE: STORMING ASGARD — HEROES & VILLAINS
HEAD WRITER/EDITOR: **JOHN RHETT THOMAS**
SPOTLIGHT BULLPEN WRITERS: **JESS HARROLD** & **DUGEN TRODGLEN**
COVER ART: **GREG LAND** & **JUSTIN PONSOR**
DESIGN: **BLAMMO! CONTENT & DESIGN, ROMMEL ALAMA** & **MIKE KRONENBERG**

COLLECTION EDITOR: **JENNIFER GRÜNWALD**
EDITORIAL ASSISTANTS: **JAMES EMMETT** & **JOE HOCHSTEIN**
ASSISTANT EDITORS: **ALEX STARBUCK** & **NELSON RIBEIRO**
EDITOR, SPECIAL PROJECTS: **MARK D. BEAZLEY**
SENIOR EDITOR, SPECIAL PROJECTS: **JEFF YOUNGQUIST**
SENIOR VICE PRESIDENT OF SALES: **DAVID GABRIEL** • BOOK DESIGNER: **RODOLFO MURAGUCHI**

EDITOR IN CHIEF: **JOE QUESADA** • PUBLISHER: **DAN BUCKLEY** • EXECUTIVE PRODUCER: **ALAN FINE**

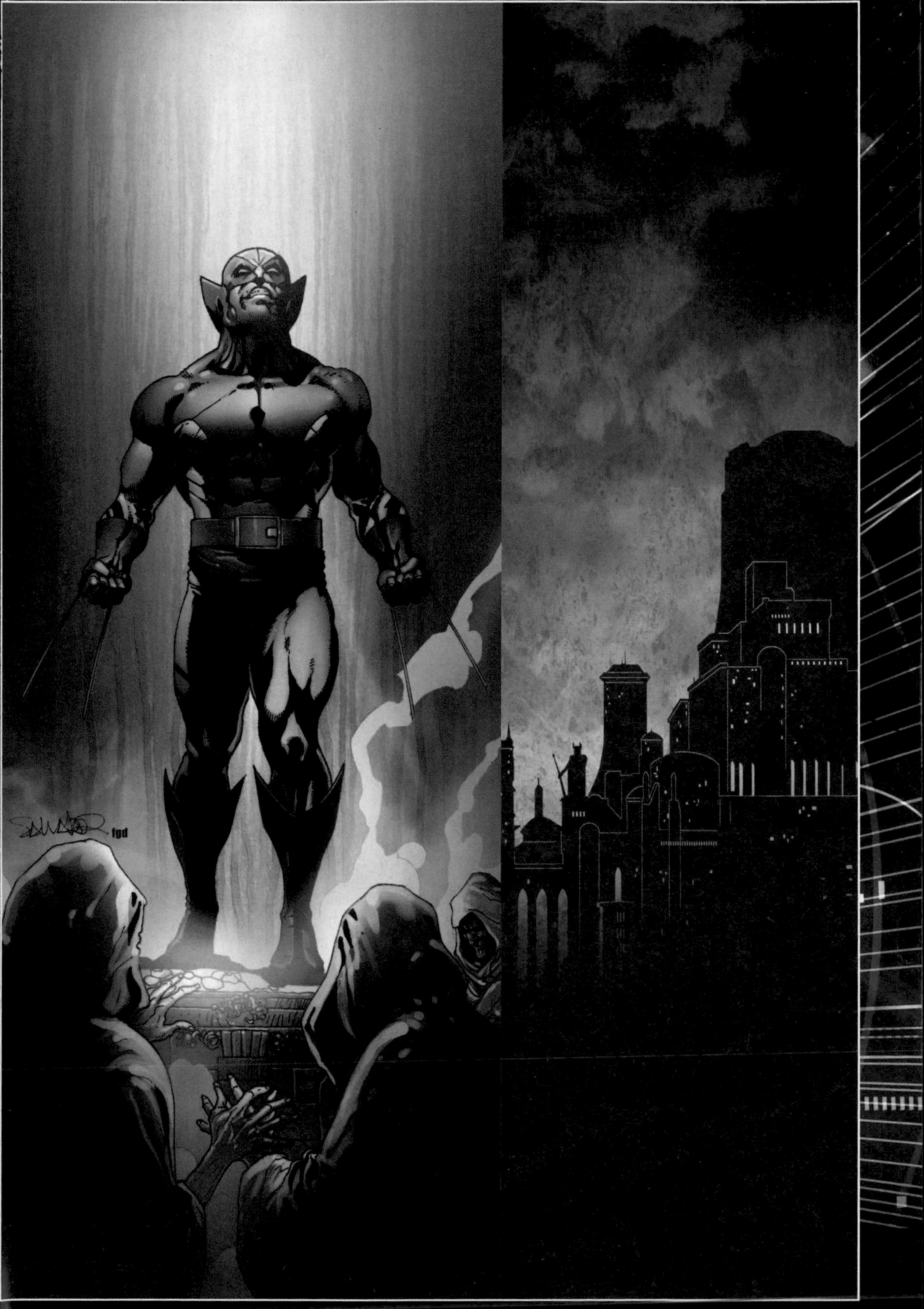

DARK WOLVERINE #82

Decades ago, the mutant known as Wolverine found peace in Japan and had a son with his wife, Itsu Akihiro. The peace was short-lived—Itsu was murdered and Wolverine believed his son died with her…but the boy lived. Like his father, the son possessed enhanced senses, a powerful healing factor, and razor-sharp claws on each hand. He became known by the name he was taunted with as a child: the Japanese term for "mongrel", Daken. As he grew, he blamed his father for his mother's death, and this resentment consumed him. Recently, Norman Osborn, the former costumed villain known as the Green Goblin, took the moniker Iron Patriot and became the Director of the U.S. government's espionage strike-team, H.A.M.M.E.R., as well as leader of its super hero team, the Avengers. Osborn then populated the Avengers with powered beings he felt he could trust along with a host of super villains and Daken as a…

DARK WOLVERINE

Norman has been using Daken and his team of Dark Avengers to remake the country's status quo into his image of justice and fairness. An image that does not include mutant, monster or vigilante. And Osborn's more than willing to bend, break, or disregard basic human rights in order to achieve his dream.

Thor, the mighty god of thunder, has recently returned to Earth and brought the golden city of Asgard— and all the gods who call it home— with him. But Norman has secretly partnered with Thor's evil half-brother Loki in a plan to overthrow the golden city, covering his tracks by rallying the troops to defend American soil from the threat of Asgard. Now Osborn, H.A.M.M.E.R. and the Dark Avengers have laid siege to Asgard…and Daken…as always…has everyone right where he wants them…

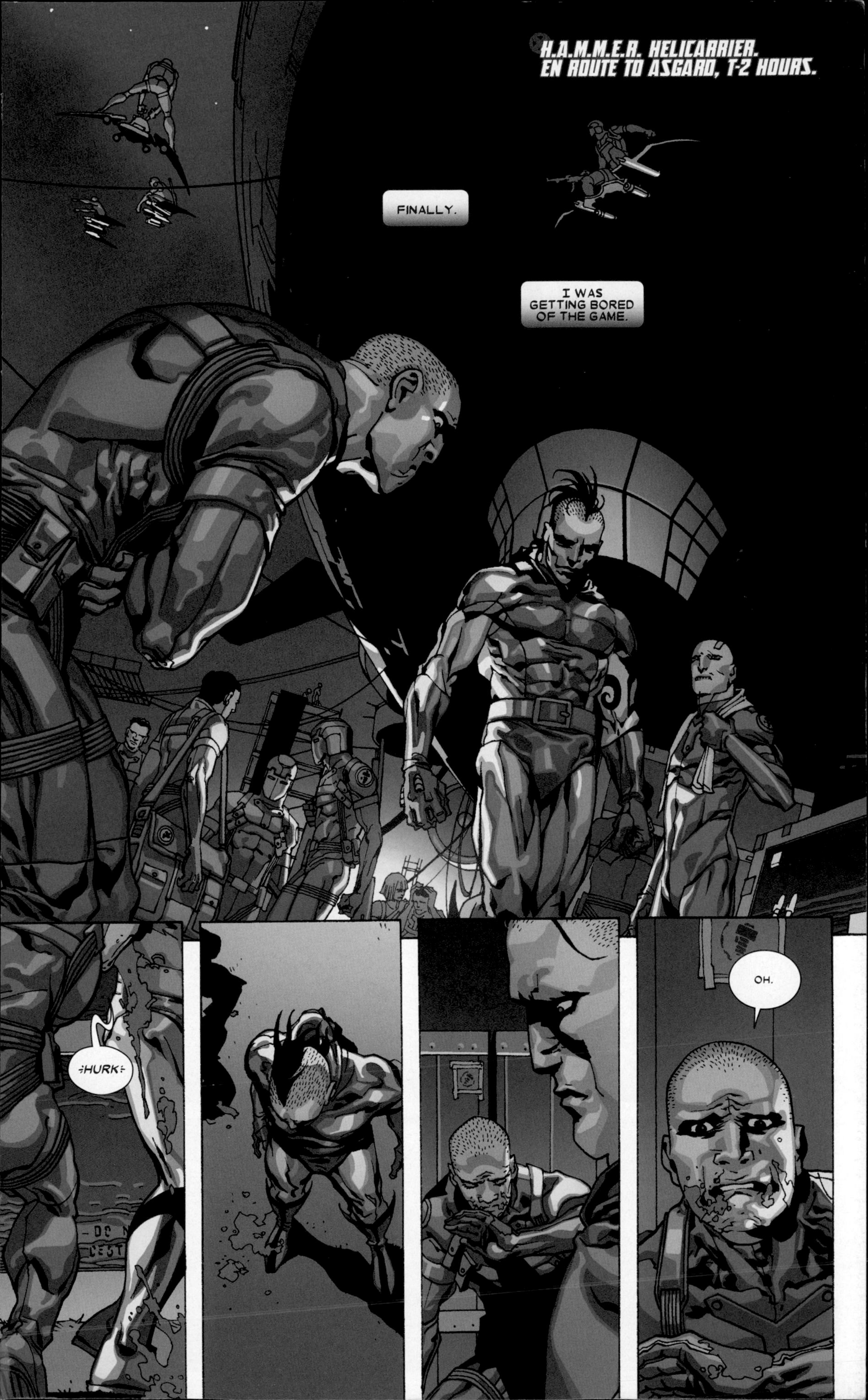
H.A.M.M.E.R. HELICARRIER.
EN ROUTE TO ASGARD, T-2 HOURS.
FINALLY.
I WAS GETTING BORED OF THE GAME.
HURK
OH.

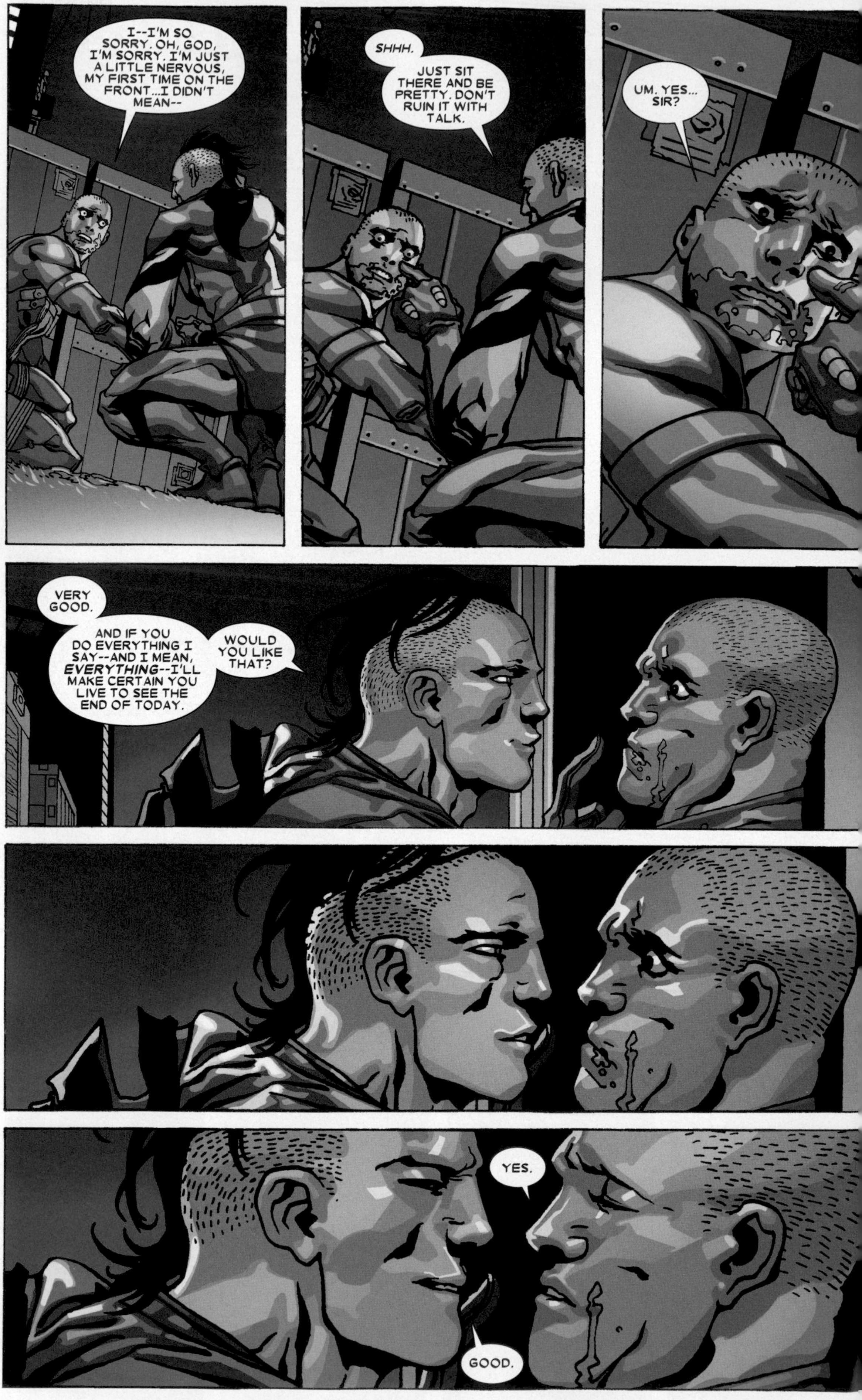
I--I'M SO SORRY. OH, GOD, I'M SORRY. I'M JUST A LITTLE NERVOUS, MY FIRST TIME ON THE FRONT...I DIDN'T MEAN--
SHHH.
JUST SIT THERE AND BE PRETTY. DON'T RUIN IT WITH TALK.
UM. YES... SIR?
VERY GOOD.
AND IF YOU DO EVERYTHING I SAY--AND I MEAN, *EVERYTHING*--I'LL MAKE CERTAIN YOU LIVE TO SEE THE END OF TODAY.
WOULD YOU LIKE THAT?
YES.
GOOD.

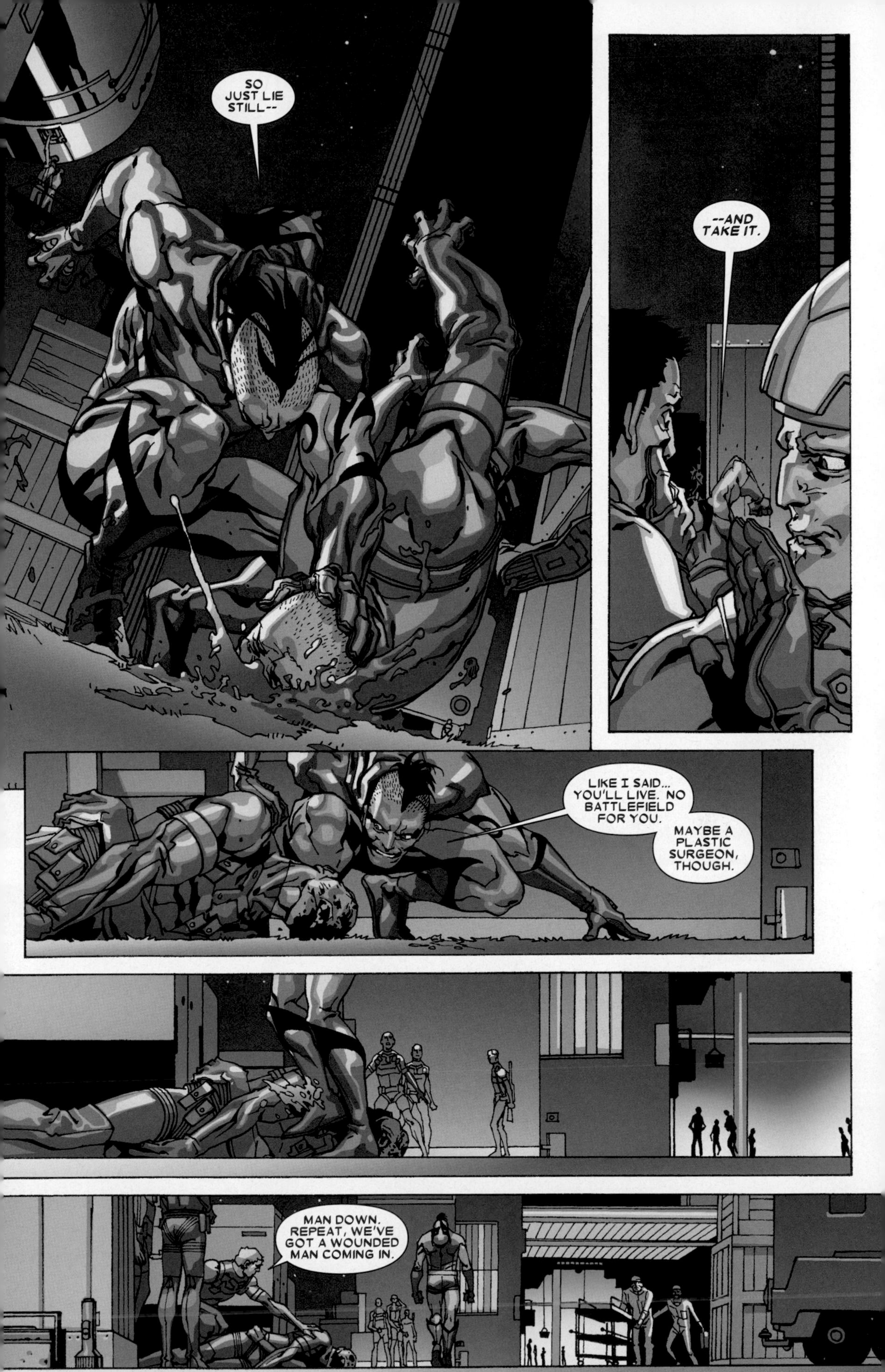
SO JUST LIE STILL--
--AND TAKE IT.
LIKE I SAID... YOU'LL LIVE. NO BATTLEFIELD FOR YOU.
MAYBE A PLASTIC SURGEON, THOUGH.
MAN DOWN. REPEAT, WE'VE GOT A WOUNDED MAN COMING IN.

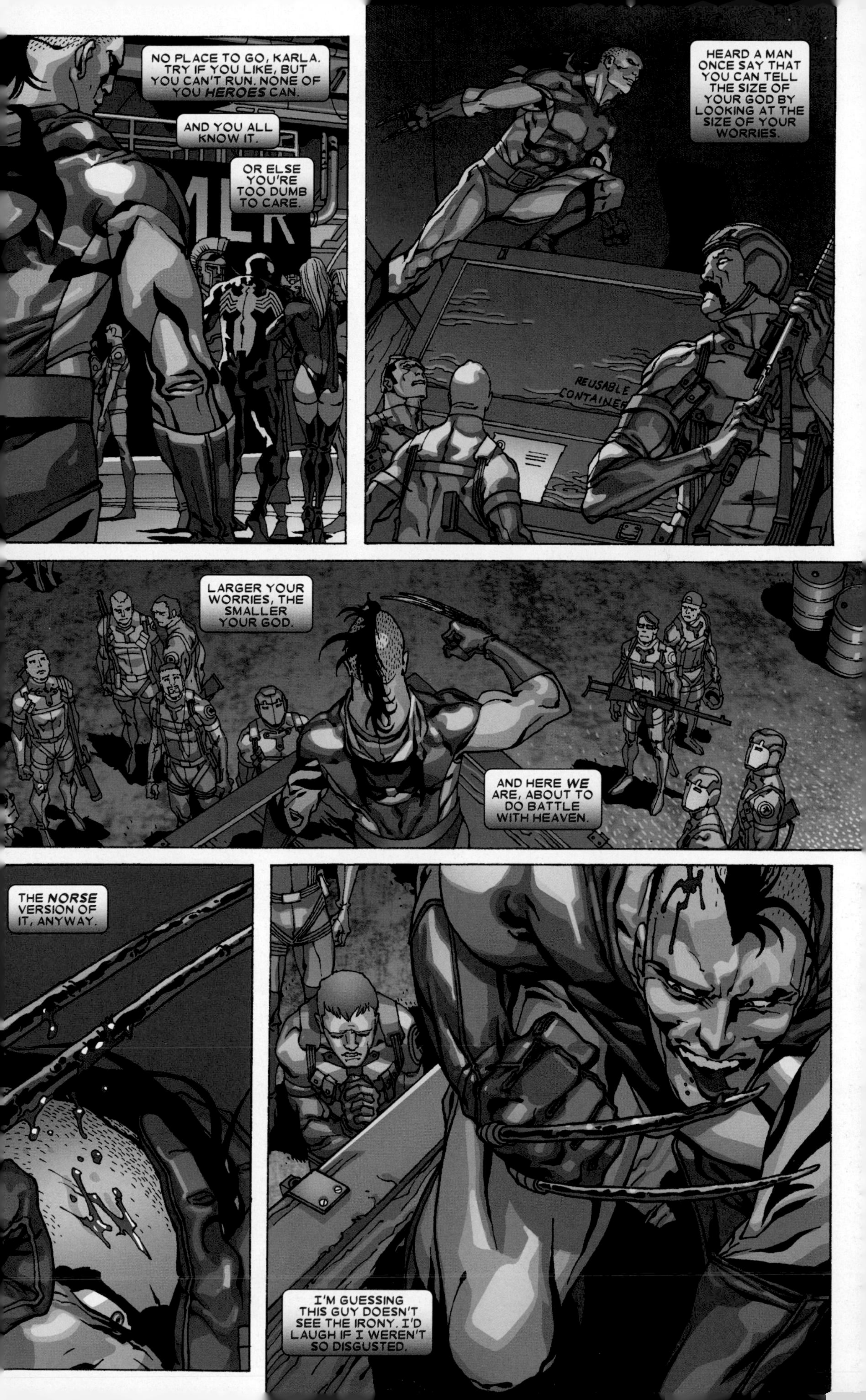
NO PLACE TO GO, KARLA. TRY IF YOU LIKE, BUT YOU CAN'T RUN. NONE OF YOU *HEROES* CAN.
AND YOU ALL KNOW IT.
OR ELSE YOU'RE TOO DUMB TO CARE.
HEARD A MAN ONCE SAY THAT YOU CAN TELL THE SIZE OF YOUR GOD BY LOOKING AT THE SIZE OF YOUR WORRIES.
REUSABLE CONTAINER
LARGER YOUR WORRIES, THE SMALLER YOUR GOD.
AND HERE *WE* ARE, ABOUT TO DO BATTLE WITH HEAVEN.
THE *NORSE* VERSION OF IT, ANYWAY.
I'M GUESSING THIS GUY DOESN'T SEE THE IRONY. I'D LAUGH IF I WEREN'T SO DISGUSTED.

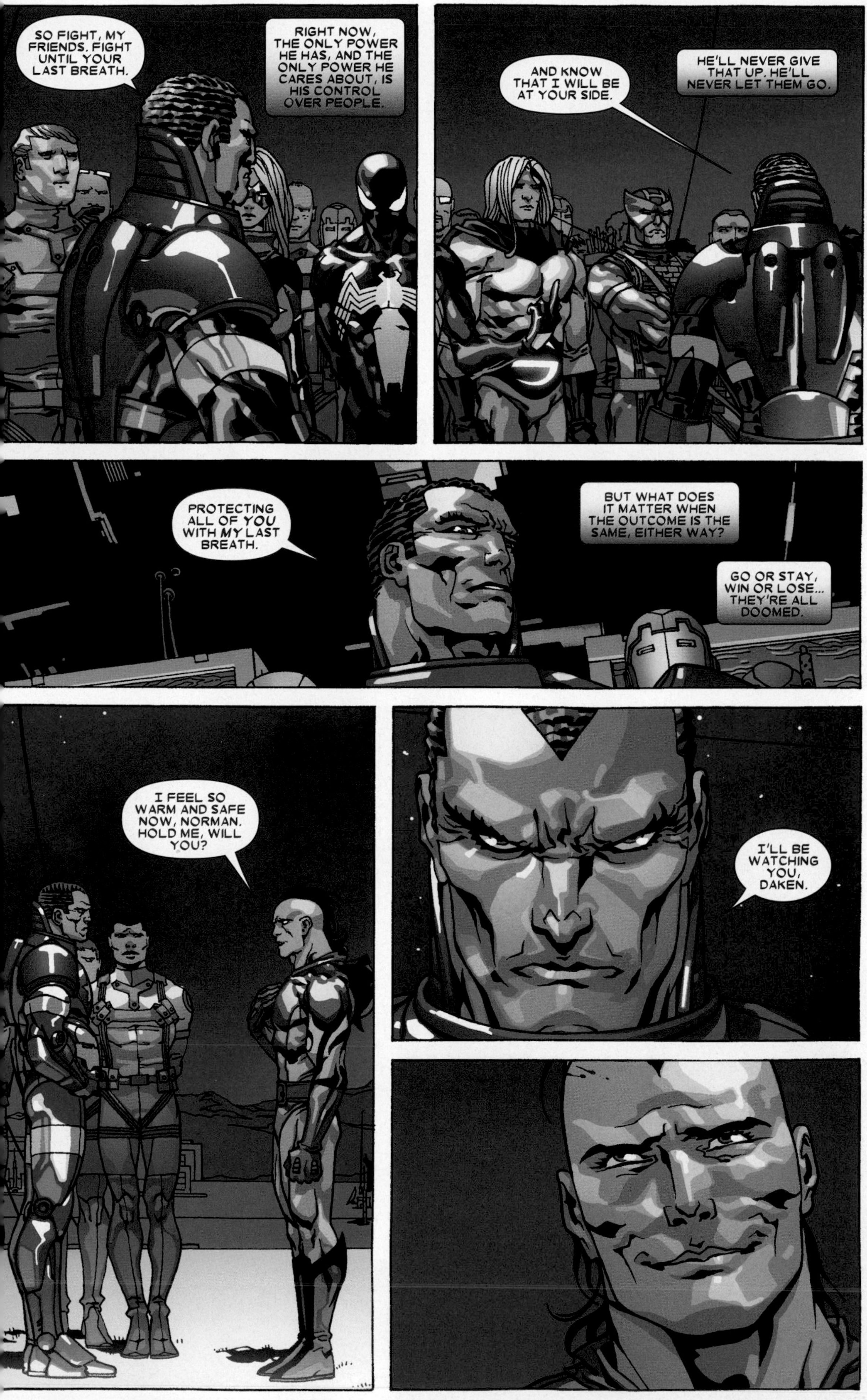

SO FIGHT, MY FRIENDS. FIGHT UNTIL YOUR LAST BREATH.
RIGHT NOW, THE ONLY POWER HE HAS, AND THE ONLY POWER HE CARES ABOUT, IS HIS CONTROL OVER PEOPLE.
AND KNOW THAT I WILL BE AT YOUR SIDE.
HE'LL NEVER GIVE THAT UP. HE'LL NEVER LET THEM GO.
PROTECTING ALL OF YOU WITH MY LAST BREATH.
BUT WHAT DOES IT MATTER WHEN THE OUTCOME IS THE SAME, EITHER WAY?
GO OR STAY, WIN OR LOSE... THEY'RE ALL DOOMED.
I FEEL SO WARM AND SAFE NOW, NORMAN. HOLD ME, WILL YOU?
I'LL BE WATCHING YOU, DAKEN.

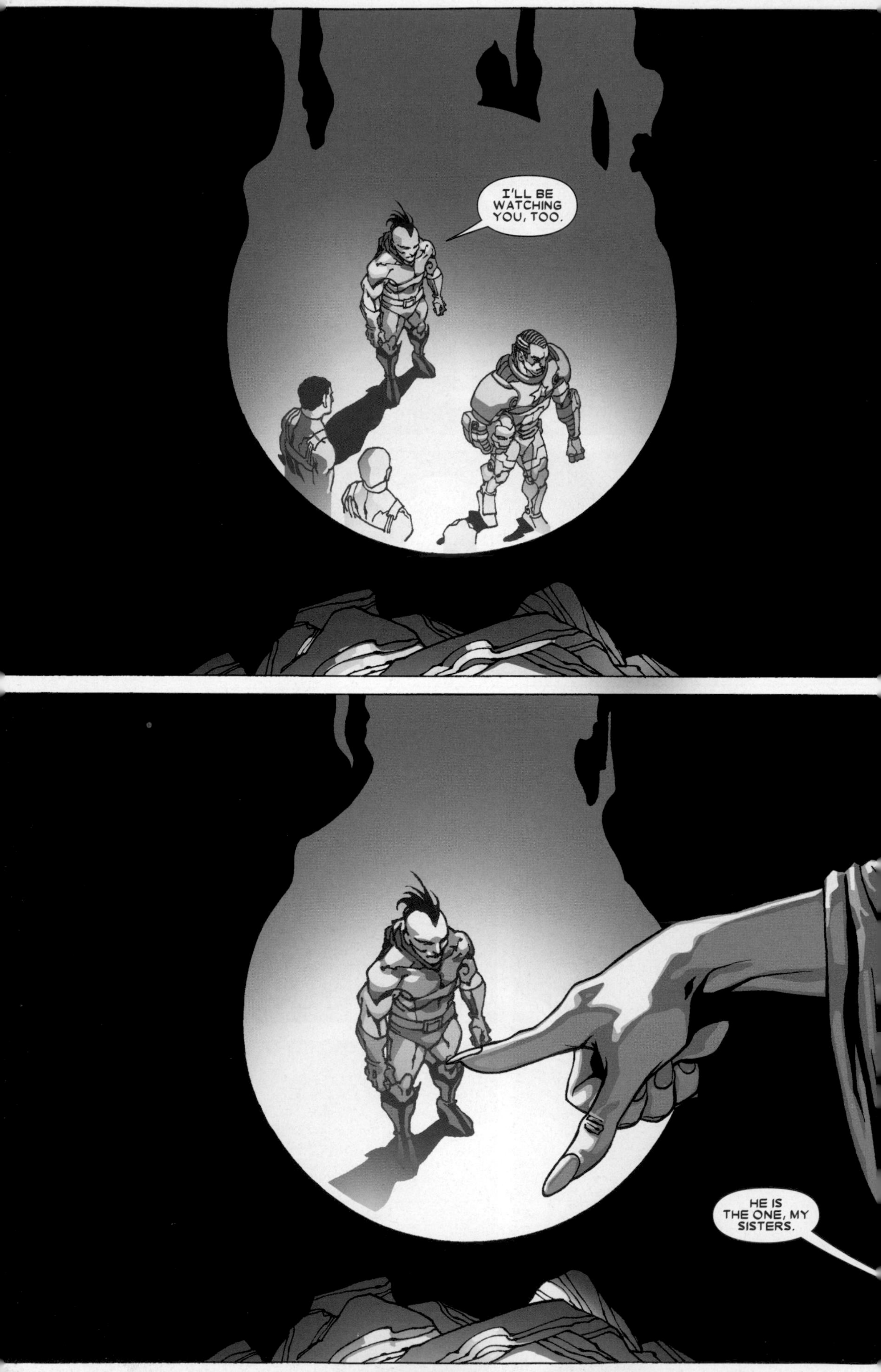
I'LL BE WATCHING YOU, TOO.
HE IS THE ONE, MY SISTERS.

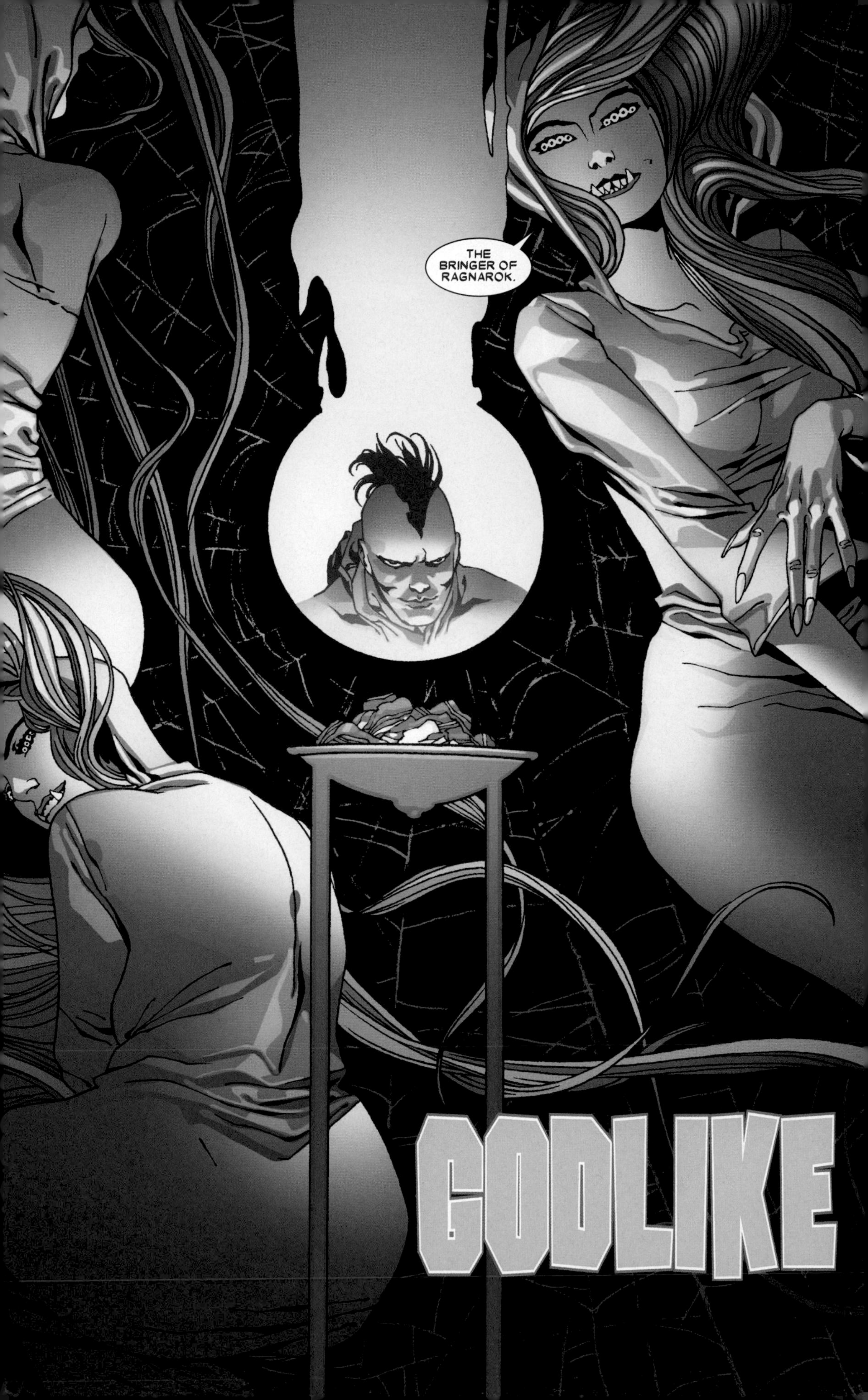
THE BRINGER OF RAGNAROK.
GODLIKE

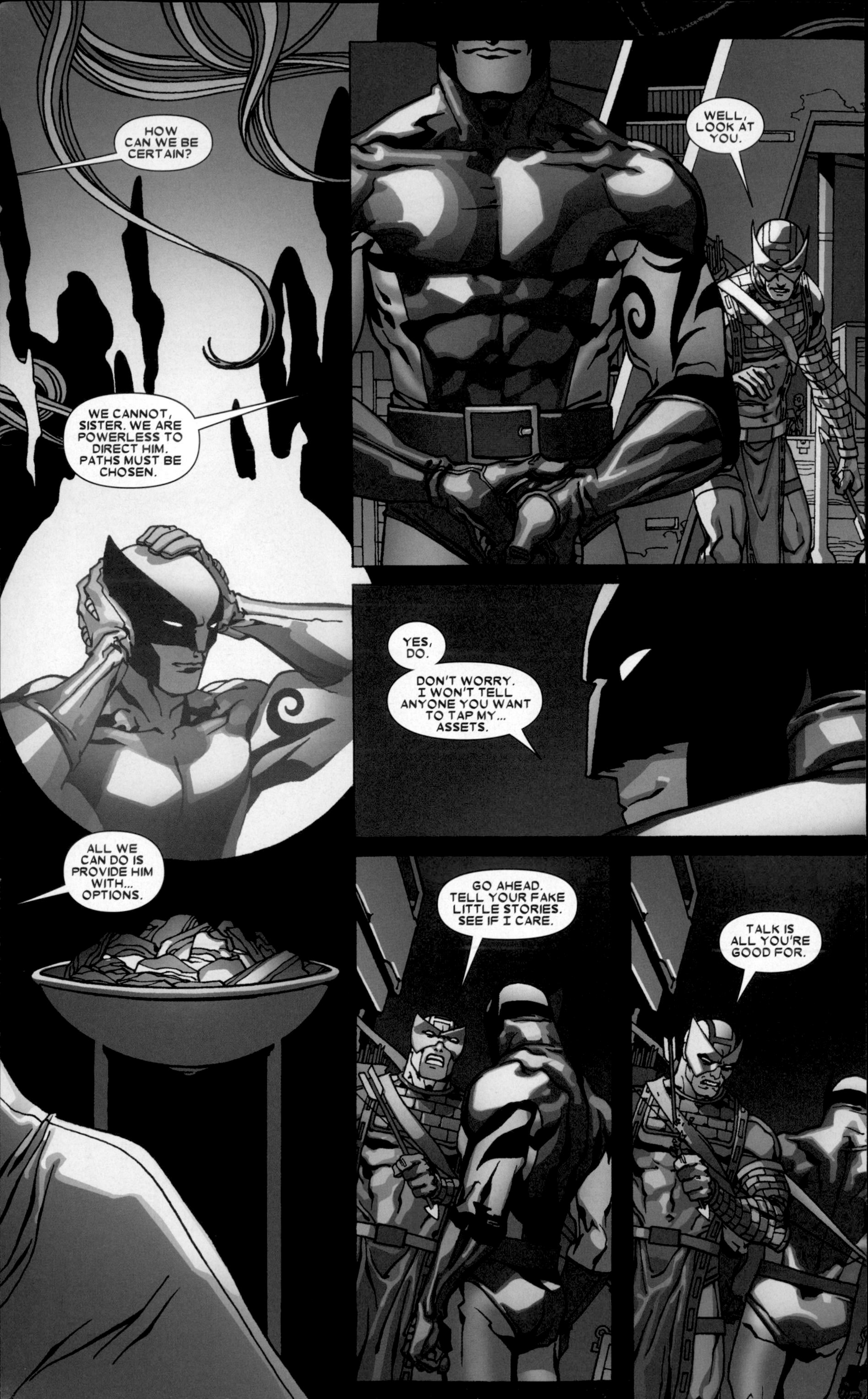

HOW CAN WE BE CERTAIN?
WELL, LOOK AT YOU.
WE CANNOT, SISTER. WE ARE POWERLESS TO DIRECT HIM. PATHS MUST BE CHOSEN.
YES, DO.
DON'T WORRY. I WON'T TELL ANYONE YOU WANT TO TAP MY... ASSETS.
ALL WE CAN DO IS PROVIDE HIM WITH... OPTIONS.
GO AHEAD. TELL YOUR FAKE LITTLE STORIES. SEE IF I CARE.
TALK IS ALL YOU'RE GOOD FOR.

OH, LESTER.

YOU KNOW THAT'S NOT TRUE.

LET ME PROVE IT TO YOU.

THIS COULD BE OUR LAST DAY ON EARTH, AFTER ALL.

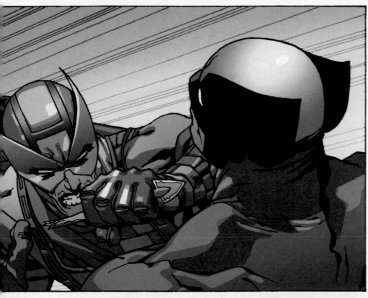

TUT TUT.

I DON'T EVEN KNOW WHY YOU'RE HERE.

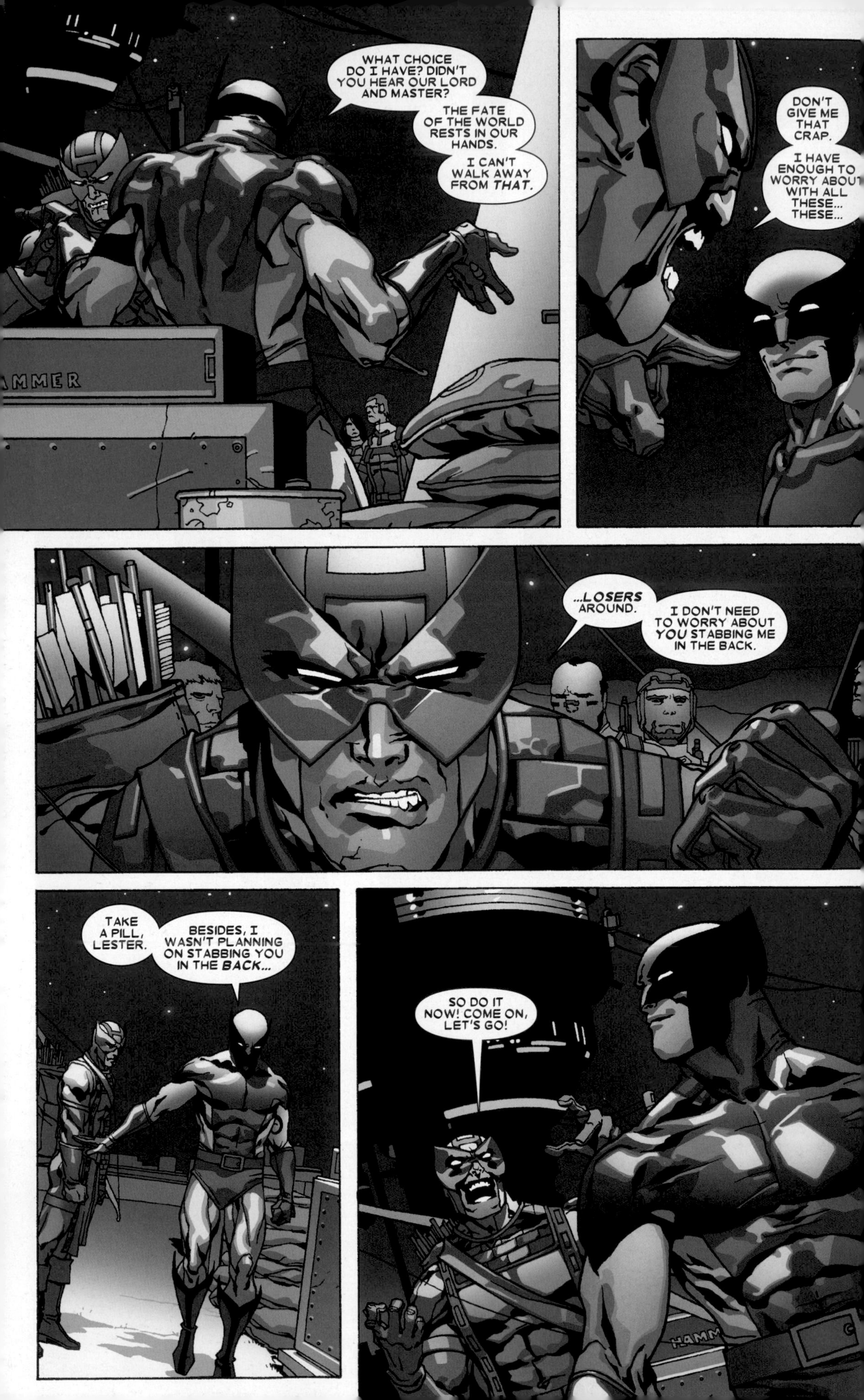
WHAT CHOICE DO I HAVE? DIDN'T YOU HEAR OUR LORD AND MASTER?
THE FATE OF THE WORLD RESTS IN OUR HANDS.
I CAN'T WALK AWAY FROM *THAT.*
MMER
DON'T GIVE ME THAT CRAP.
I HAVE ENOUGH TO WORRY ABOUT WITH ALL THESE... THESE...
...*LOSERS* AROUND.
I DON'T NEED TO WORRY ABOUT *YOU* STABBING ME IN THE BACK.
TAKE A PILL, LESTER.
BESIDES, I WASN'T PLANNING ON STABBING YOU IN THE *BACK*...
SO DO IT NOW! COME ON, LET'S GO!
HAMM

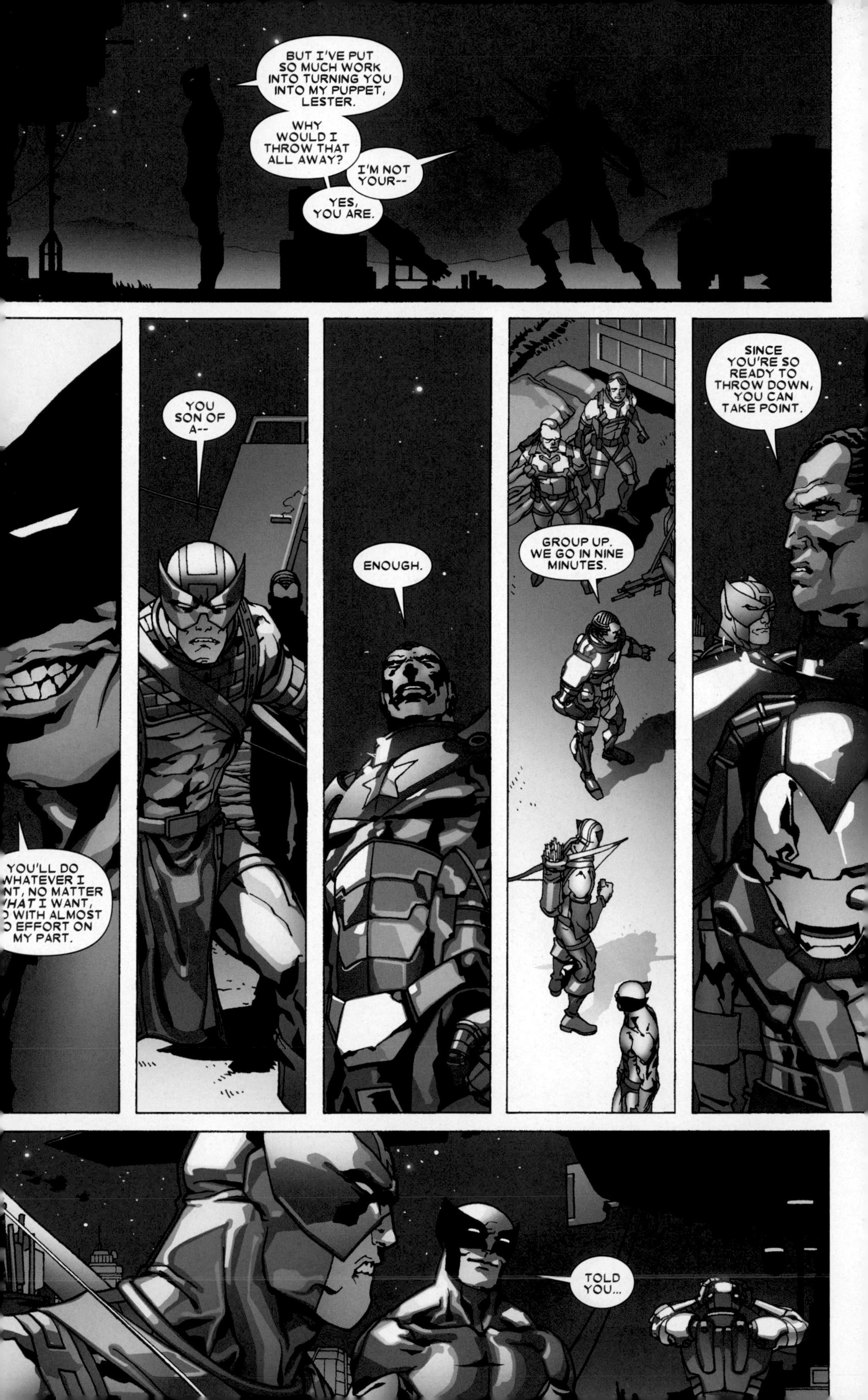
BUT I'VE PUT SO MUCH WORK INTO TURNING YOU INTO MY PUPPET, LESTER.
WHY WOULD I THROW THAT ALL AWAY?
I'M NOT YOUR--
YES, YOU ARE.
YOU'LL DO WHATEVER I WANT, NO MATTER WHAT I WANT, AND WITH ALMOST NO EFFORT ON MY PART.
YOU SON OF A--
ENOUGH.
GROUP UP. WE GO IN NINE MINUTES.
SINCE YOU'RE SO READY TO THROW DOWN, YOU CAN TAKE POINT.
TOLD YOU...

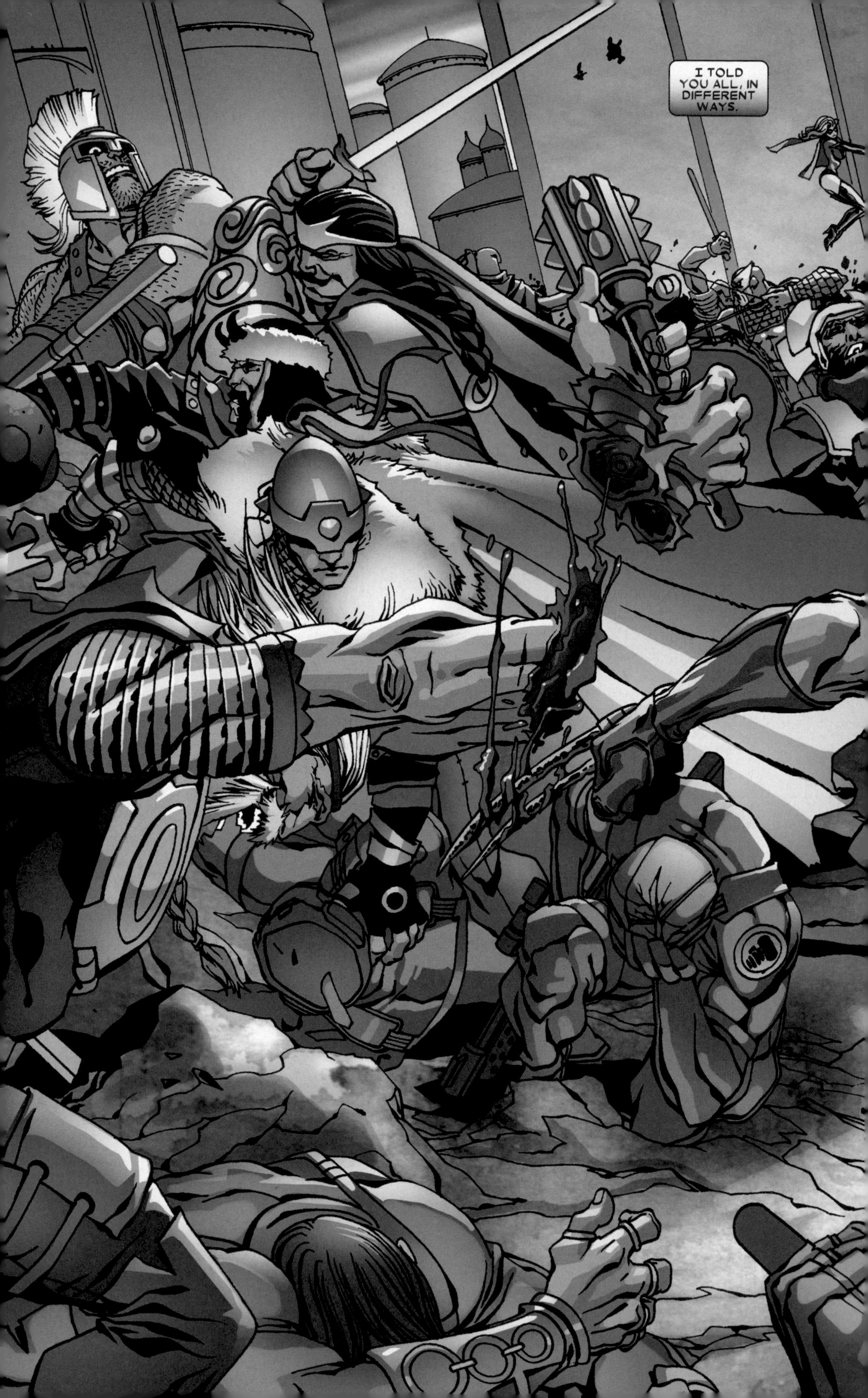
I TOLD YOU ALL, IN DIFFERENT WAYS.

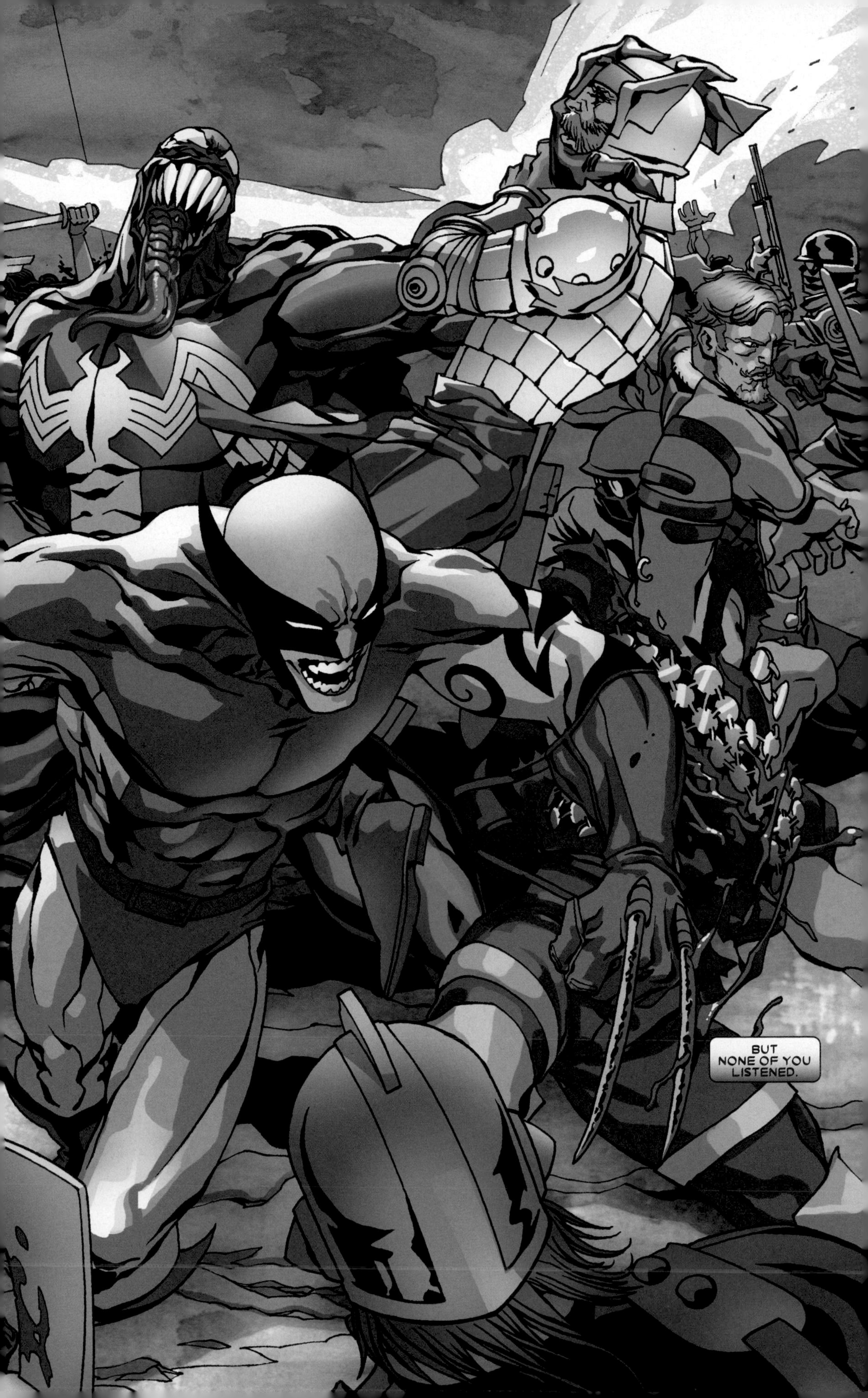
BUT NONE OF YOU LISTENED.

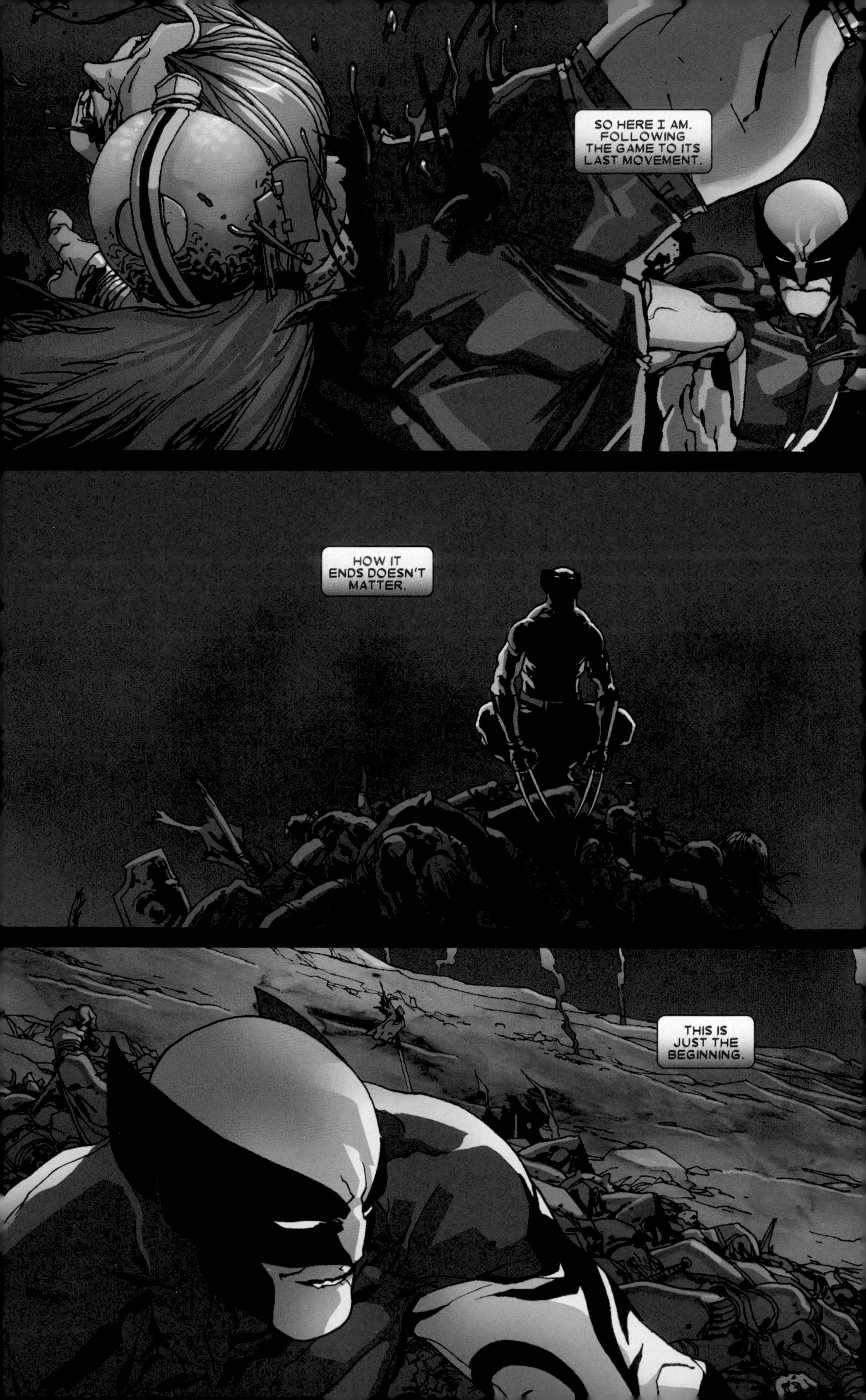
SO HERE I AM. FOLLOWING THE GAME TO ITS LAST MOVEMENT.
HOW IT ENDS DOESN'T MATTER.
THIS IS JUST THE BEGINNING.

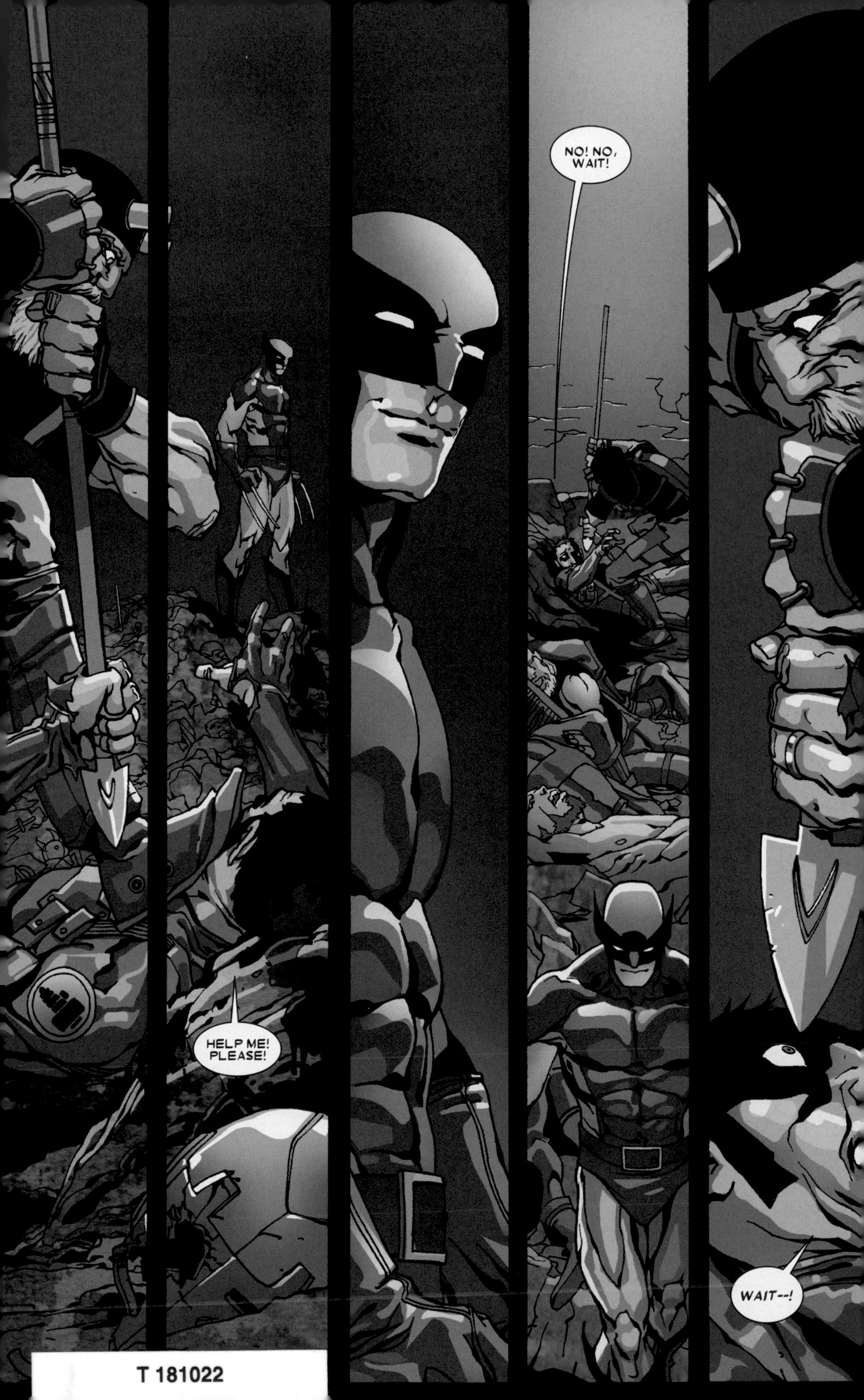
HELP ME! PLEASE!
NO! NO, WAIT!
WAIT--!

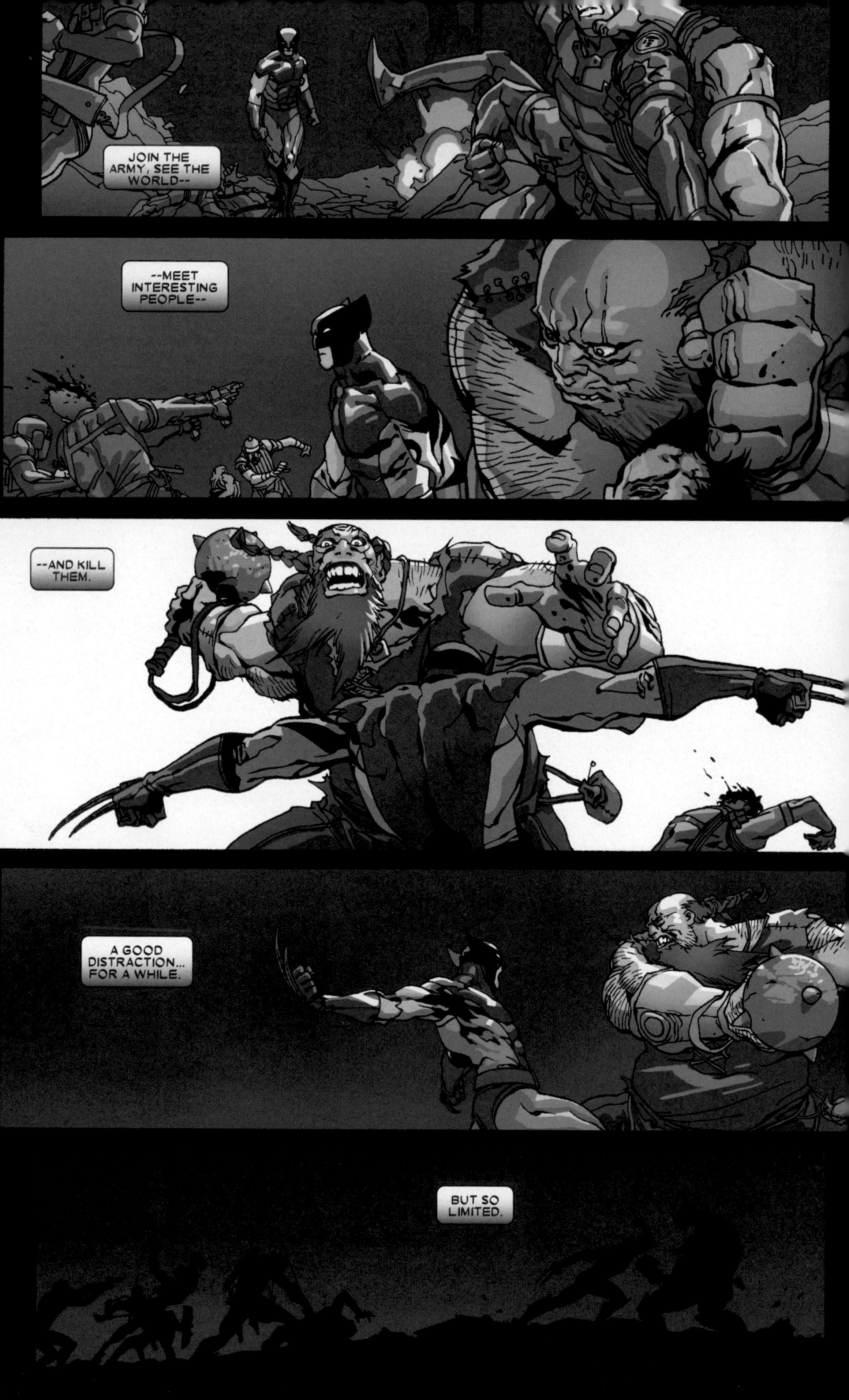
JOIN THE ARMY, SEE THE WORLD--
--MEET INTERESTING PEOPLE--
--AND KILL THEM.
A GOOD DISTRACTION... FOR A WHILE.
BUT SO LIMITED.

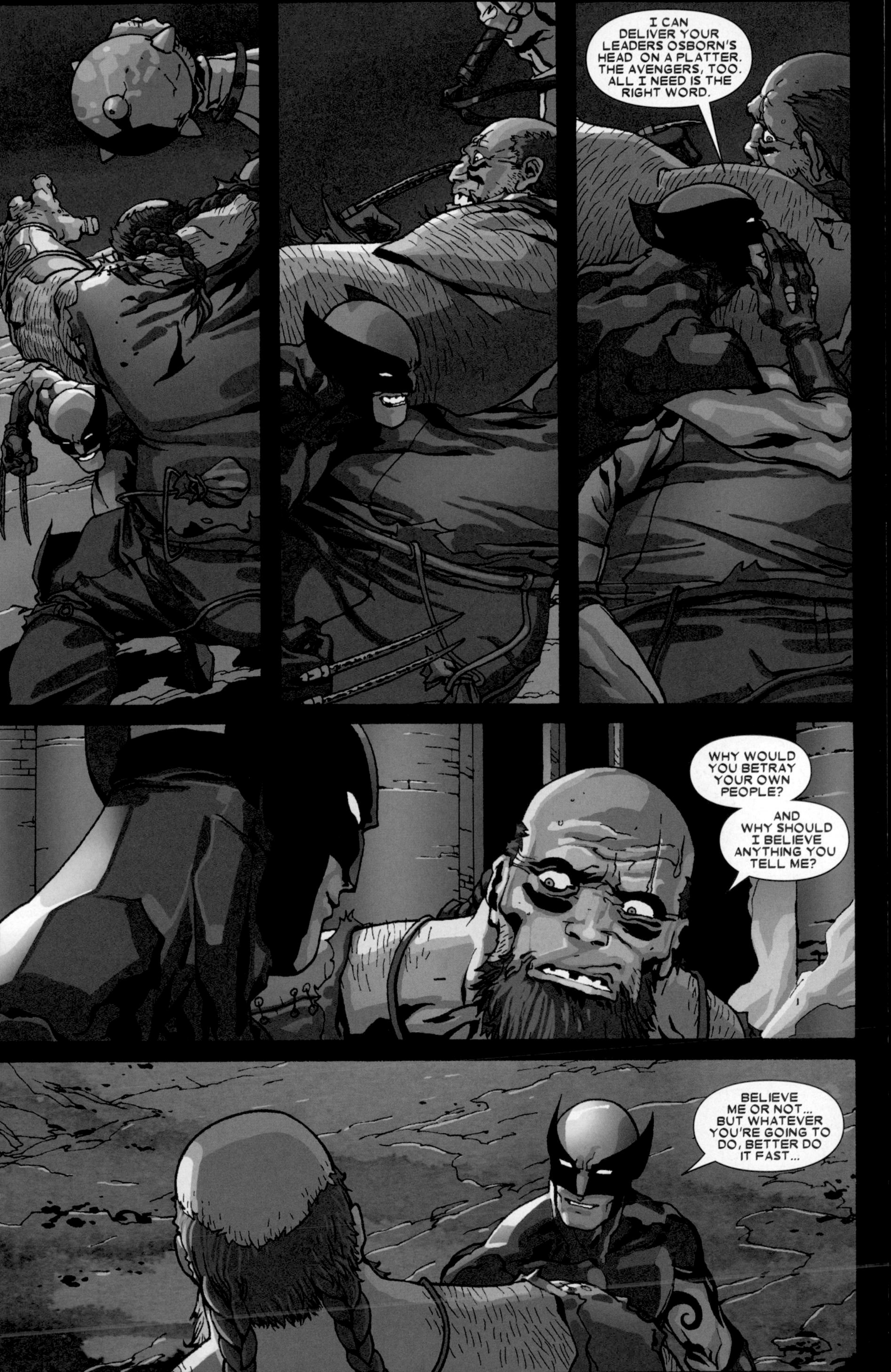
I CAN DELIVER YOUR LEADERS OSBORN'S HEAD ON A PLATTER. THE AVENGERS, TOO. ALL I NEED IS THE RIGHT WORD.
WHY WOULD YOU BETRAY YOUR OWN PEOPLE?
AND WHY SHOULD I BELIEVE ANYTHING YOU TELL ME?
BELIEVE ME OR NOT... BUT WHATEVER YOU'RE GOING TO DO, BETTER DO IT FAST...

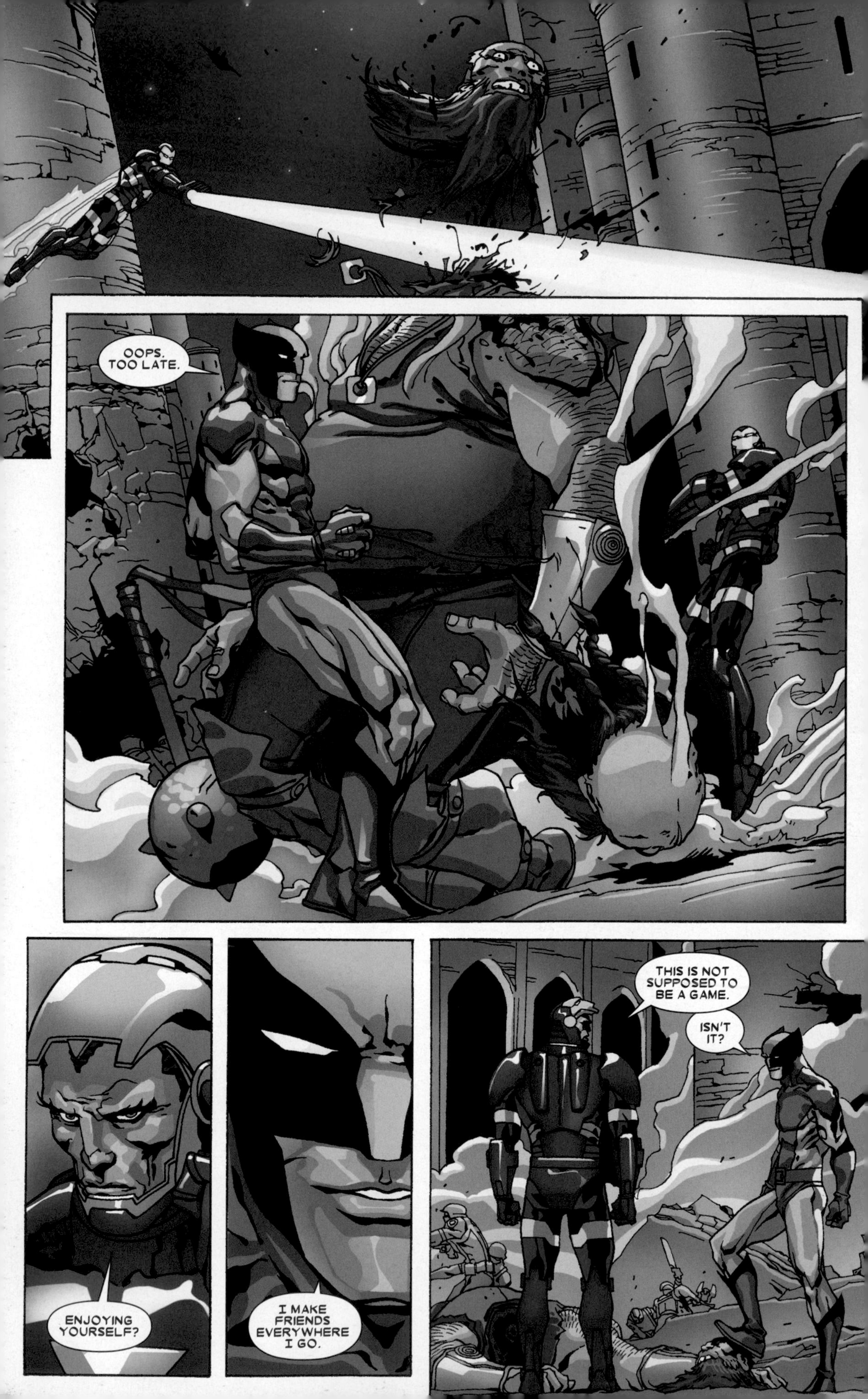
OOPS. TOO LATE.
ENJOYING YOURSELF?
I MAKE FRIENDS EVERYWHERE I GO.
THIS IS NOT SUPPOSED TO BE A GAME.
ISN'T IT?

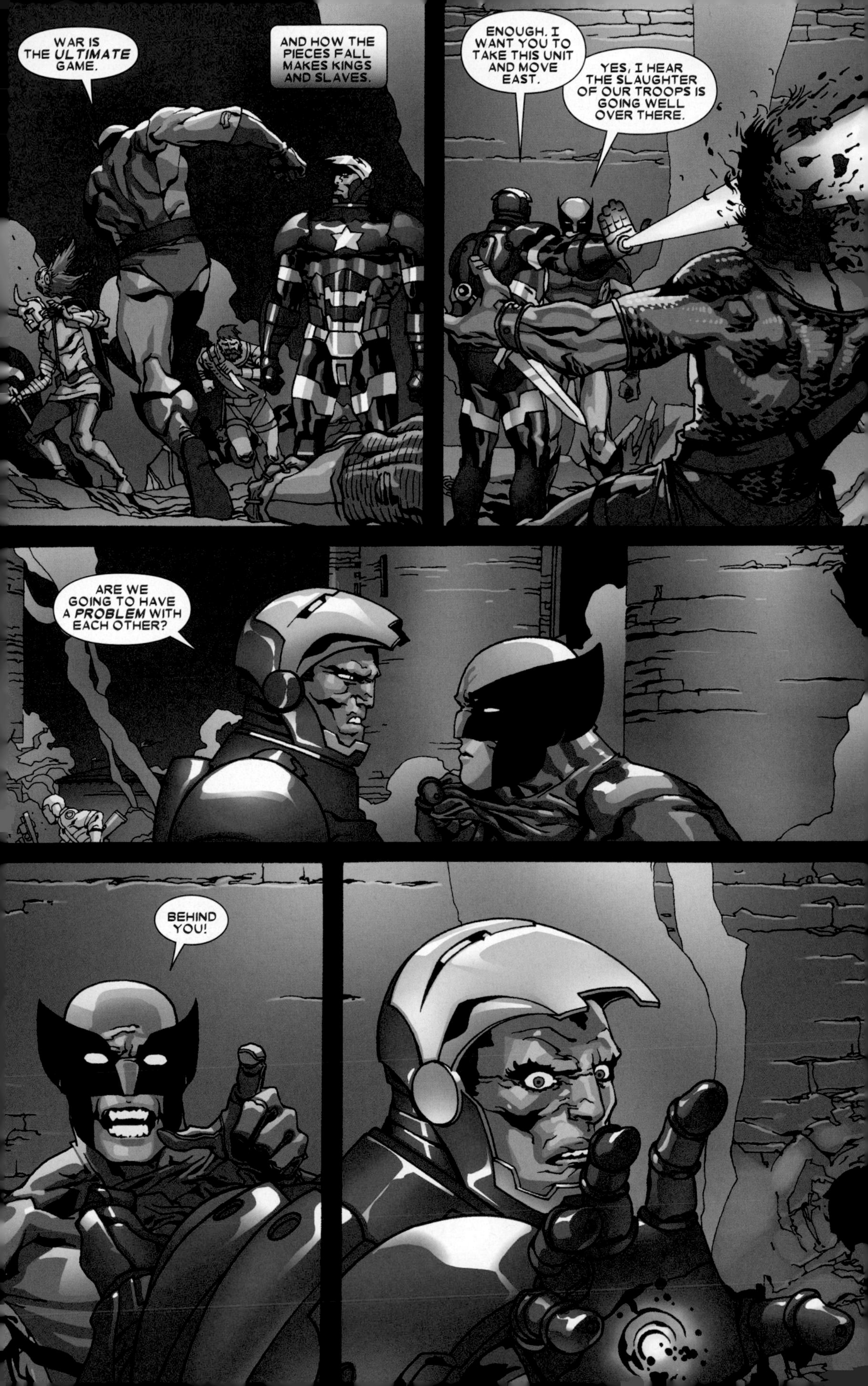
WAR IS THE *ULTIMATE* GAME.
AND HOW THE PIECES FALL MAKES KINGS AND SLAVES.
ENOUGH. I WANT YOU TO TAKE THIS UNIT AND MOVE EAST.
YES, I HEAR THE SLAUGHTER OF OUR TROOPS IS GOING WELL OVER THERE.
ARE WE GOING TO HAVE A *PROBLEM* WITH EACH OTHER?
BEHIND YOU!

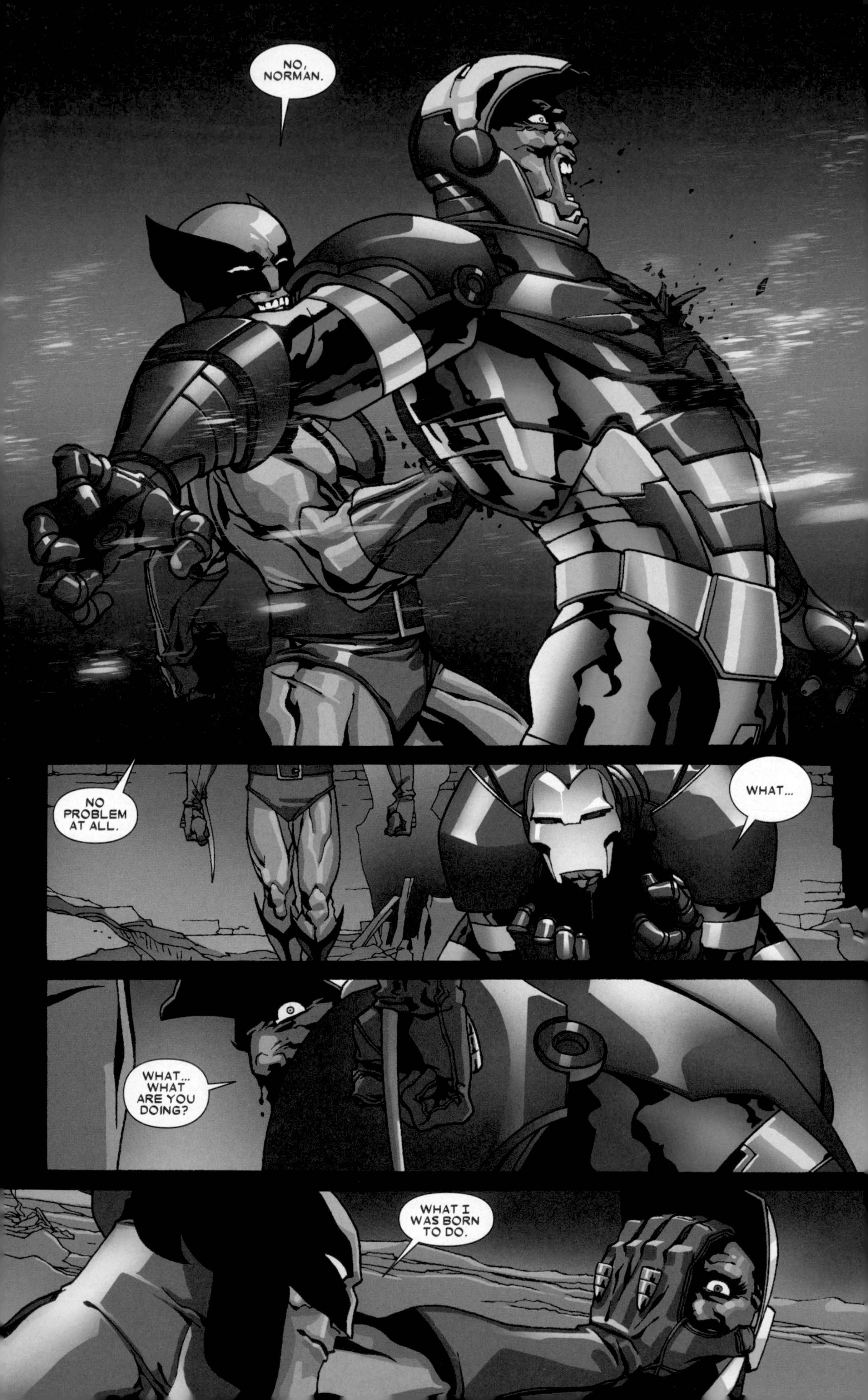
NO, NORMAN.
NO PROBLEM AT ALL.
WHAT...
WHAT... WHAT ARE YOU DOING?
WHAT I WAS BORN TO DO.

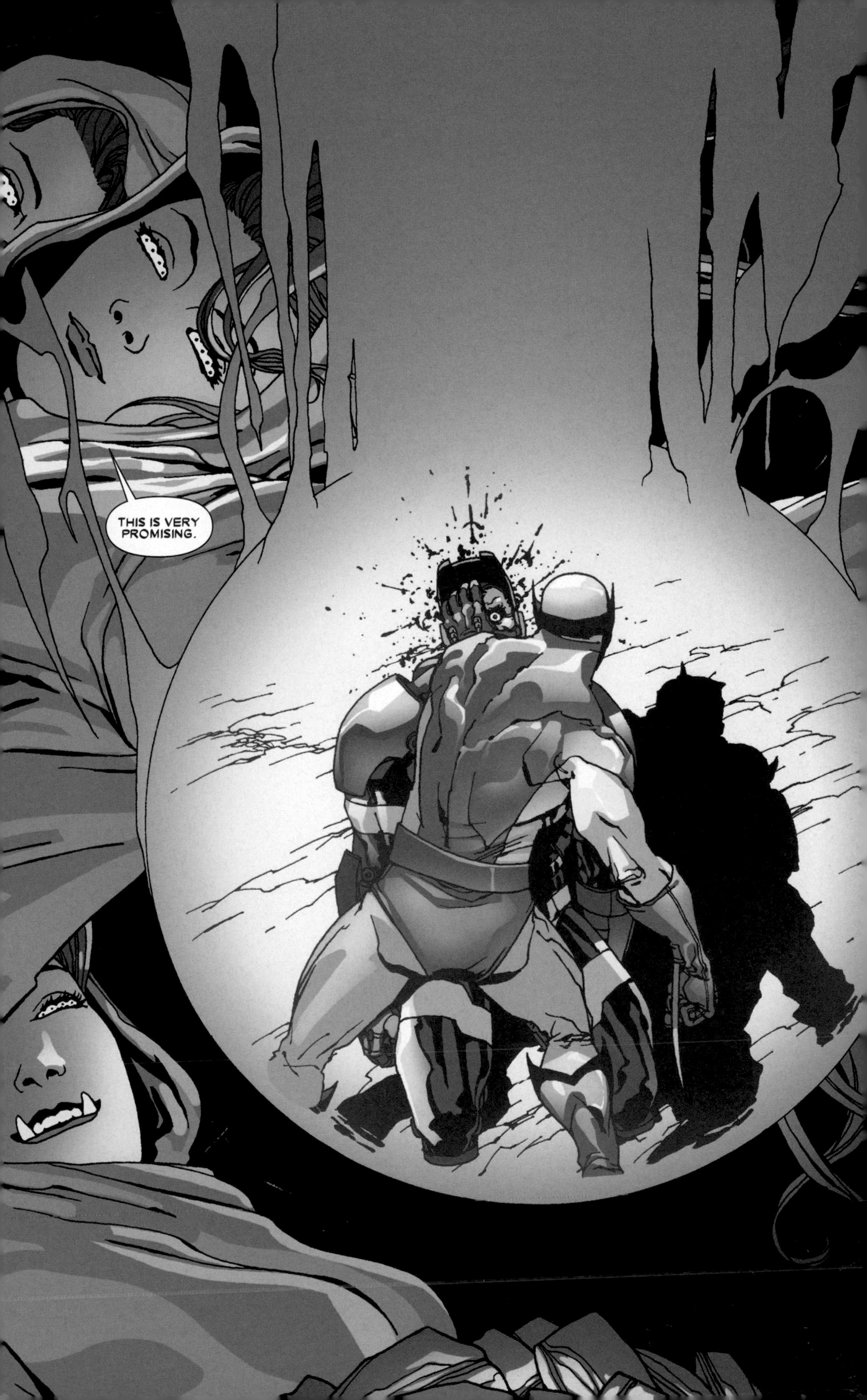
THIS IS VERY PROMISING.

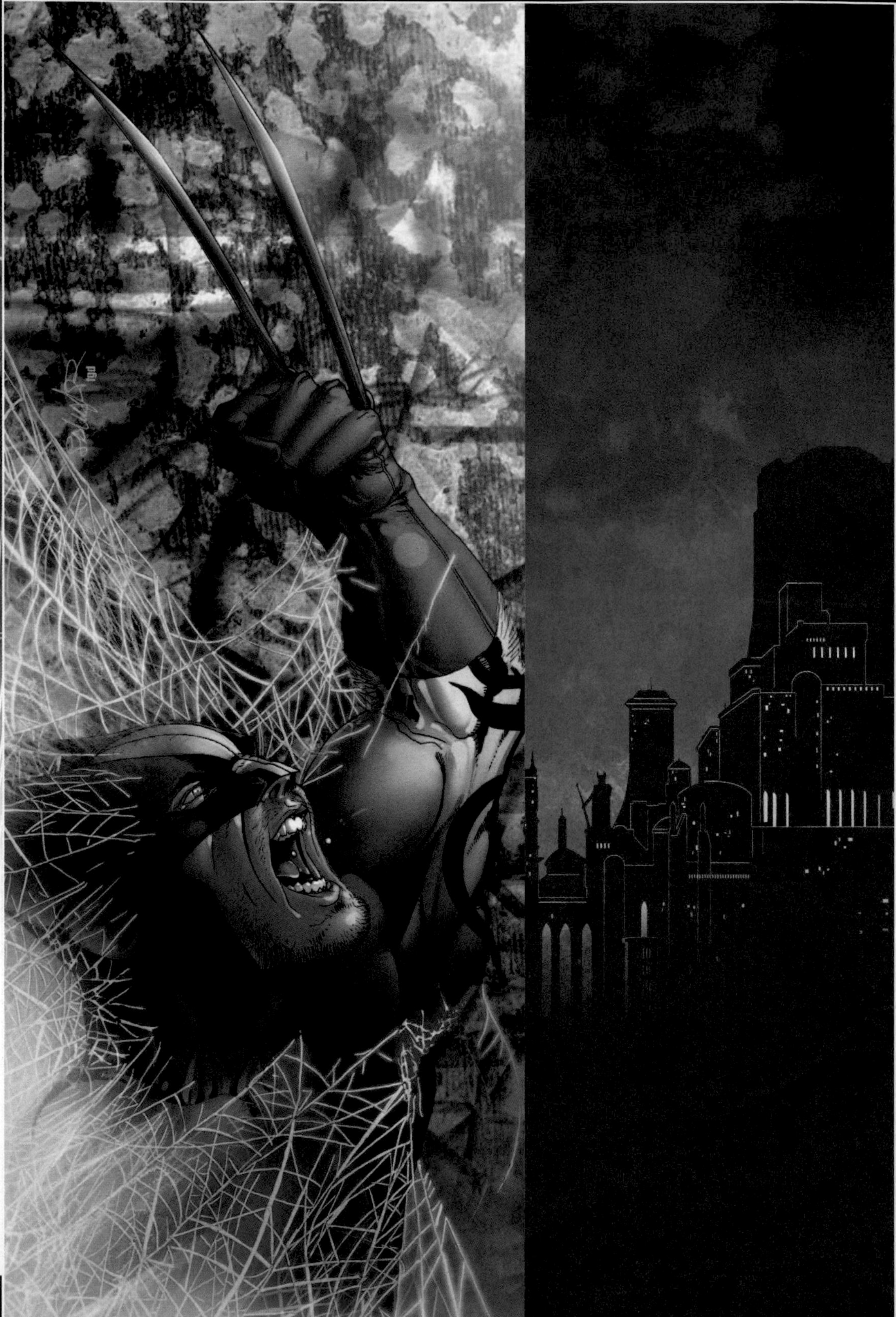

DARK WOLVERINE #83

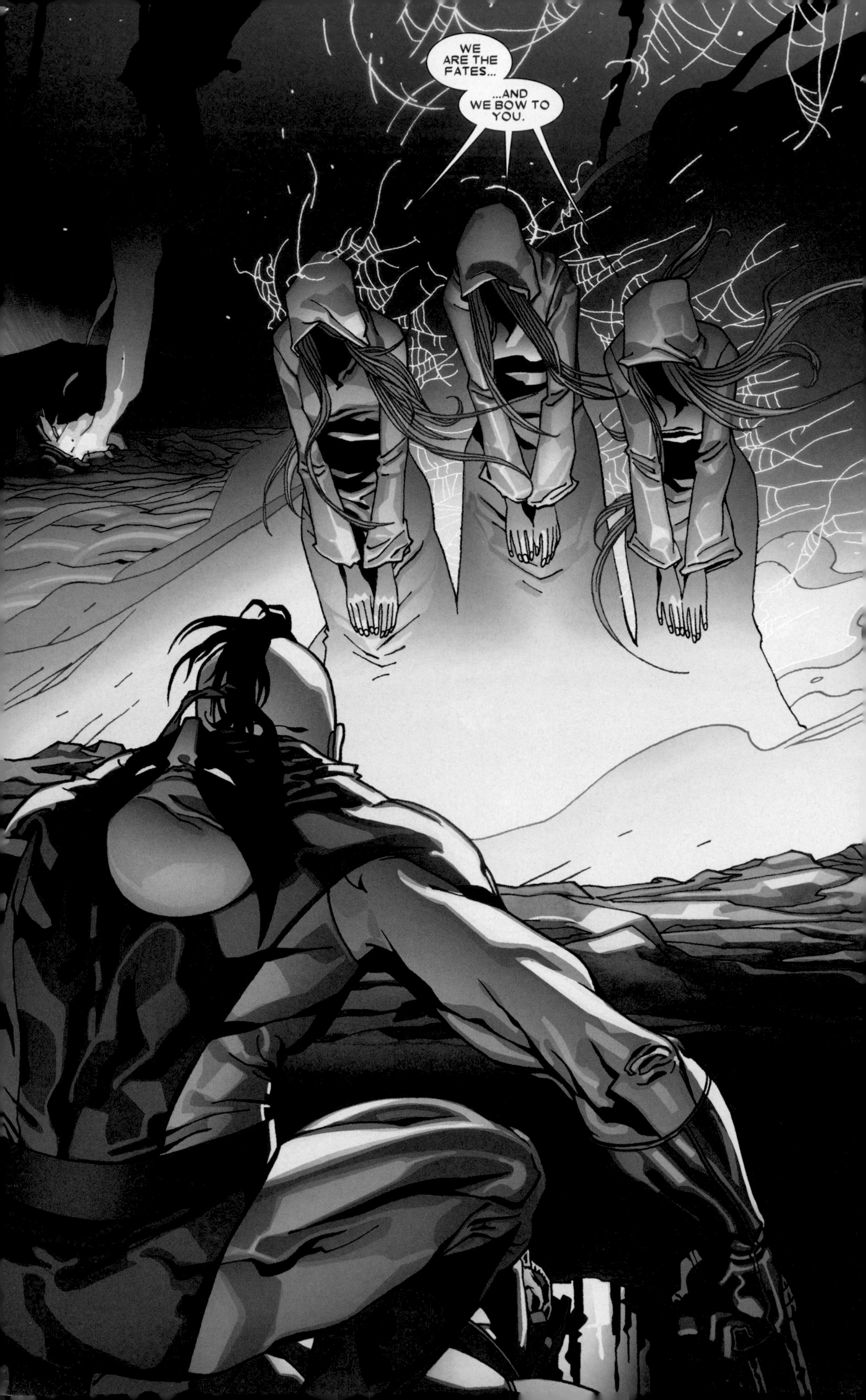
WE ARE THE FATES...
...AND WE BOW TO YOU.

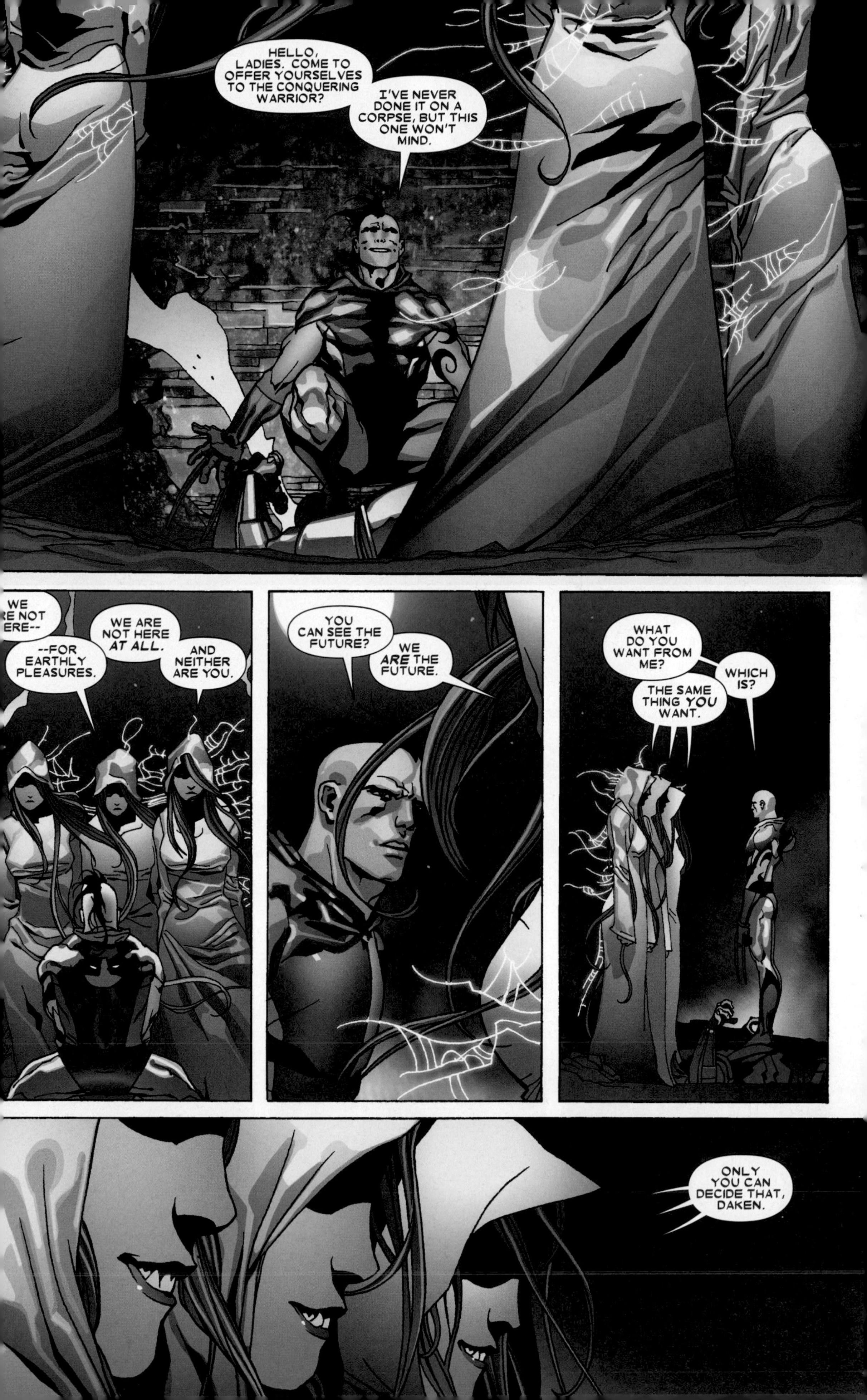
HELLO, LADIES. COME TO OFFER YOURSELVES TO THE CONQUERING WARRIOR?
I'VE NEVER DONE IT ON A CORPSE, BUT THIS ONE WON'T MIND.
WE ...E NOT ...ERE--
--FOR EARTHLY PLEASURES.
WE ARE NOT HERE AT ALL.
AND NEITHER ARE YOU.
YOU CAN SEE THE FUTURE?
WE ARE THE FUTURE.
WHAT DO YOU WANT FROM ME?
THE SAME THING YOU WANT.
WHICH IS?
ONLY YOU CAN DECIDE THAT, DAKEN.

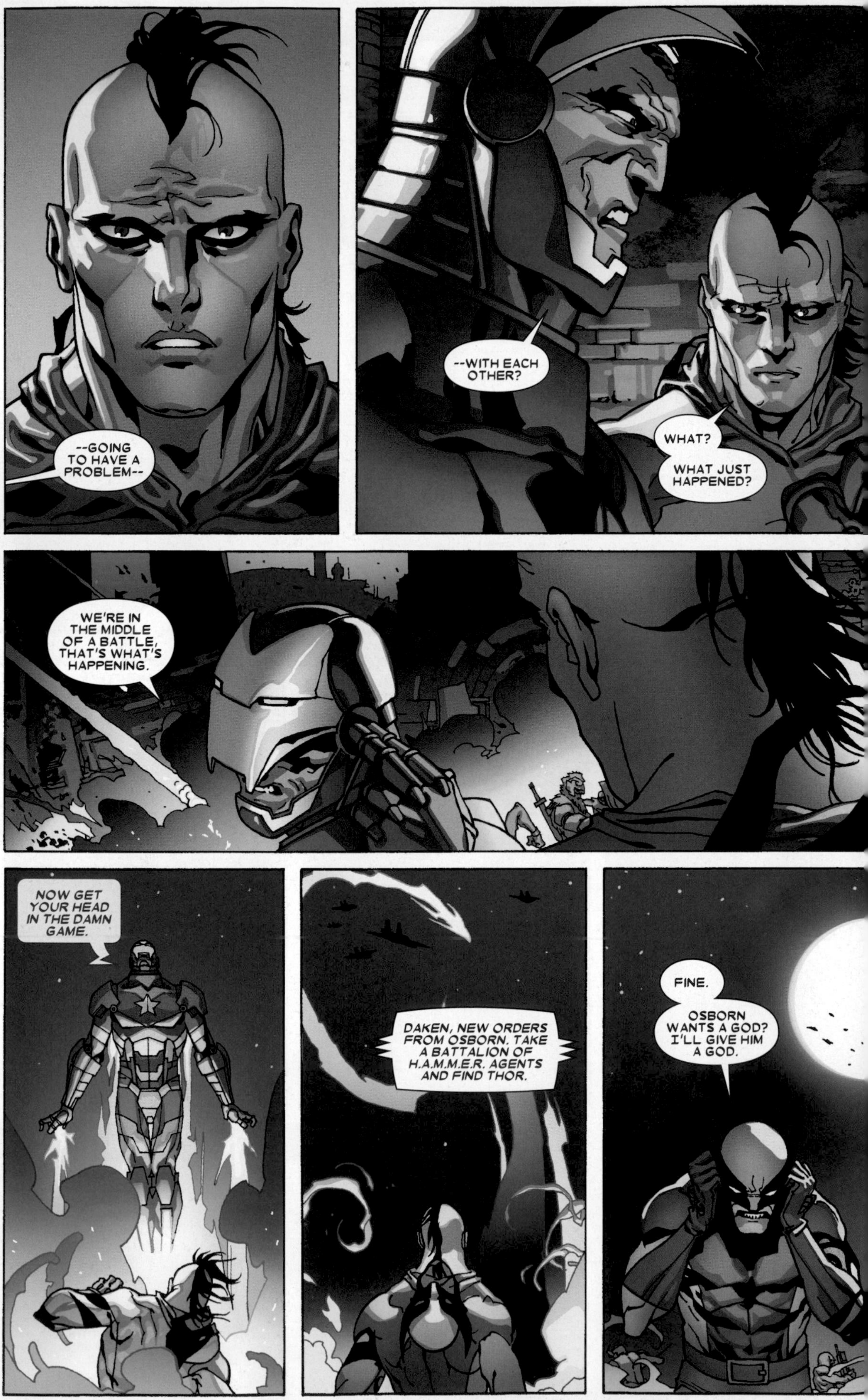
--GOING TO HAVE A PROBLEM--
--WITH EACH OTHER?
WHAT?
WHAT JUST HAPPENED?
WE'RE IN THE MIDDLE OF A BATTLE, THAT'S WHAT'S HAPPENING.
NOW GET YOUR HEAD IN THE DAMN GAME.
DAKEN, NEW ORDERS FROM OSBORN. TAKE A BATTALION OF H.A.M.M.E.R. AGENTS AND FIND THOR.
FINE.
OSBORN WANTS A GOD? I'LL GIVE HIM A GOD.

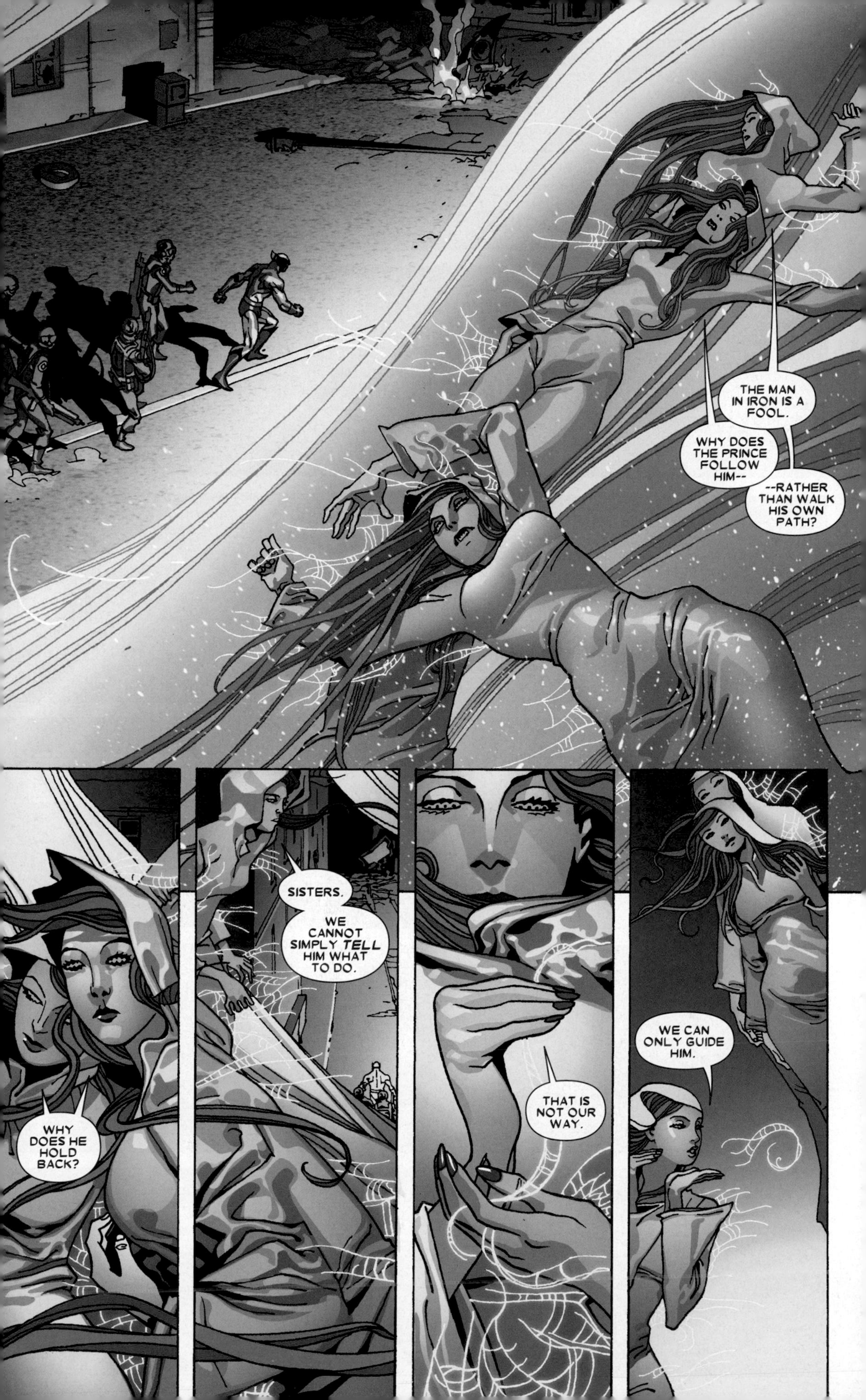
THE MAN IN IRON IS A FOOL.
WHY DOES THE PRINCE FOLLOW HIM--
--RATHER THAN WALK HIS OWN PATH?
WHY DOES HE HOLD BACK?
SISTERS.
WE CANNOT SIMPLY TELL HIM WHAT TO DO.
THAT IS NOT OUR WAY.
WE CAN ONLY GUIDE HIM.

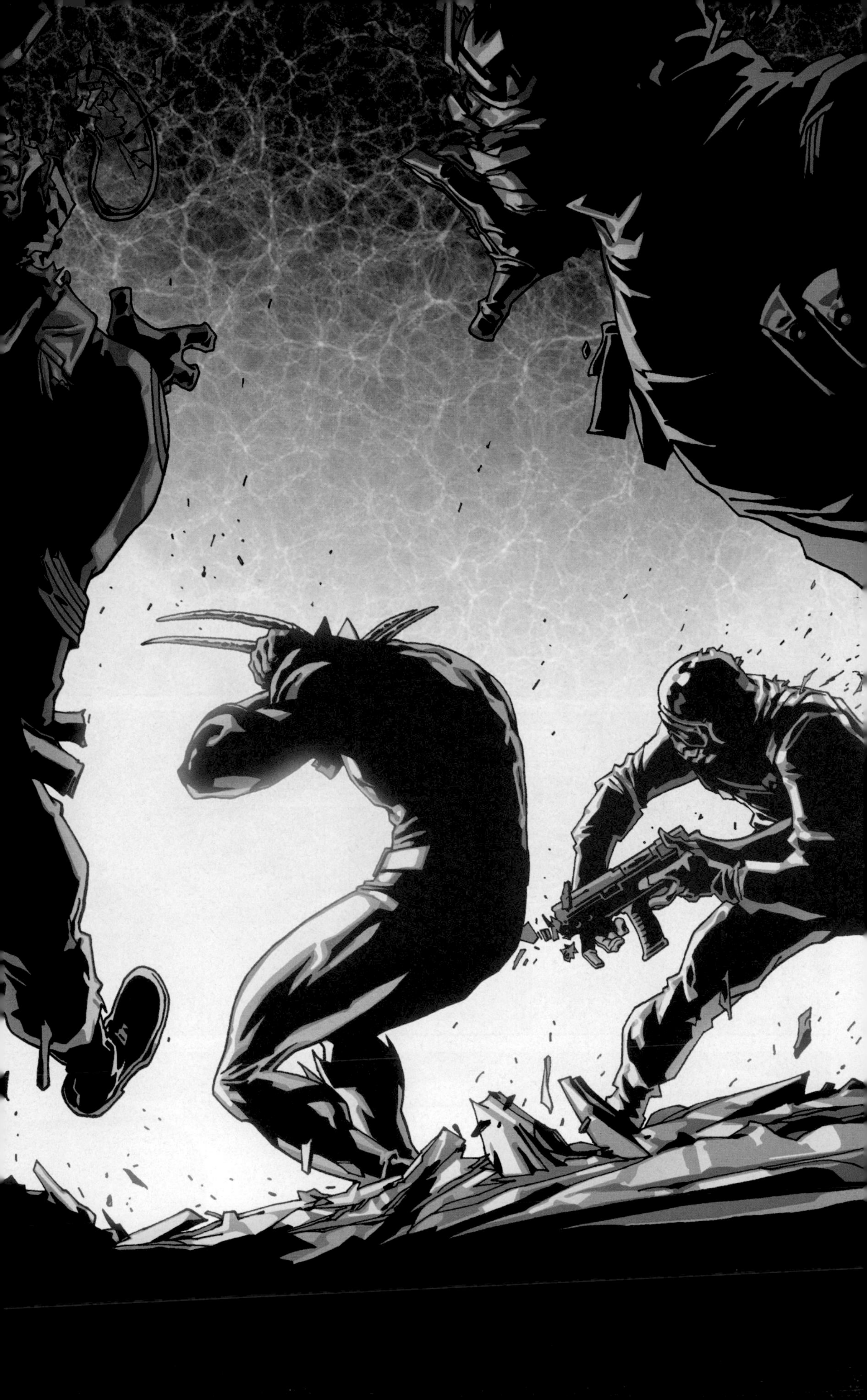

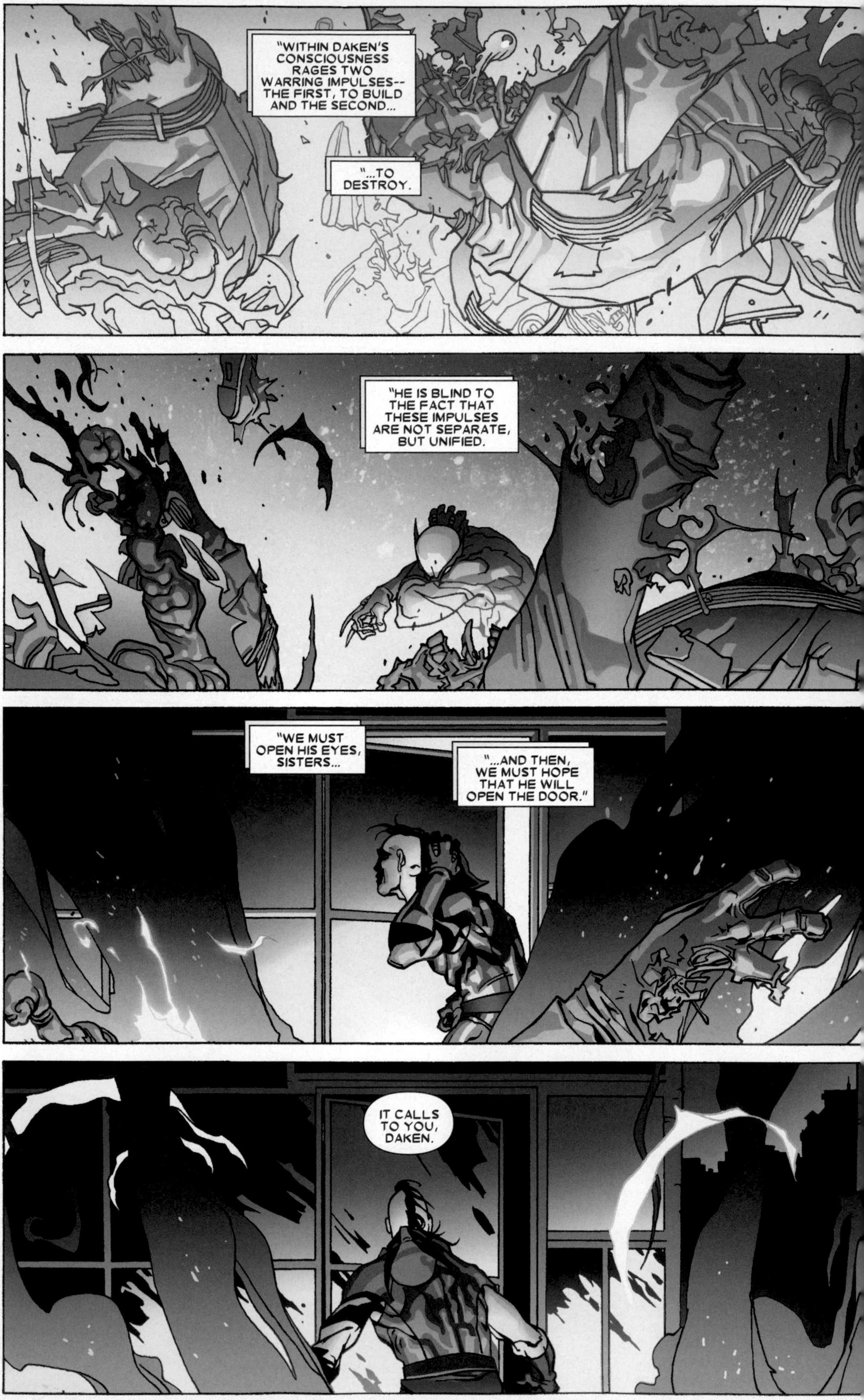
"WITHIN DAKEN'S CONSCIOUSNESS RAGES TWO WARRING IMPULSES-- THE FIRST, TO BUILD AND THE SECOND...
"...TO DESTROY.
"HE IS BLIND TO THE FACT THAT THESE IMPULSES ARE NOT SEPARATE, BUT UNIFIED.
"WE MUST OPEN HIS EYES, SISTERS...
"...AND THEN, WE MUST HOPE THAT HE WILL OPEN THE DOOR."
IT CALLS TO YOU, DAKEN.

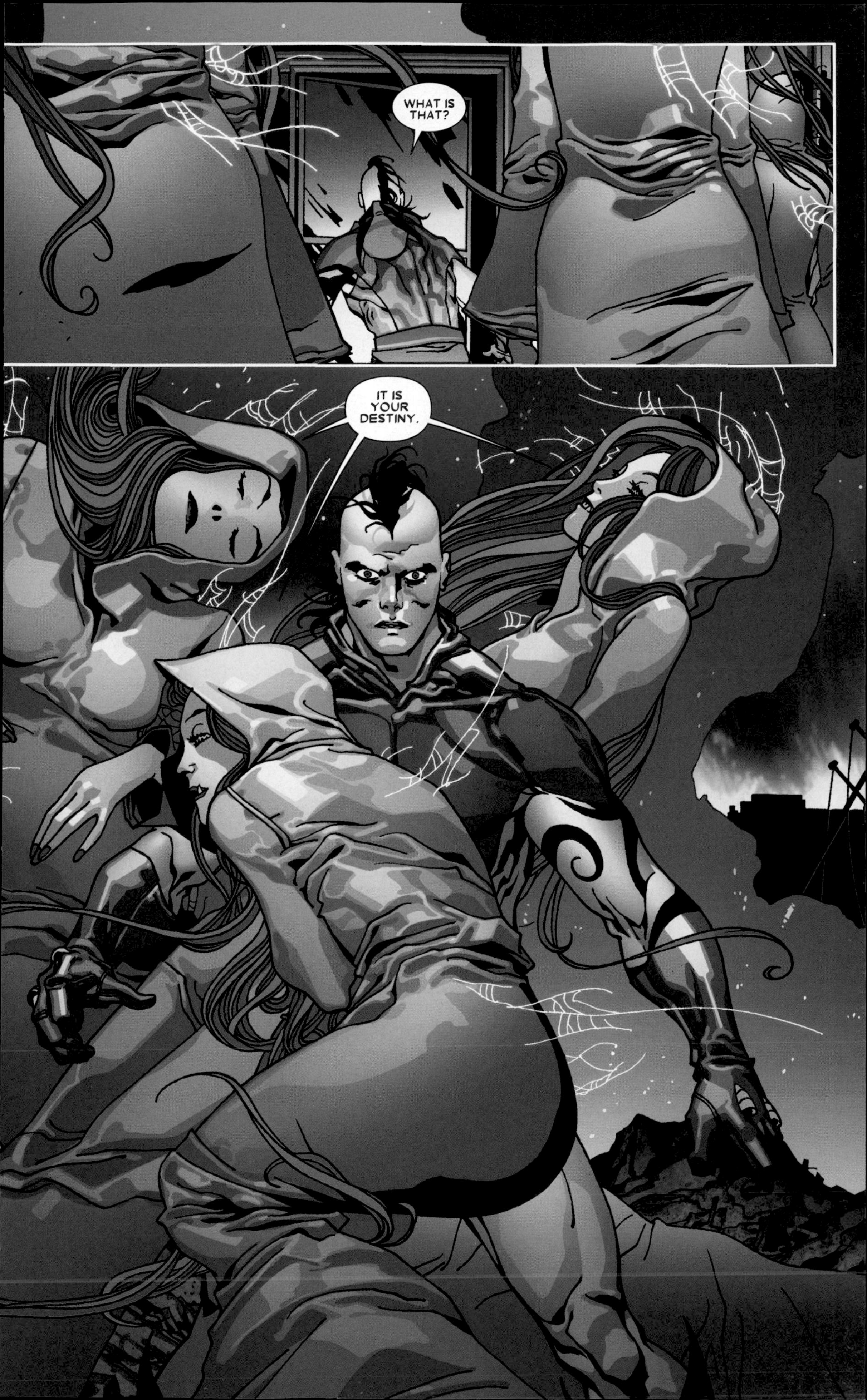
WHAT IS THAT?
IT IS YOUR DESTINY.

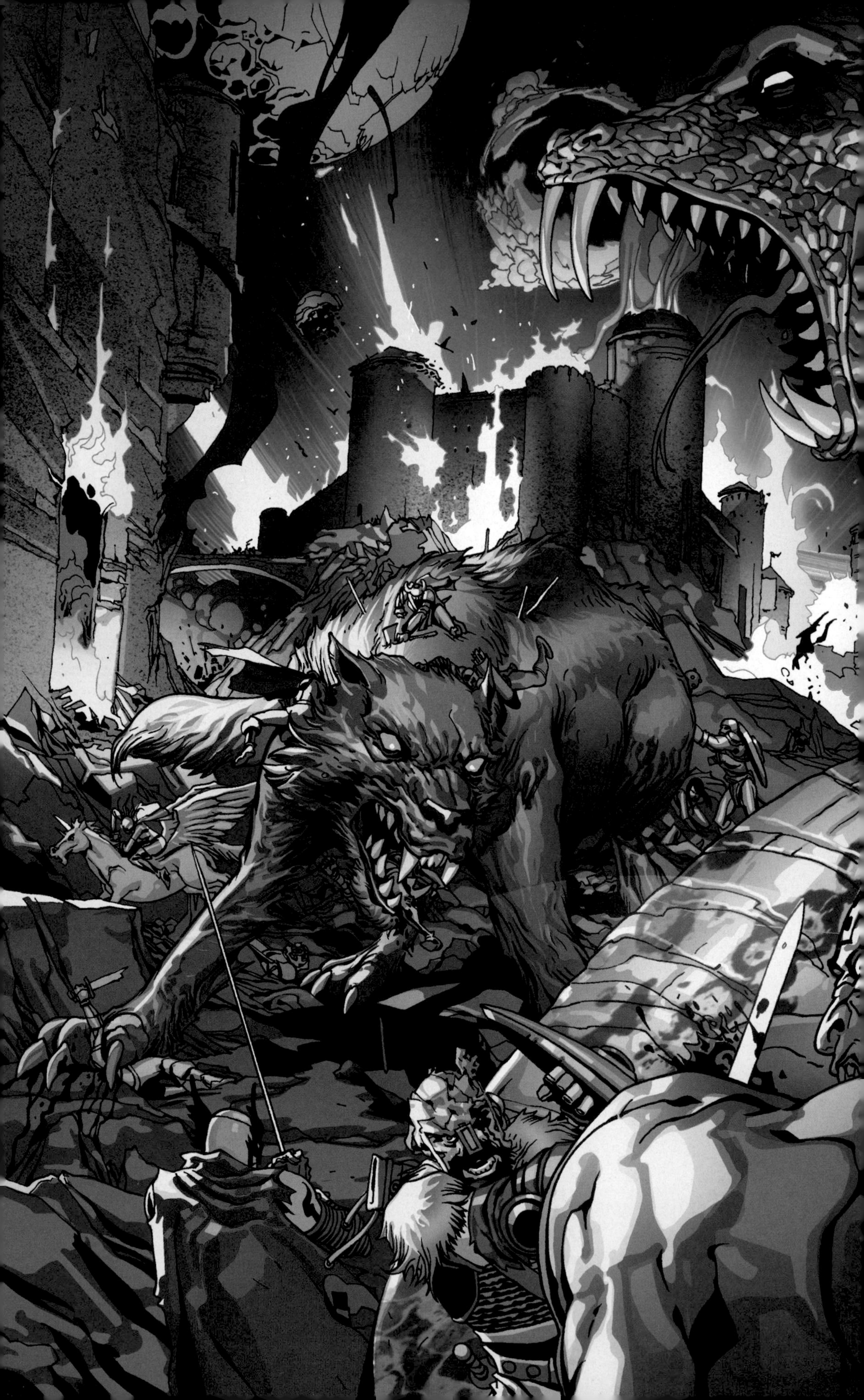

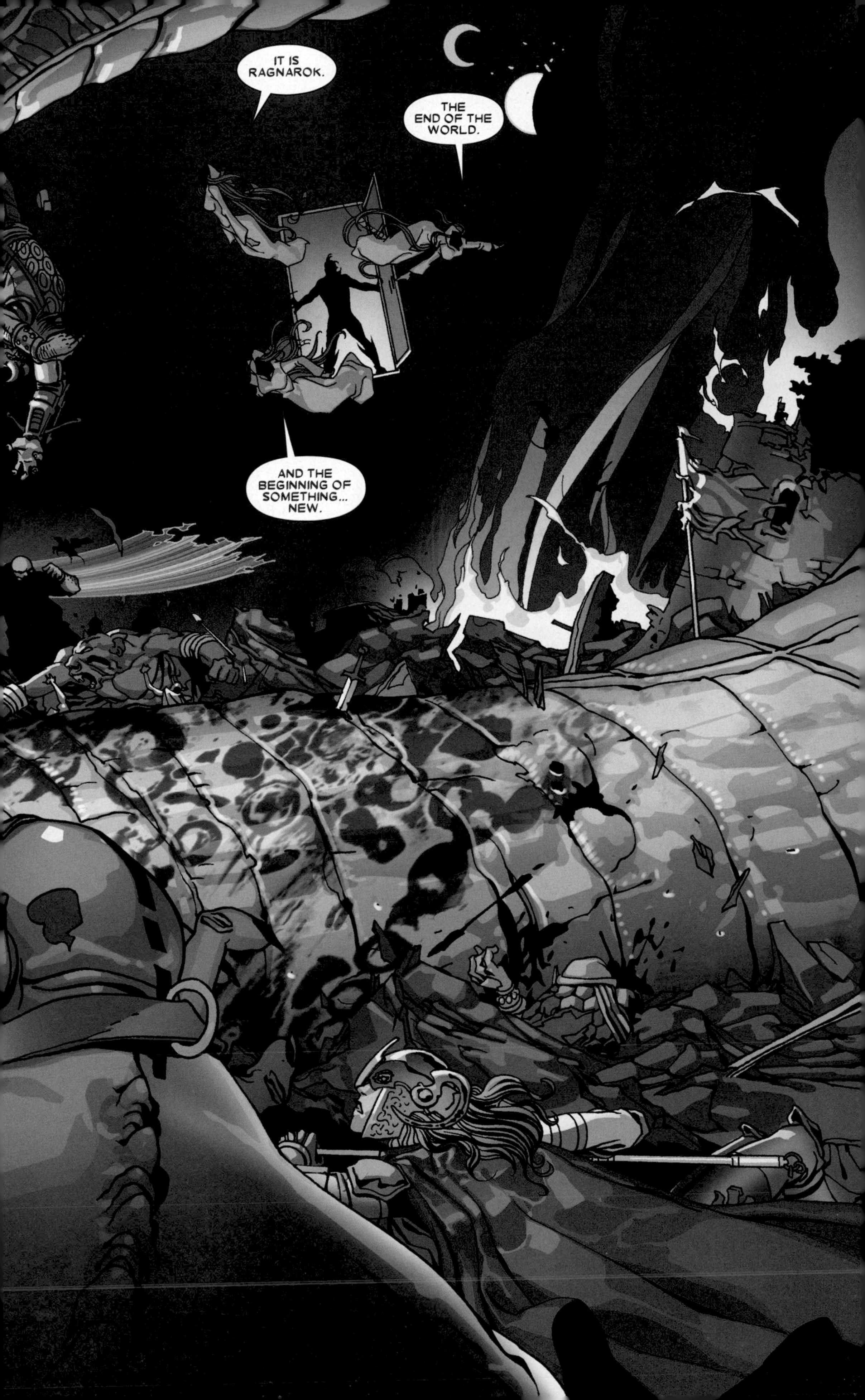
IT IS RAGNAROK.
THE END OF THE WORLD.
AND THE BEGINNING OF SOMETHING... NEW.

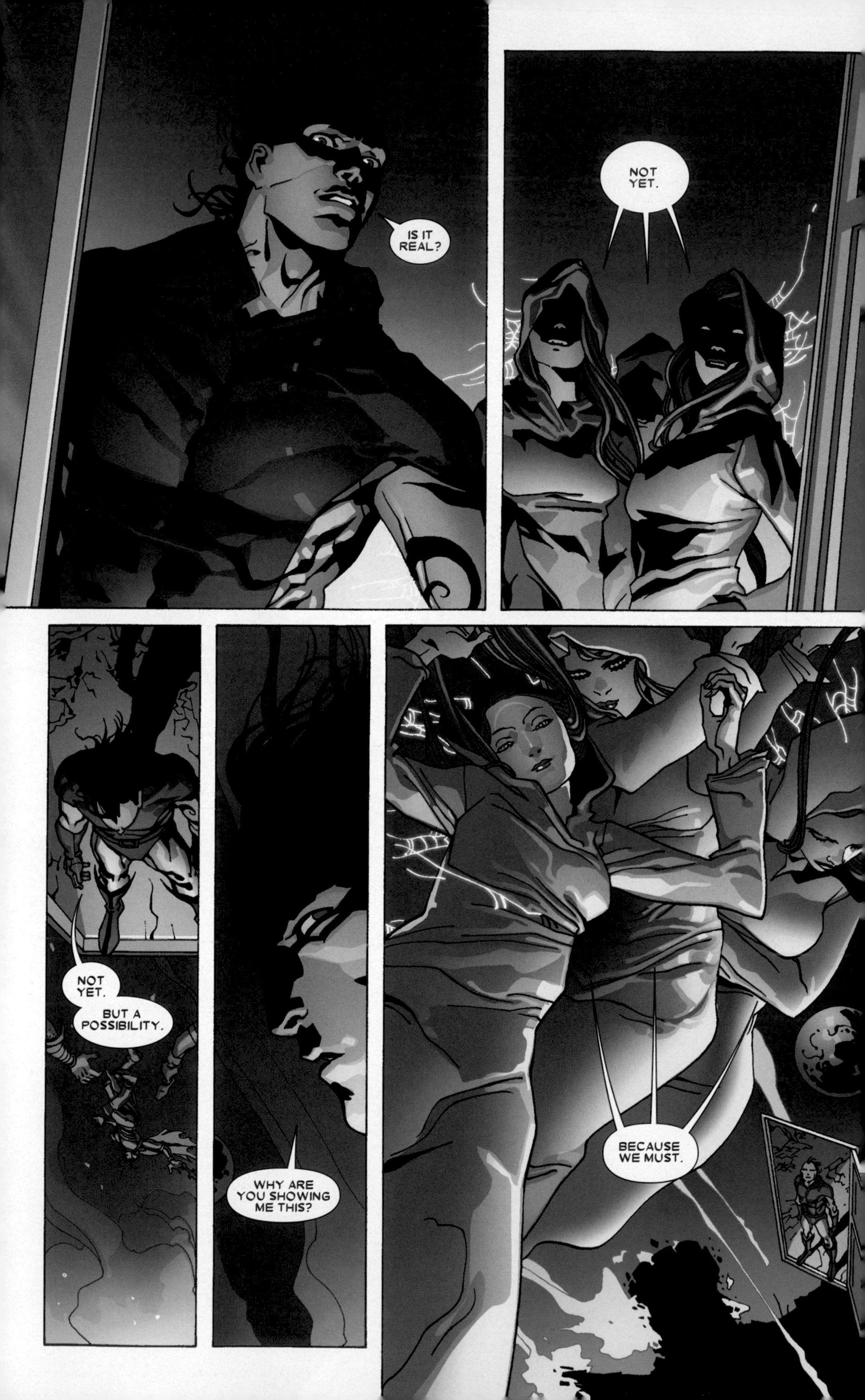
IS IT REAL?
NOT YET.
NOT YET.
BUT A POSSIBILITY.
WHY ARE YOU SHOWING ME THIS?
BECAUSE WE MUST.

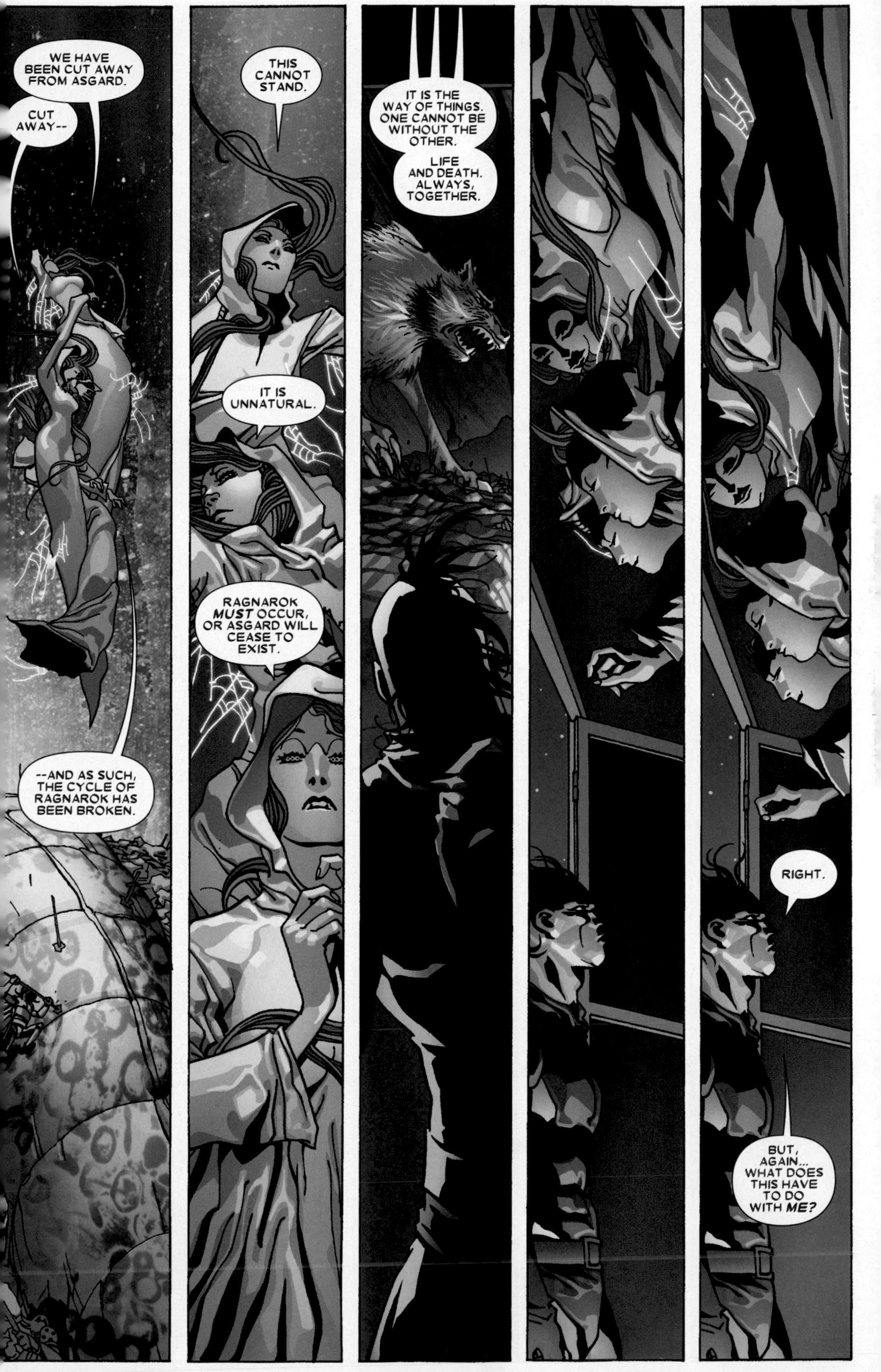
WE HAVE BEEN CUT AWAY FROM ASGARD.
CUT AWAY--
--AND AS SUCH, THE CYCLE OF RAGNAROK HAS BEEN BROKEN.
THIS CANNOT STAND.
IT IS UNNATURAL.
RAGNAROK *MUST* OCCUR, OR ASGARD WILL CEASE TO EXIST.
IT IS THE WAY OF THINGS. ONE CANNOT BE WITHOUT THE OTHER.
LIFE AND DEATH. ALWAYS, TOGETHER.
RIGHT.
BUT, AGAIN... WHAT DOES THIS HAVE TO DO WITH *ME?*

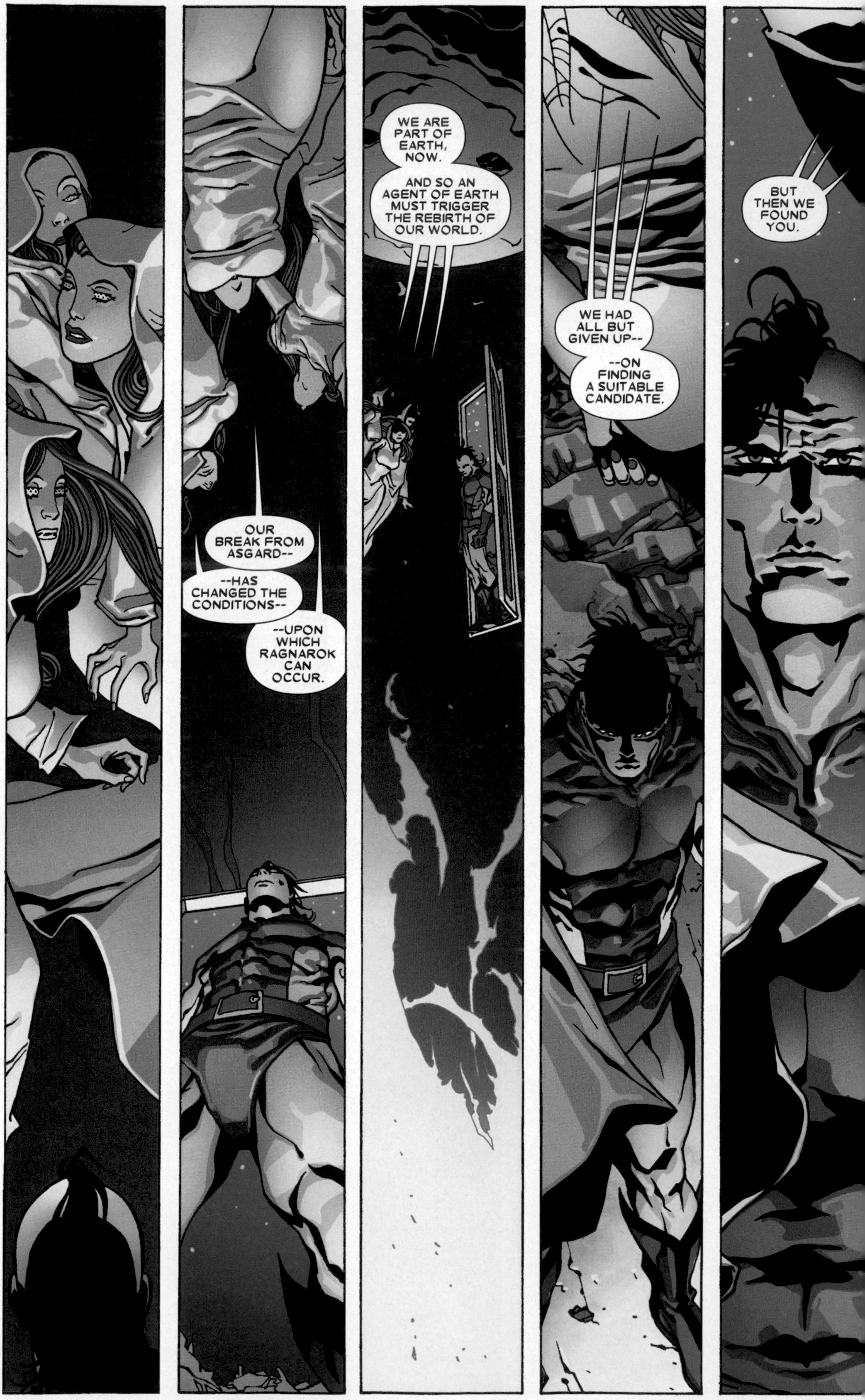
OUR BREAK FROM ASGARD--
--HAS CHANGED THE CONDITIONS--
--UPON WHICH RAGNAROK CAN OCCUR.
WE ARE PART OF EARTH, NOW.
AND SO AN AGENT OF EARTH MUST TRIGGER THE REBIRTH OF OUR WORLD.
WE HAD ALL BUT GIVEN UP--
--ON FINDING A SUITABLE CANDIDATE.
BUT THEN WE FOUND YOU.

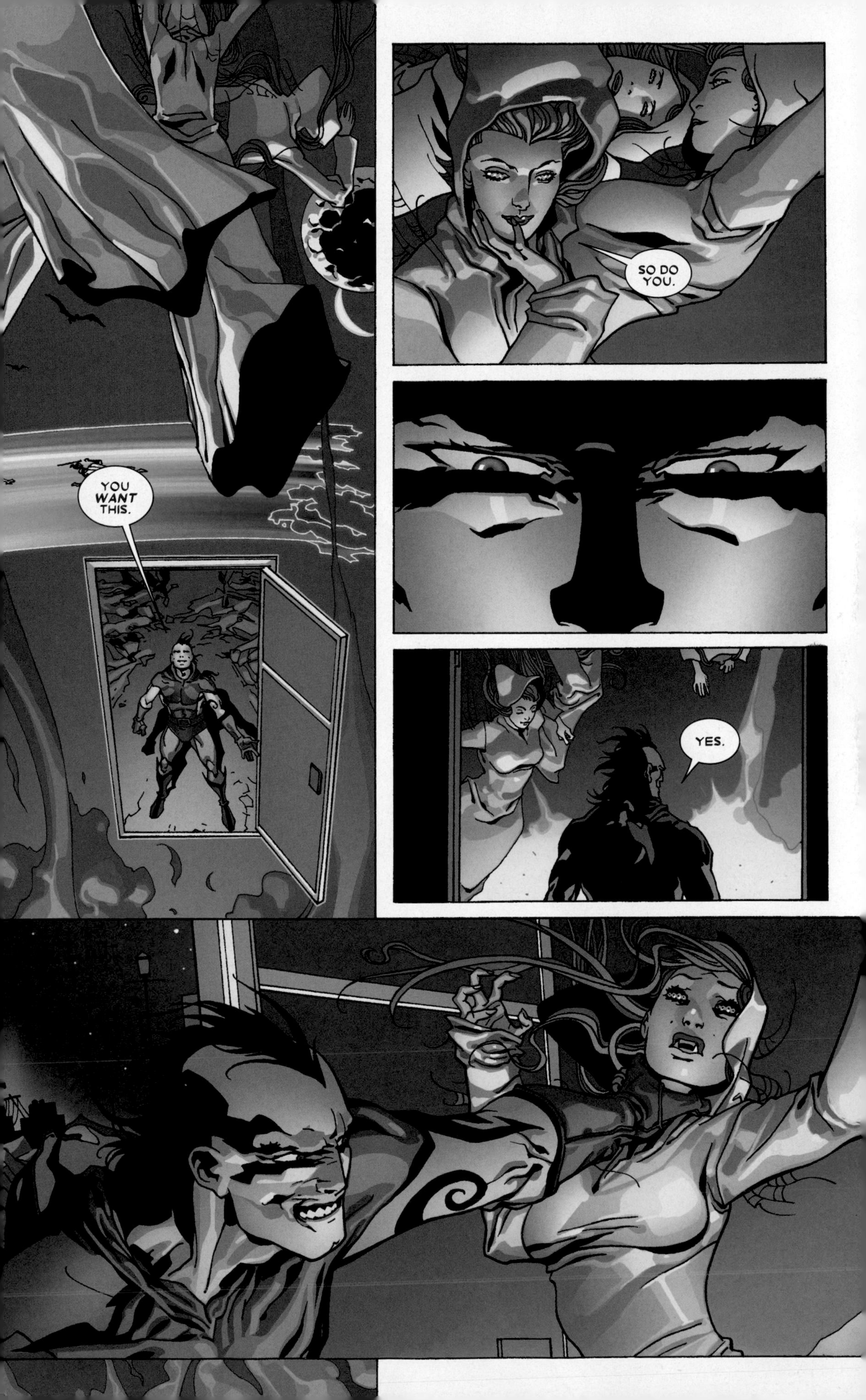
YOU WANT THIS.
SO DO YOU.
YES.

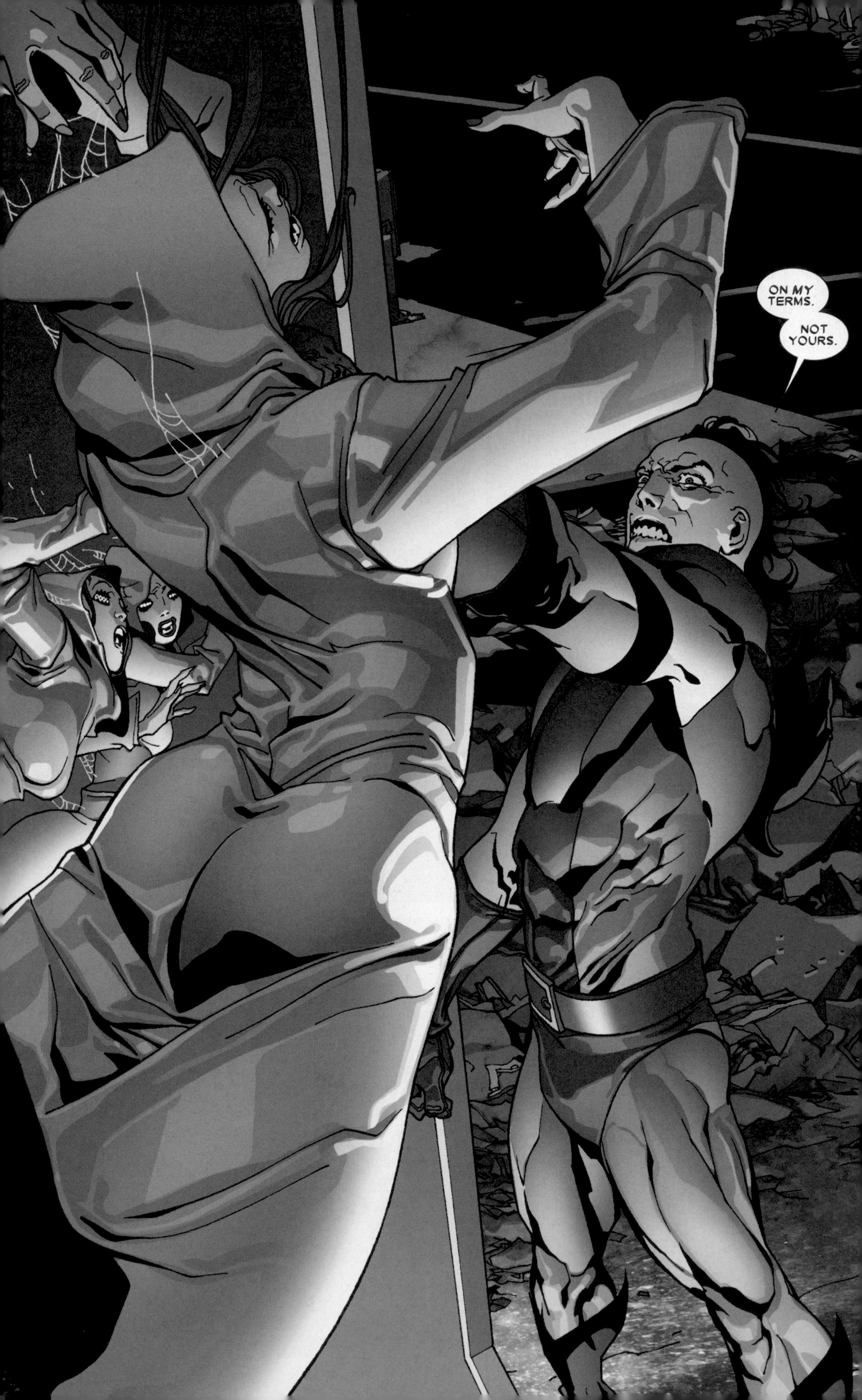
ON MY TERMS.
NOT YOURS.

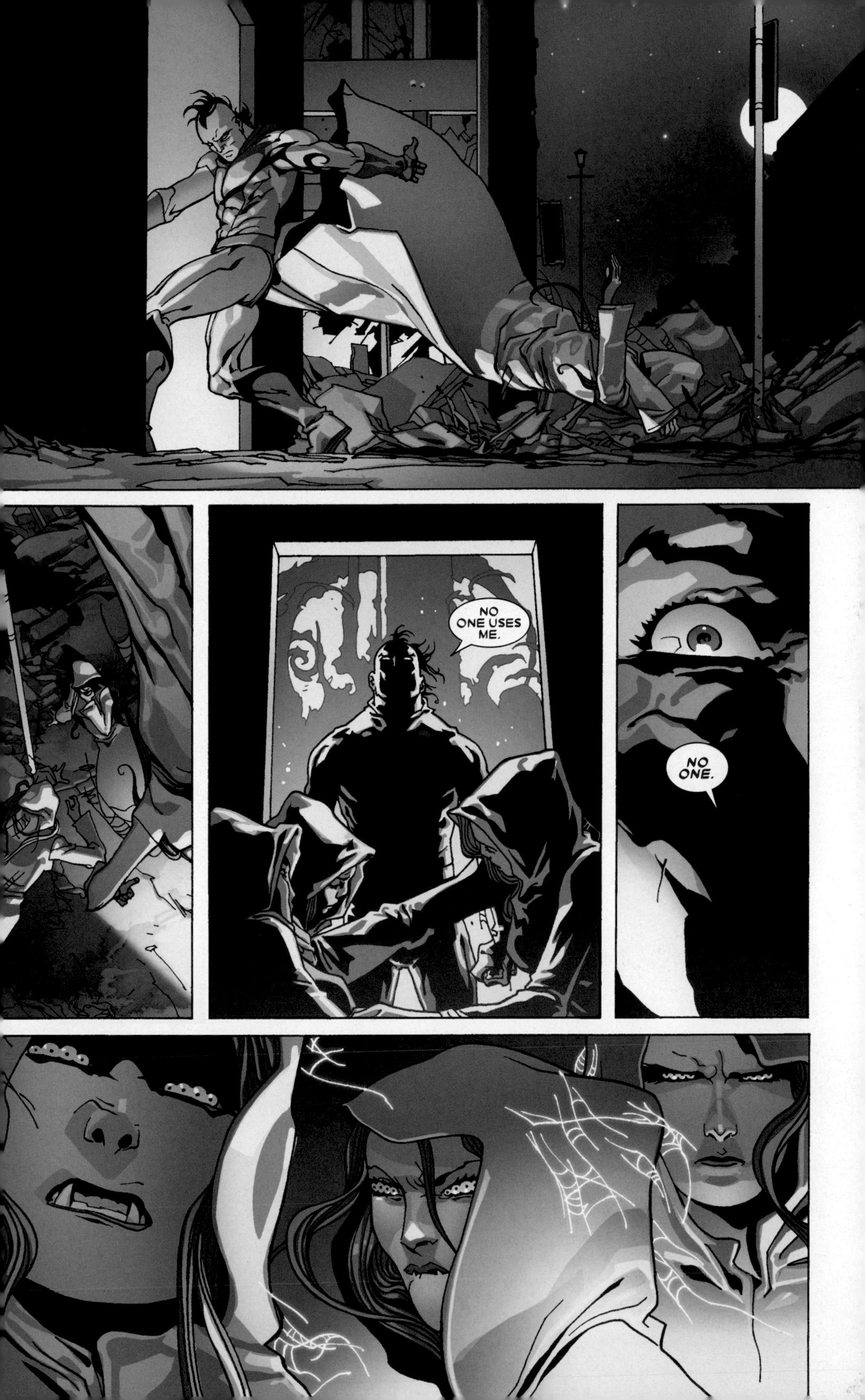
NO ONE USES ME.
NO ONE.

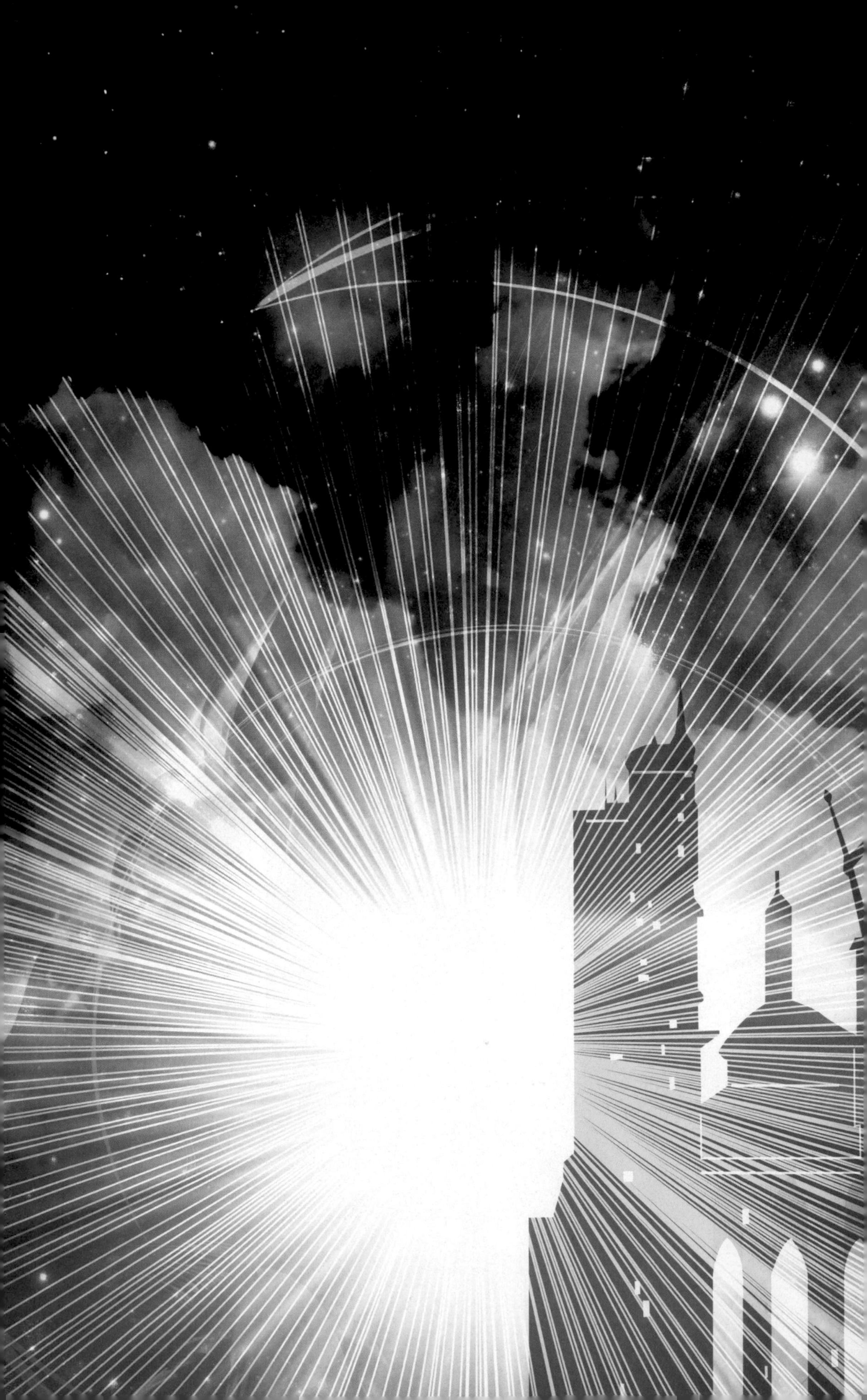

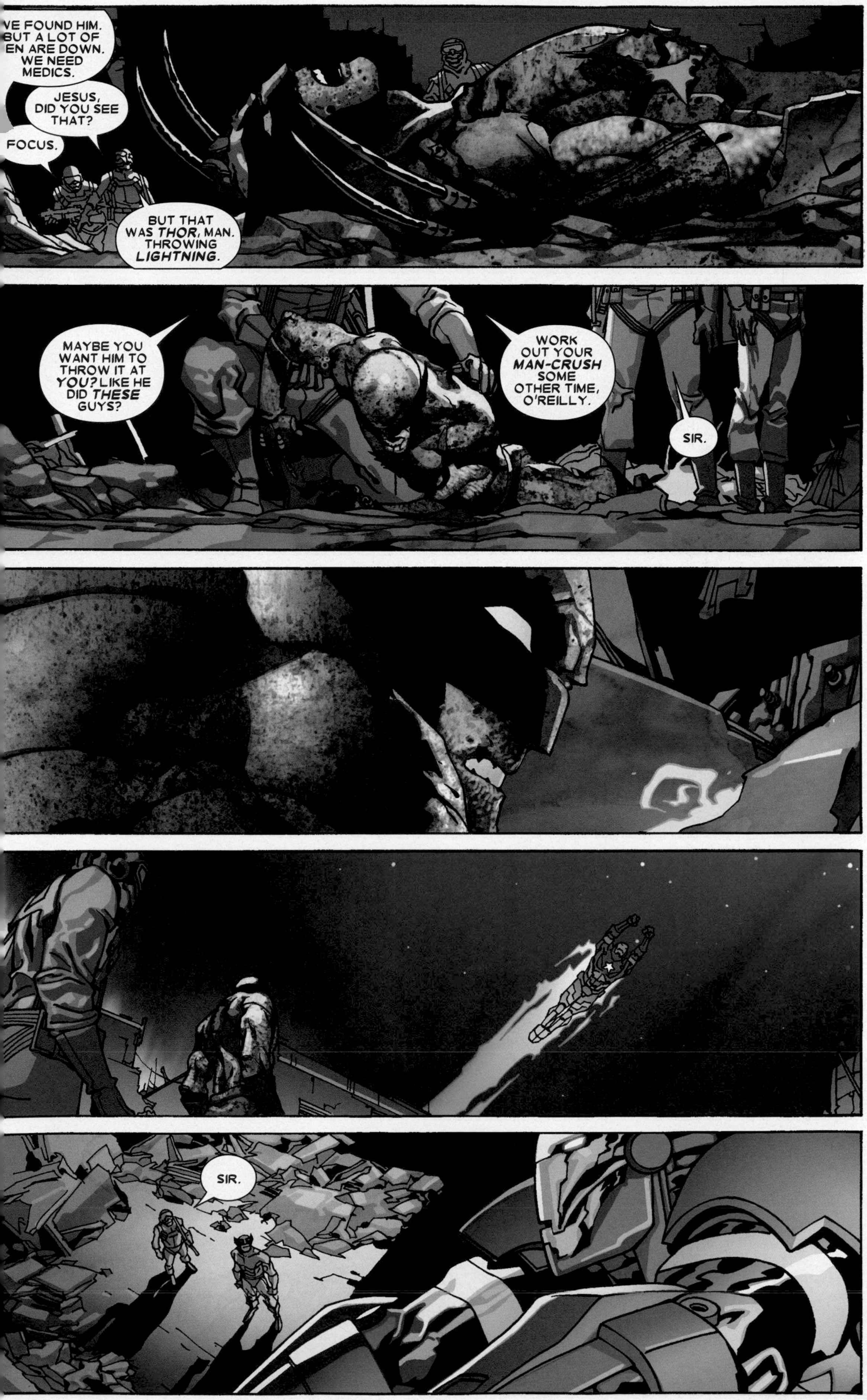

VE FOUND HIM. BUT A LOT OF EN ARE DOWN. WE NEED MEDICS.
JESUS, DID YOU SEE THAT?
FOCUS.
BUT THAT WAS THOR, MAN. THROWING LIGHTNING.
MAYBE YOU WANT HIM TO THROW IT AT YOU? LIKE HE DID THESE GUYS?
WORK OUT YOUR MAN-CRUSH SOME OTHER TIME, O'REILLY.
SIR.
SIR.

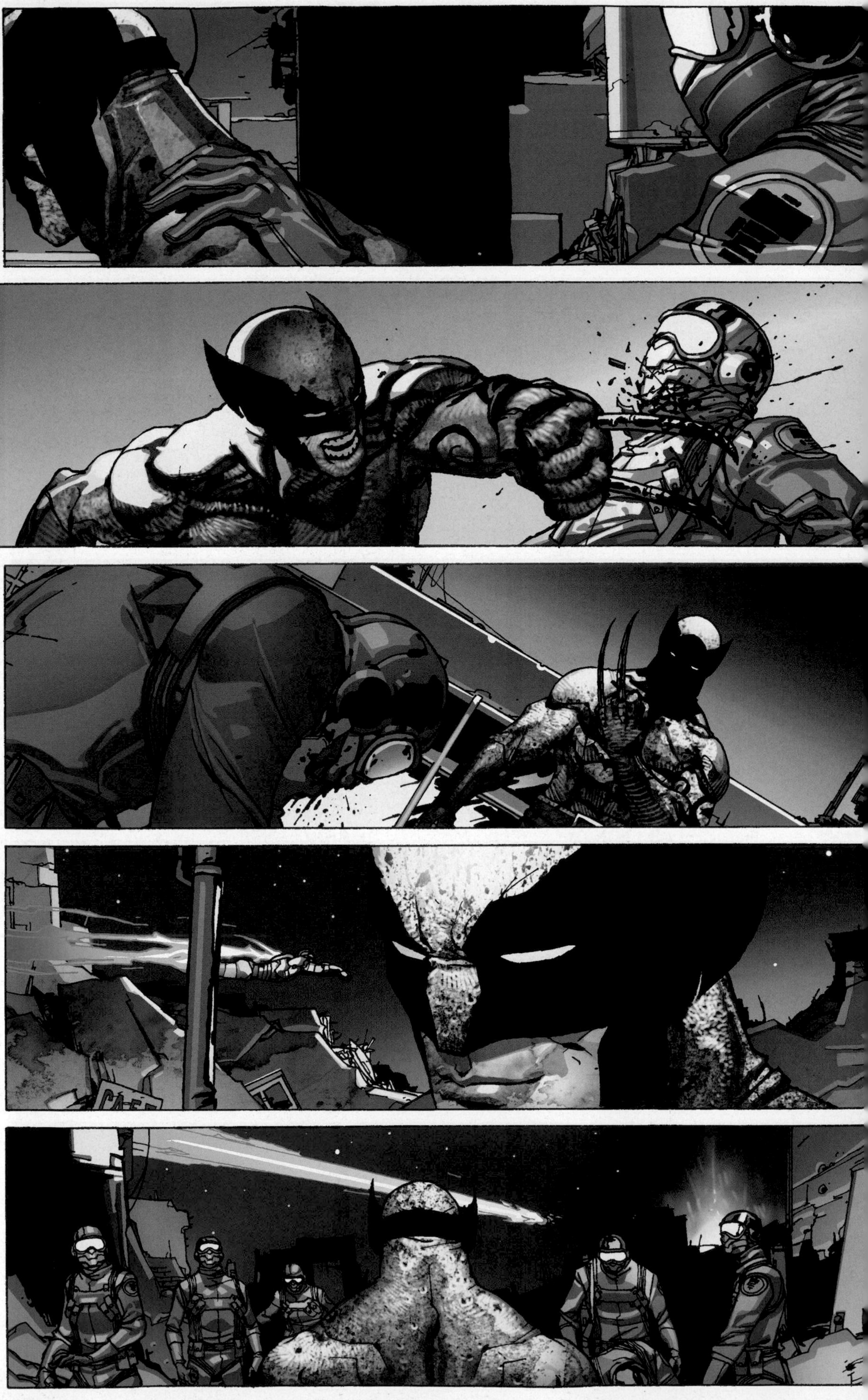

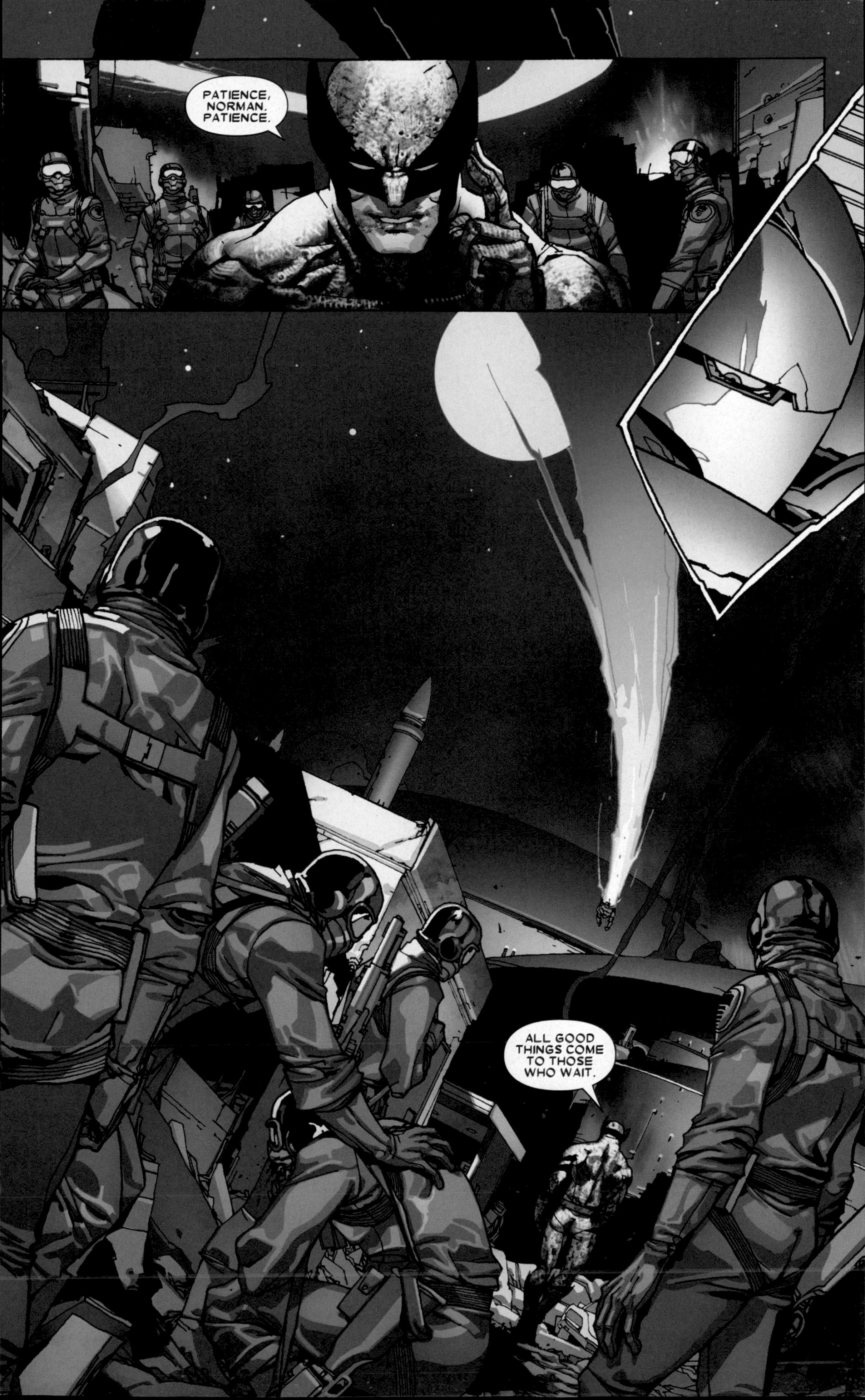
PATIENCE, NORMAN. PATIENCE.
ALL GOOD THINGS COME TO THOSE WHO WAIT.

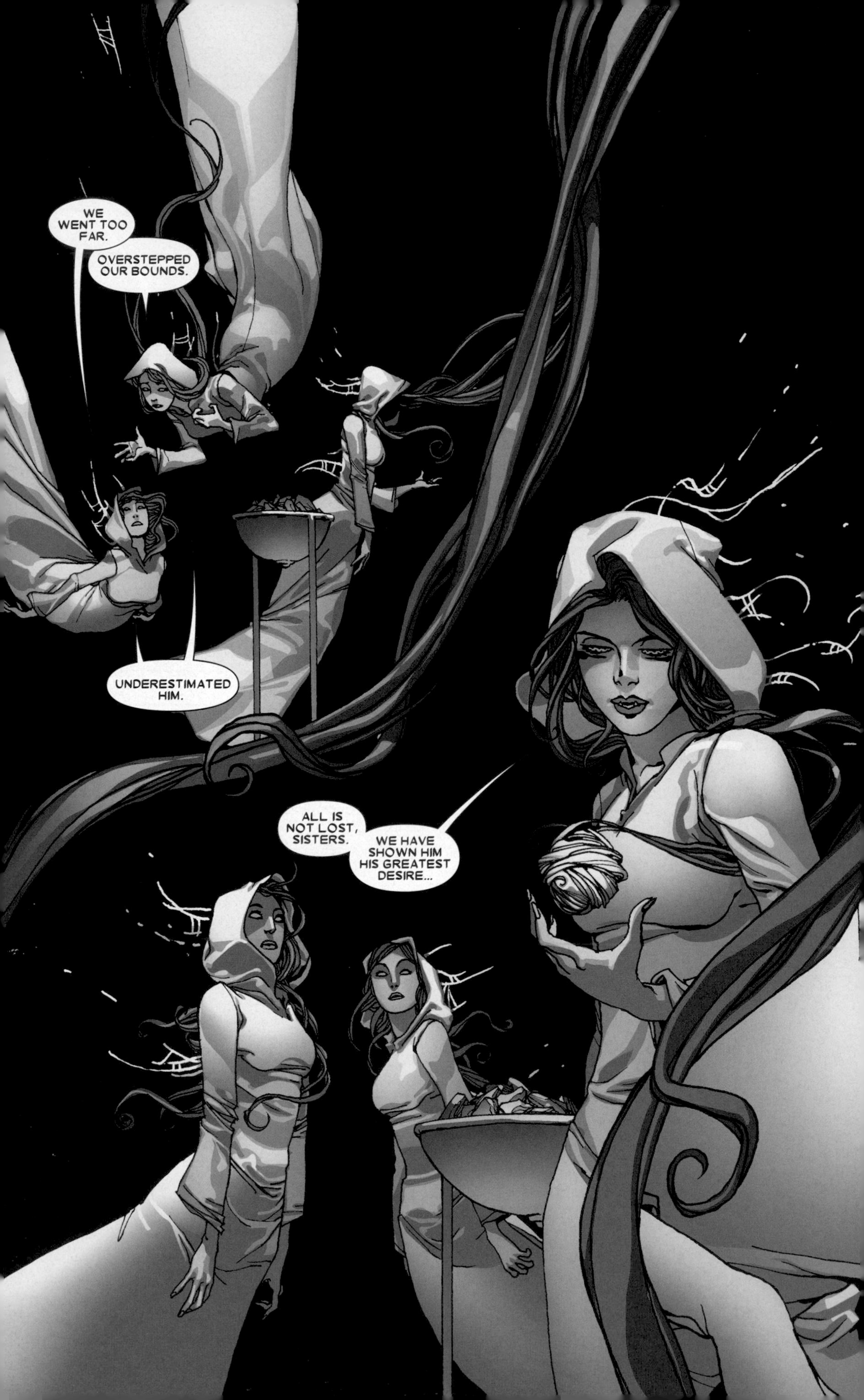
WE WENT TOO FAR.
OVERSTEPPED OUR BOUNDS.
UNDERESTIMATED HIM.
ALL IS NOT LOST, SISTERS.
WE HAVE SHOWN HIM HIS GREATEST DESIRE...

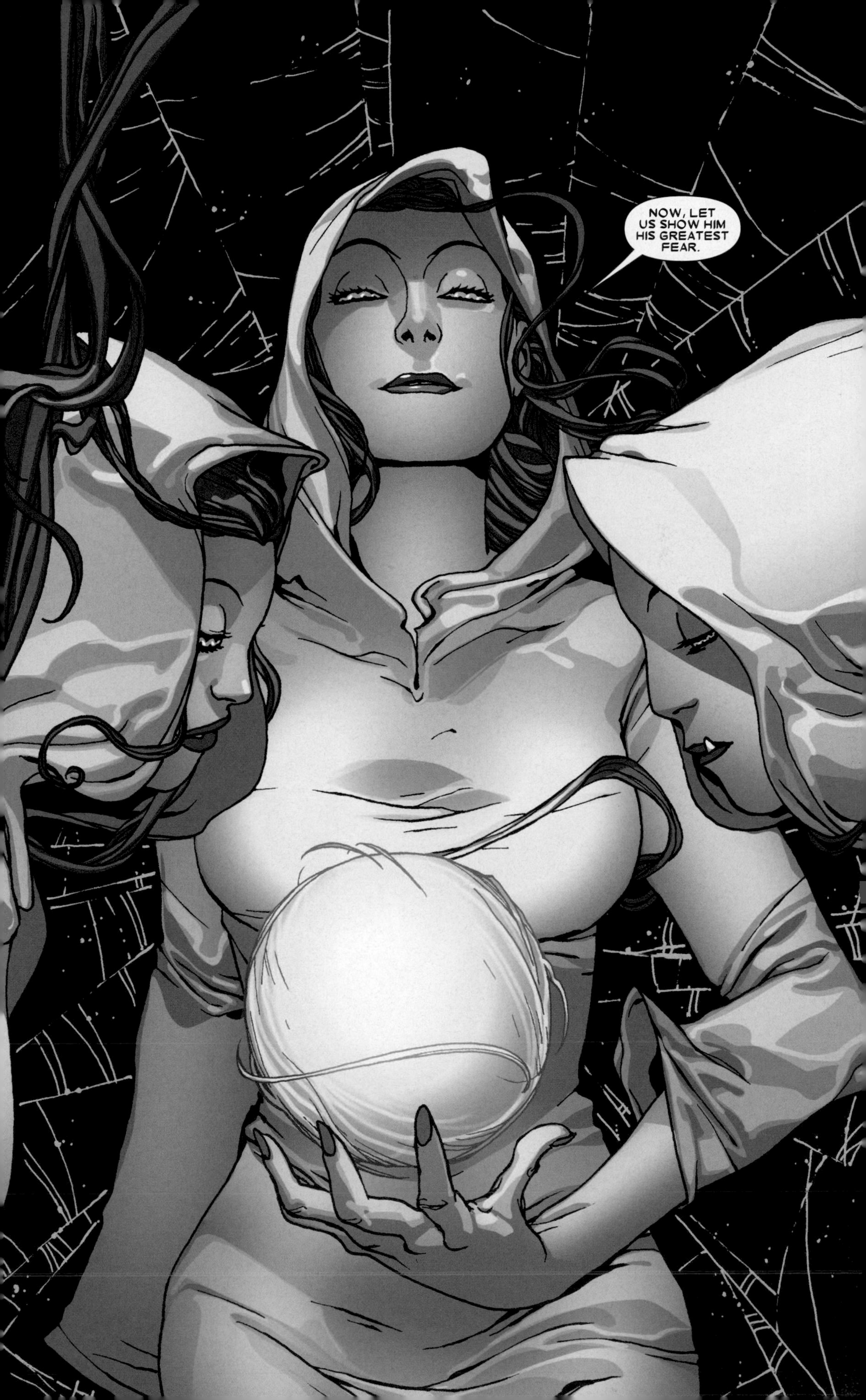
NOW, LET US SHOW HIM HIS GREATEST FEAR.

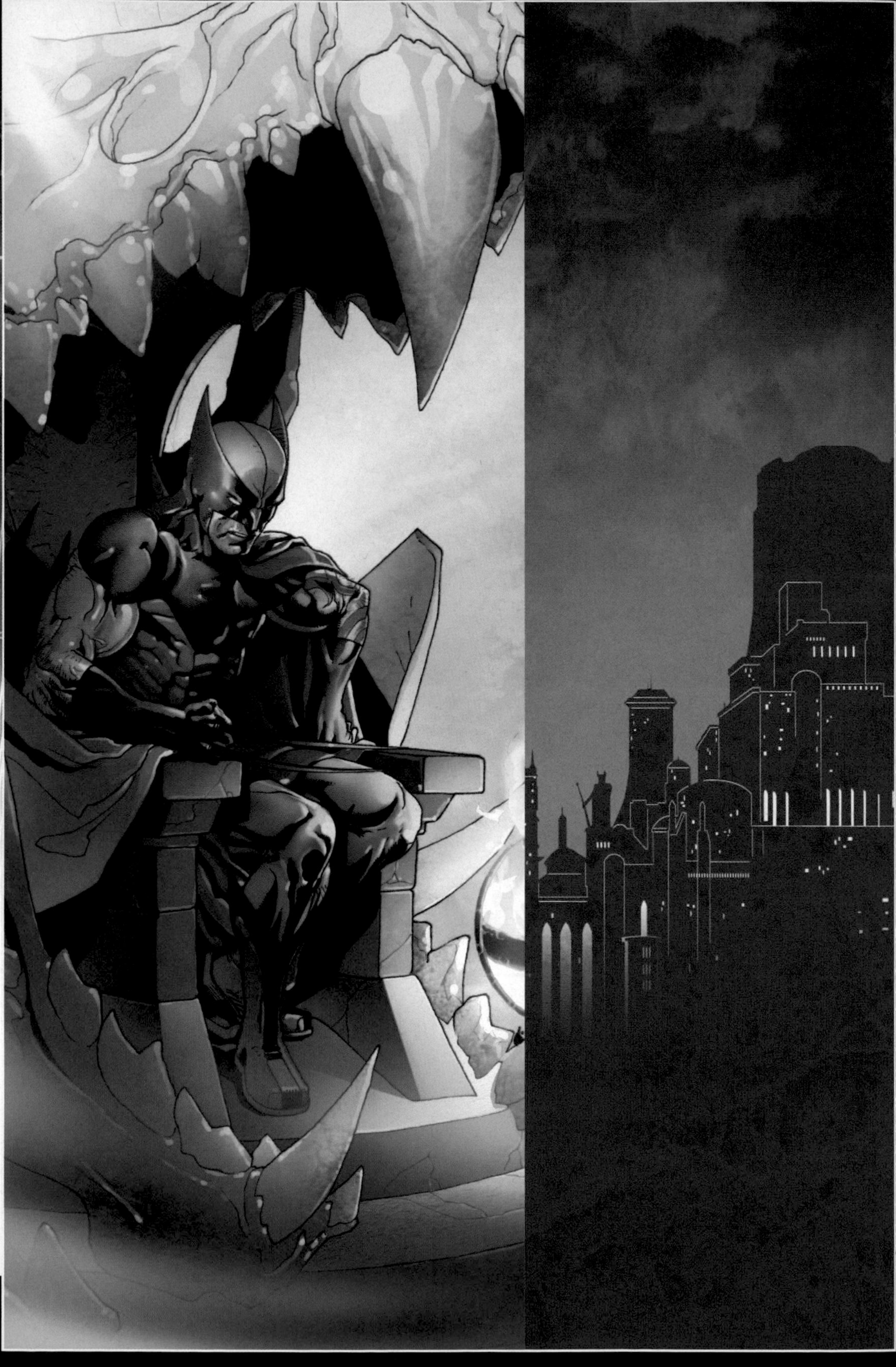

DARK WOLVERINE #84

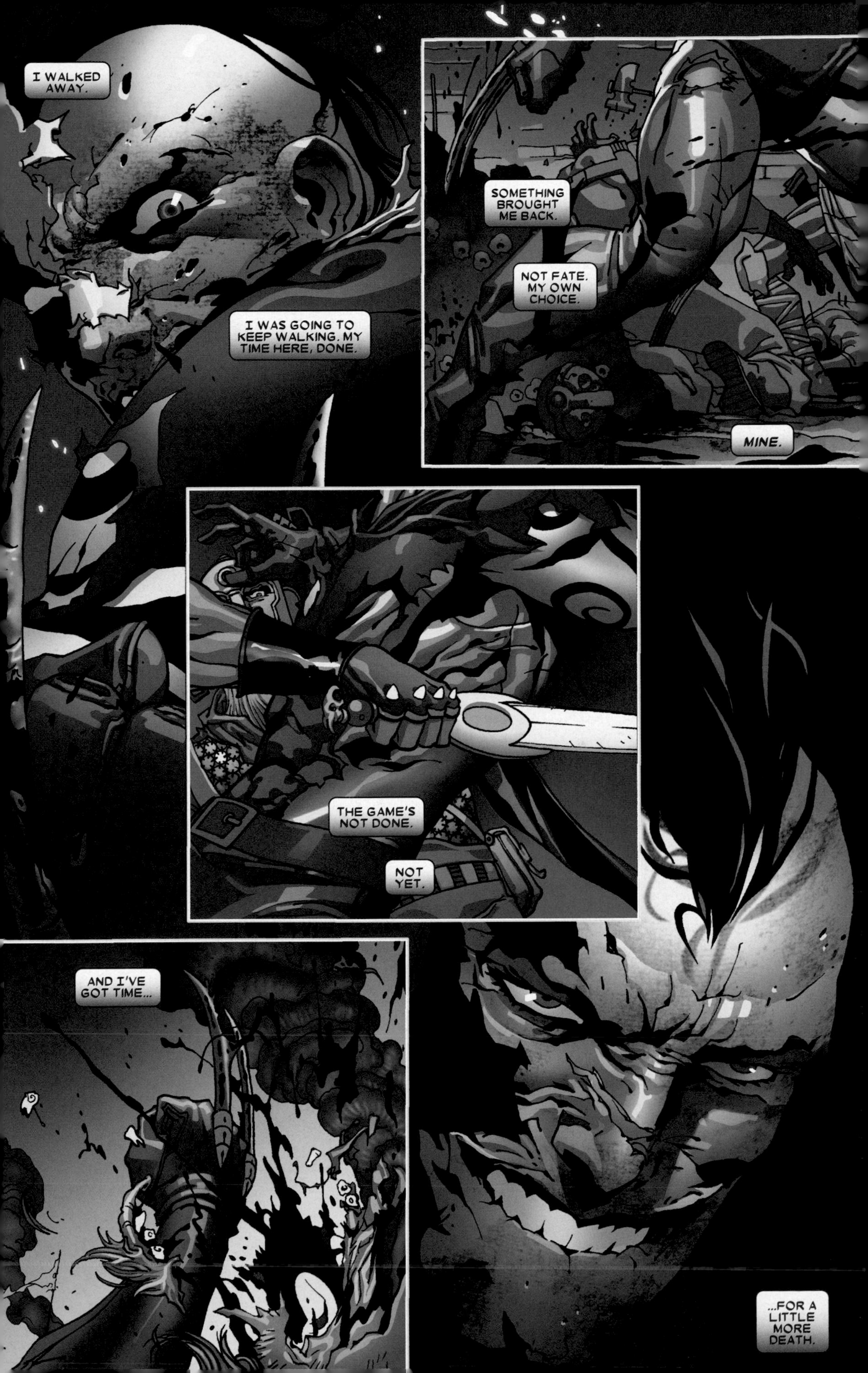
I WALKED AWAY.
I WAS GOING TO KEEP WALKING. MY TIME HERE, DONE.
SOMETHING BROUGHT ME BACK.
NOT FATE. MY OWN CHOICE.
MINE.
THE GAME'S NOT DONE.
NOT YET.
AND I'VE GOT TIME...
...FOR A LITTLE MORE DEATH.

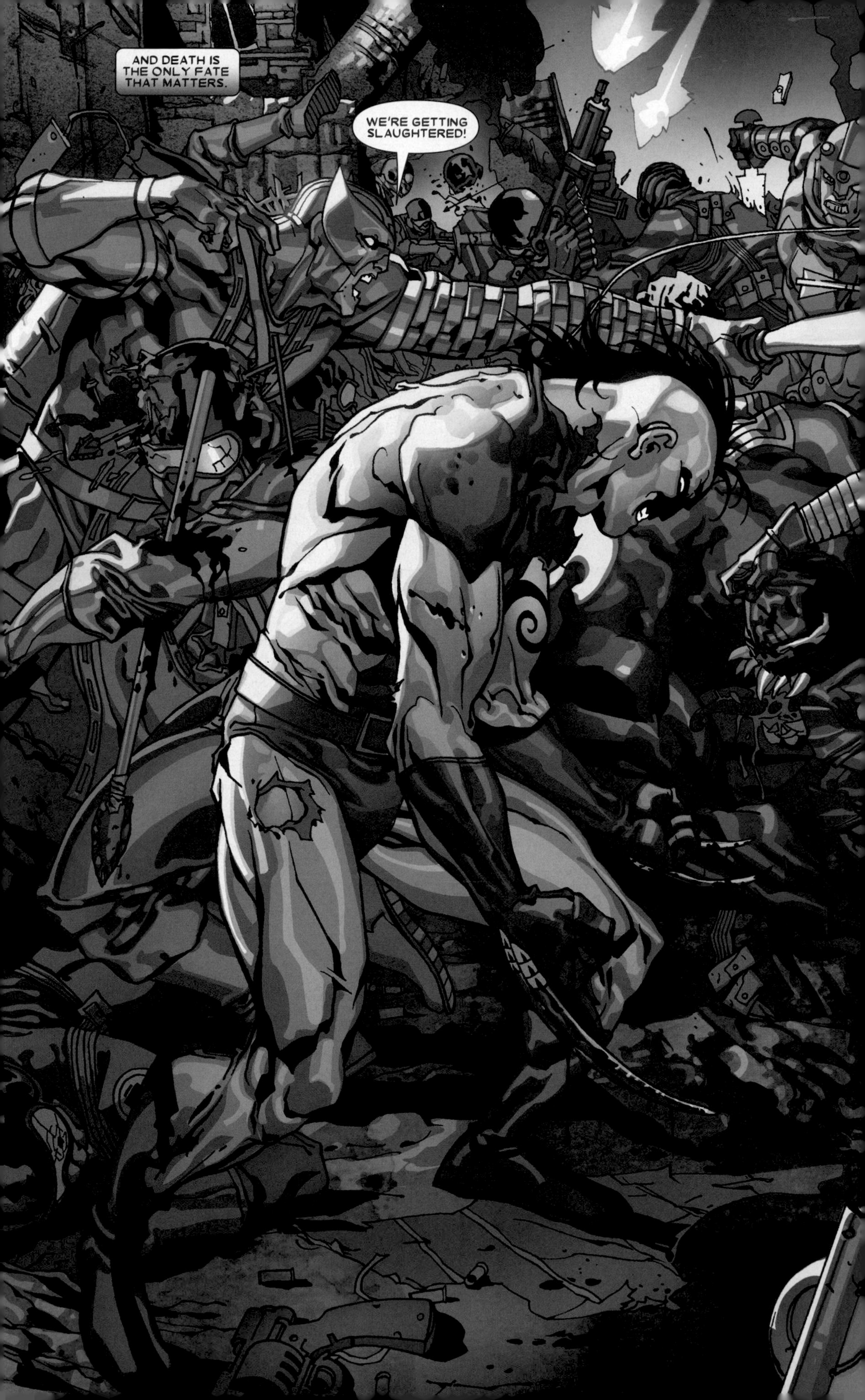
AND DEATH IS THE ONLY FATE THAT MATTERS.
WE'RE GETTING SLAUGHTERED!

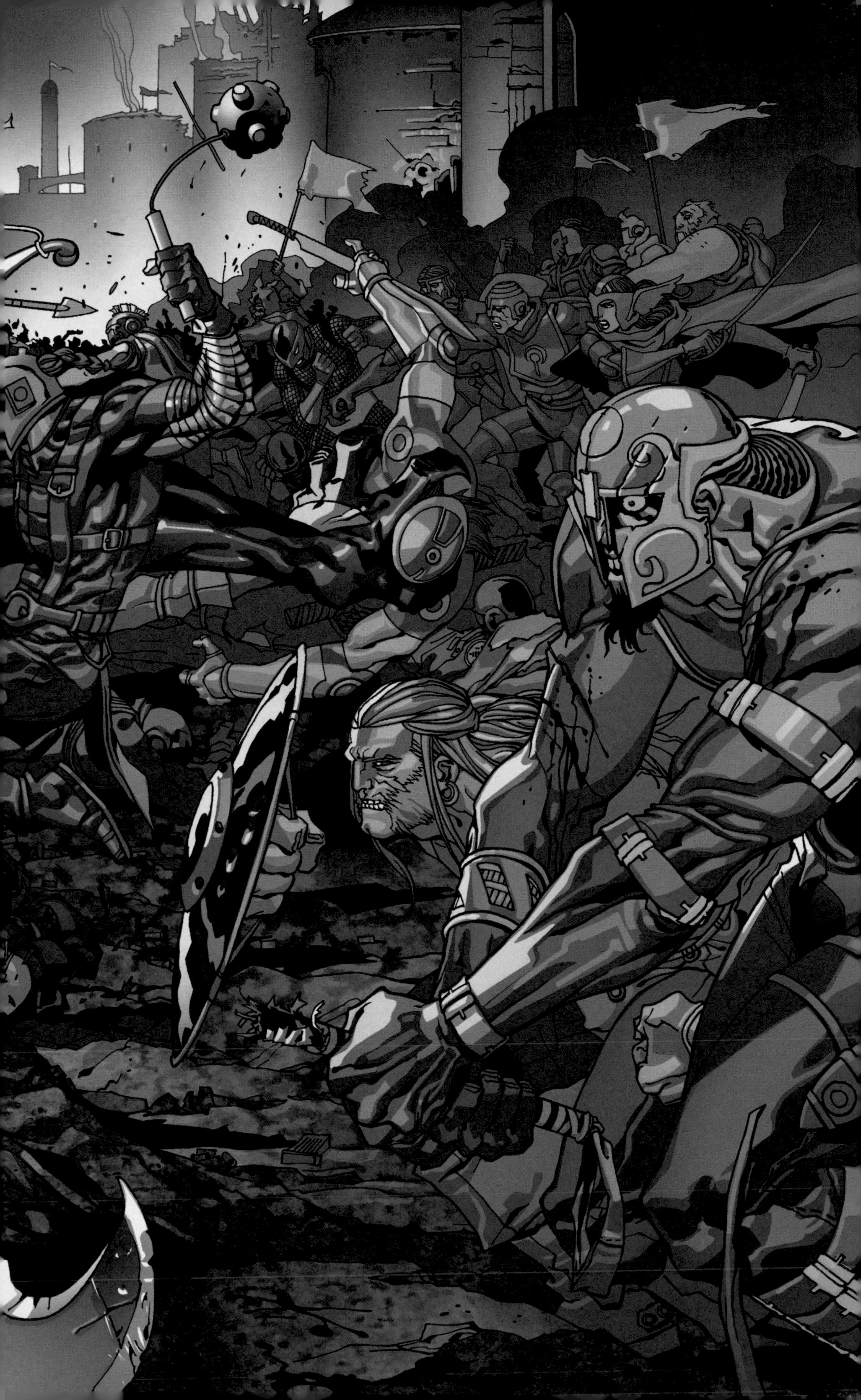

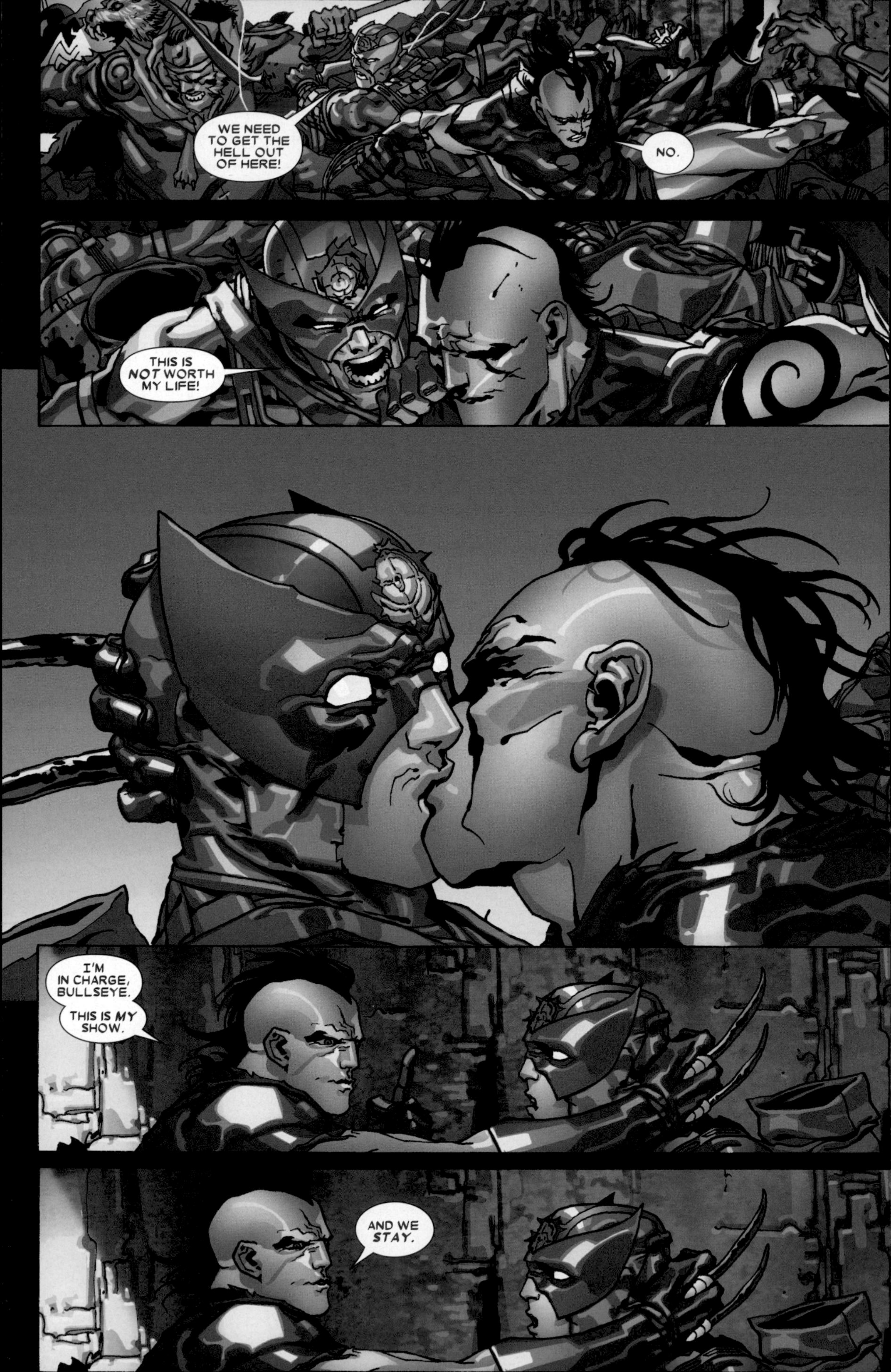
WE NEED TO GET THE HELL OUT OF HERE!
NO.
THIS IS *NOT* WORTH MY LIFE!
I'M IN CHARGE, BULLSEYE.
THIS IS *MY* SHOW.
AND WE *STAY*.

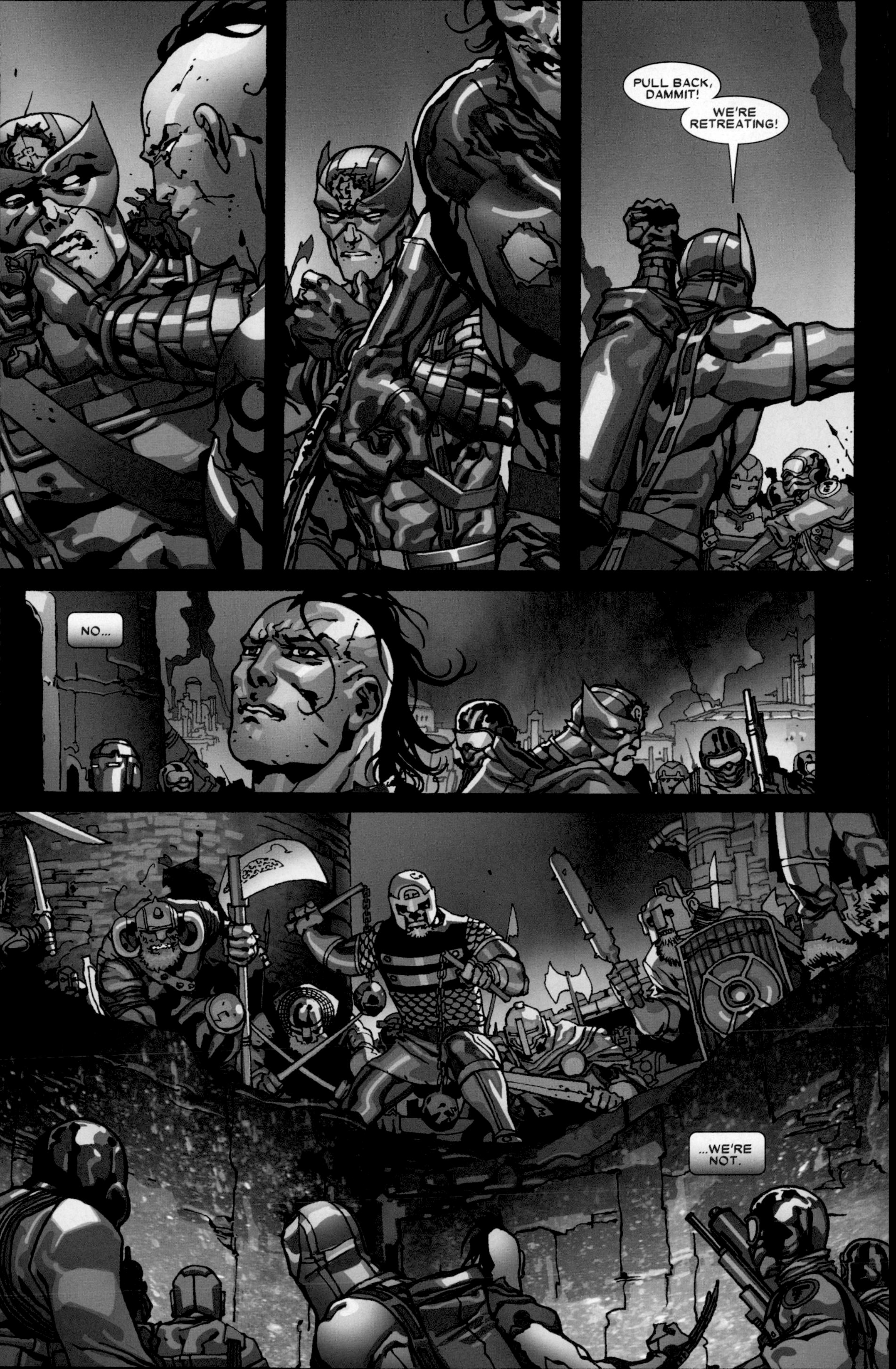
PULL BACK, DAMMIT!
WE'RE RETREATING!
NO...
...WE'RE NOT.

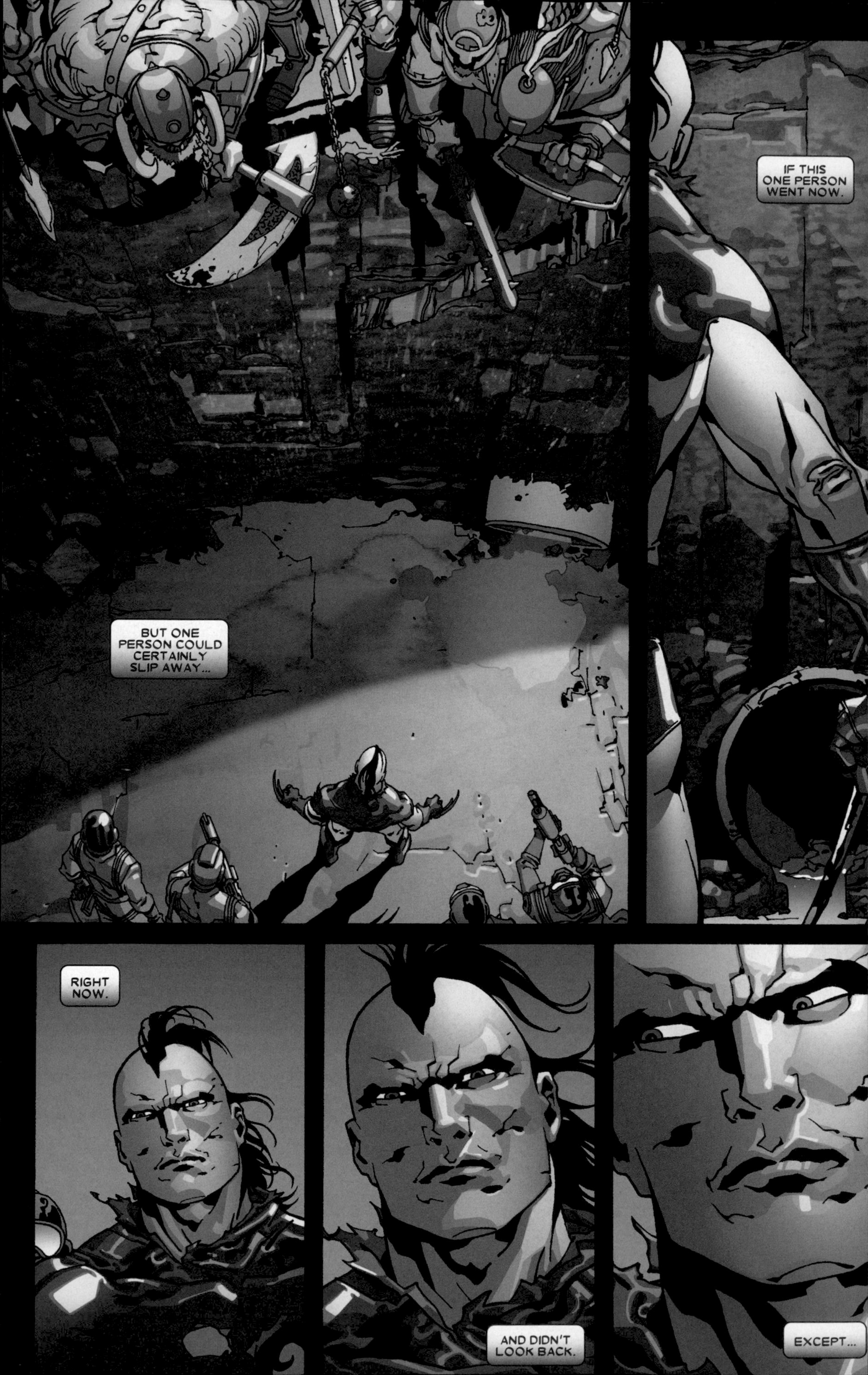
BUT ONE PERSON COULD CERTAINLY SLIP AWAY...
IF THIS ONE PERSON WENT NOW.
RIGHT NOW.
AND DIDN'T LOOK BACK.
EXCEPT...

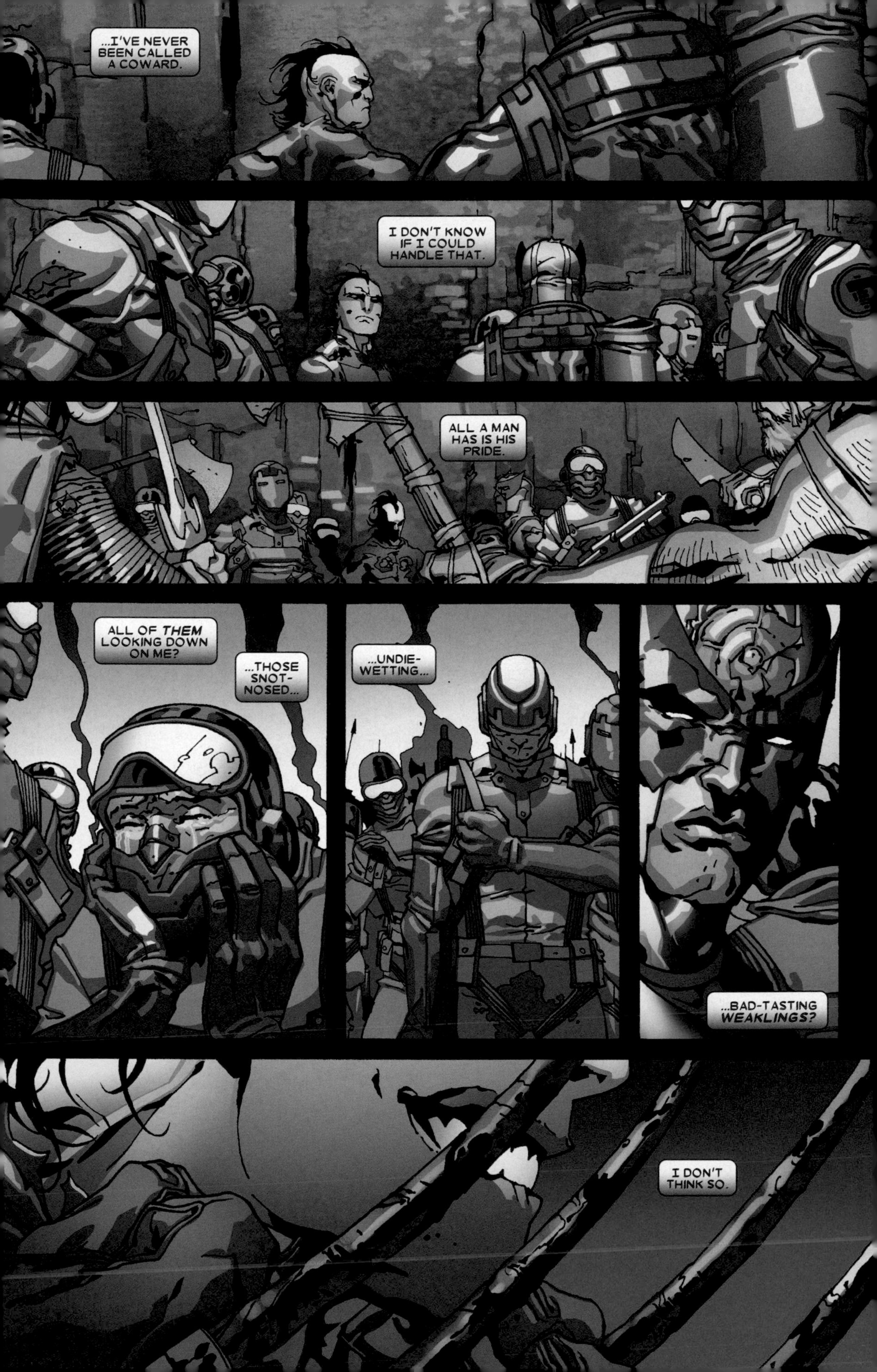
...I'VE NEVER BEEN CALLED A COWARD.
I DON'T KNOW IF I COULD HANDLE THAT.
ALL A MAN HAS IS HIS PRIDE.
ALL OF *THEM* LOOKING DOWN ON ME?
...THOSE SNOT-NOSED...
...UNDIE-WETTING...
...BAD-TASTING *WEAKLINGS?*
I DON'T THINK SO.

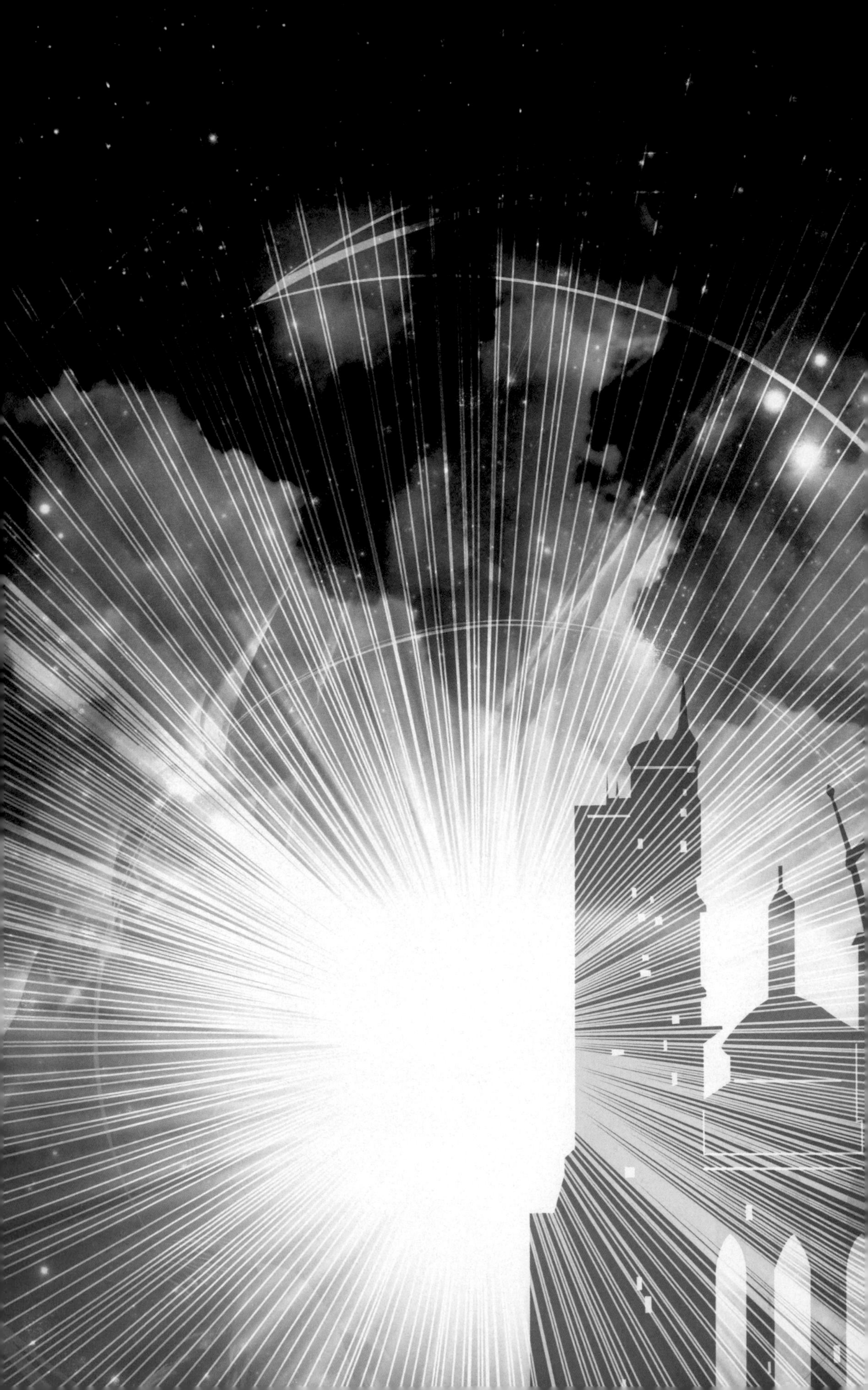

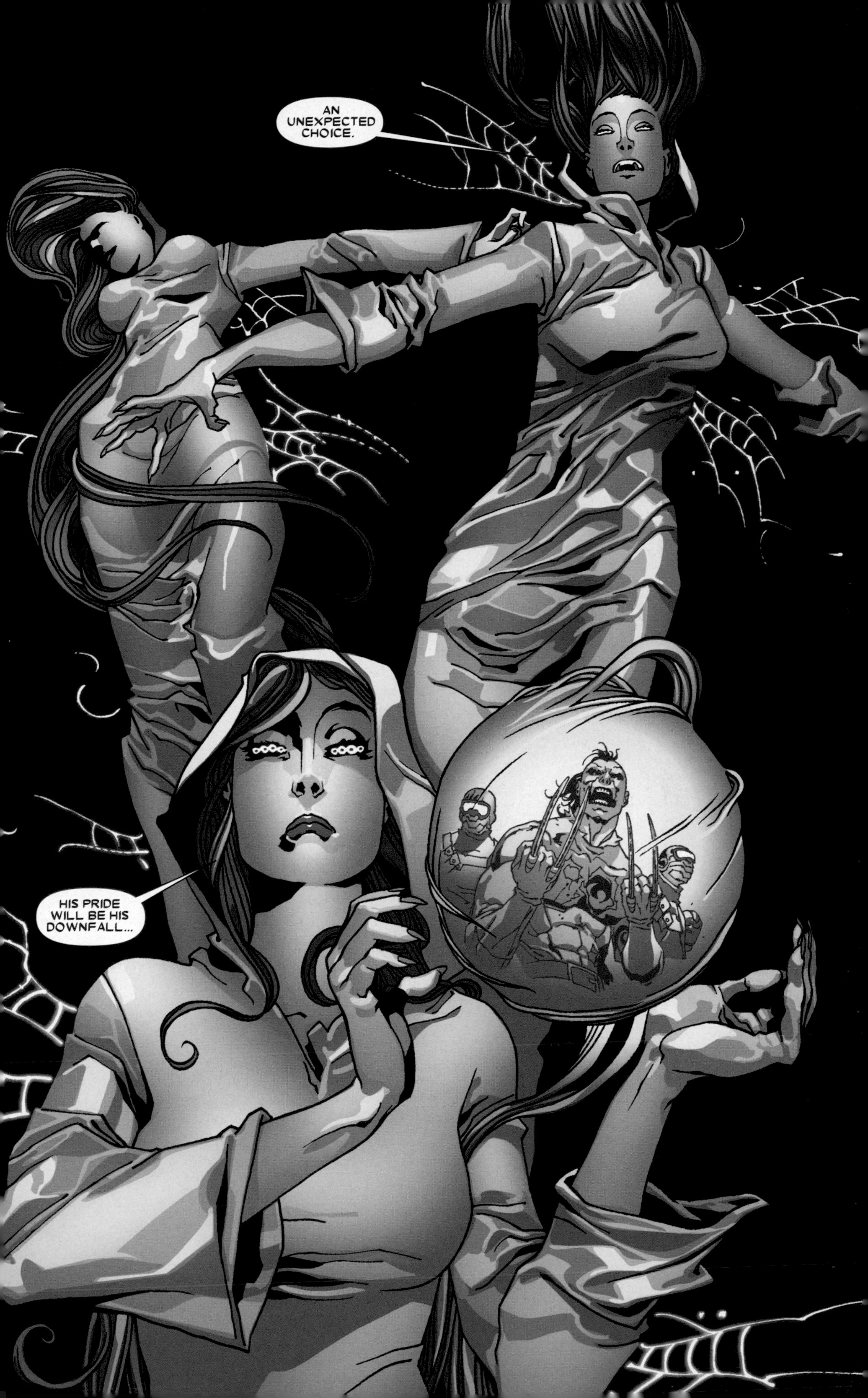
AN UNEXPECTED CHOICE.
HIS PRIDE WILL BE HIS DOWNFALL...

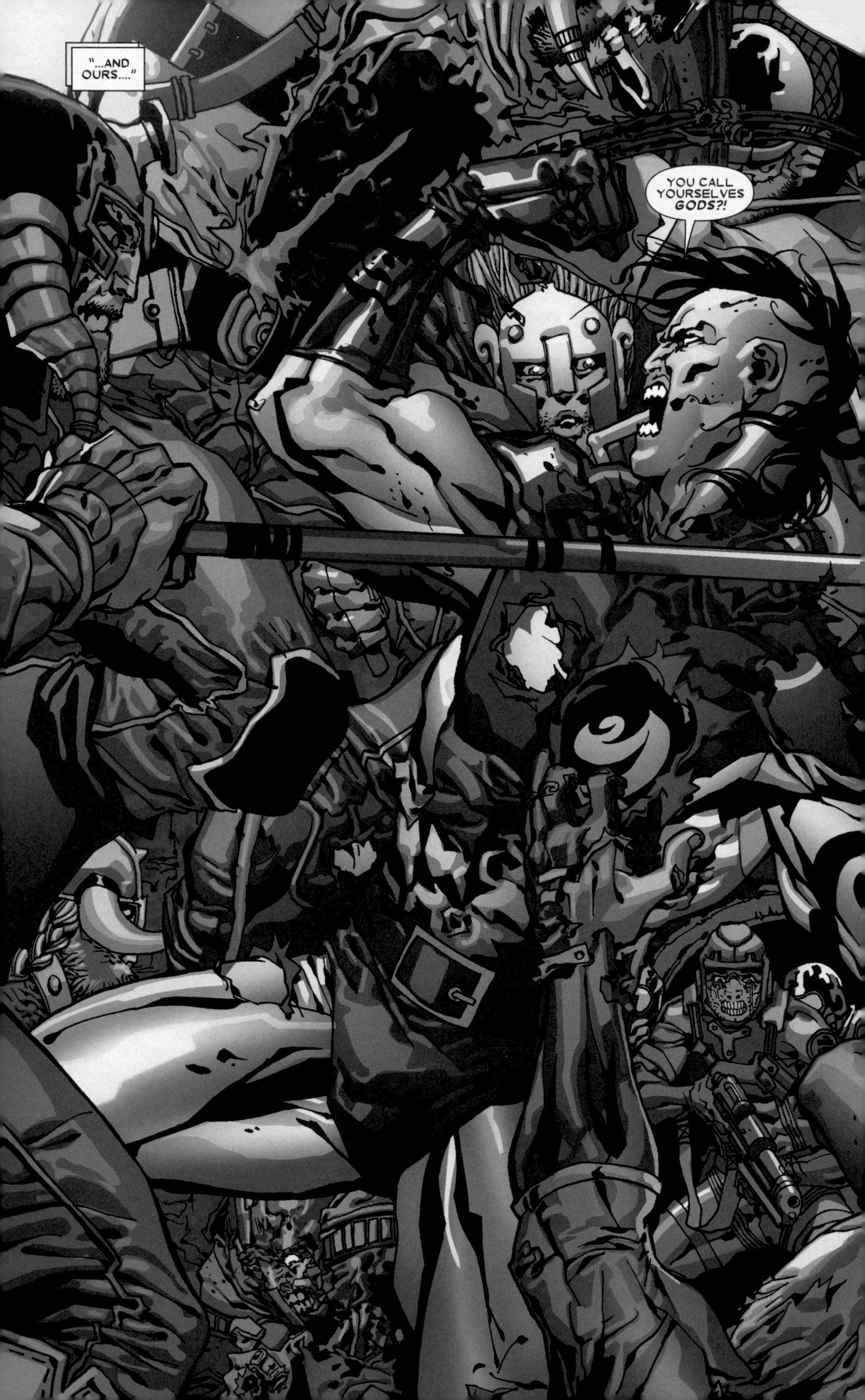
"...AND OURS...."
YOU CALL YOURSELVES GODS?!

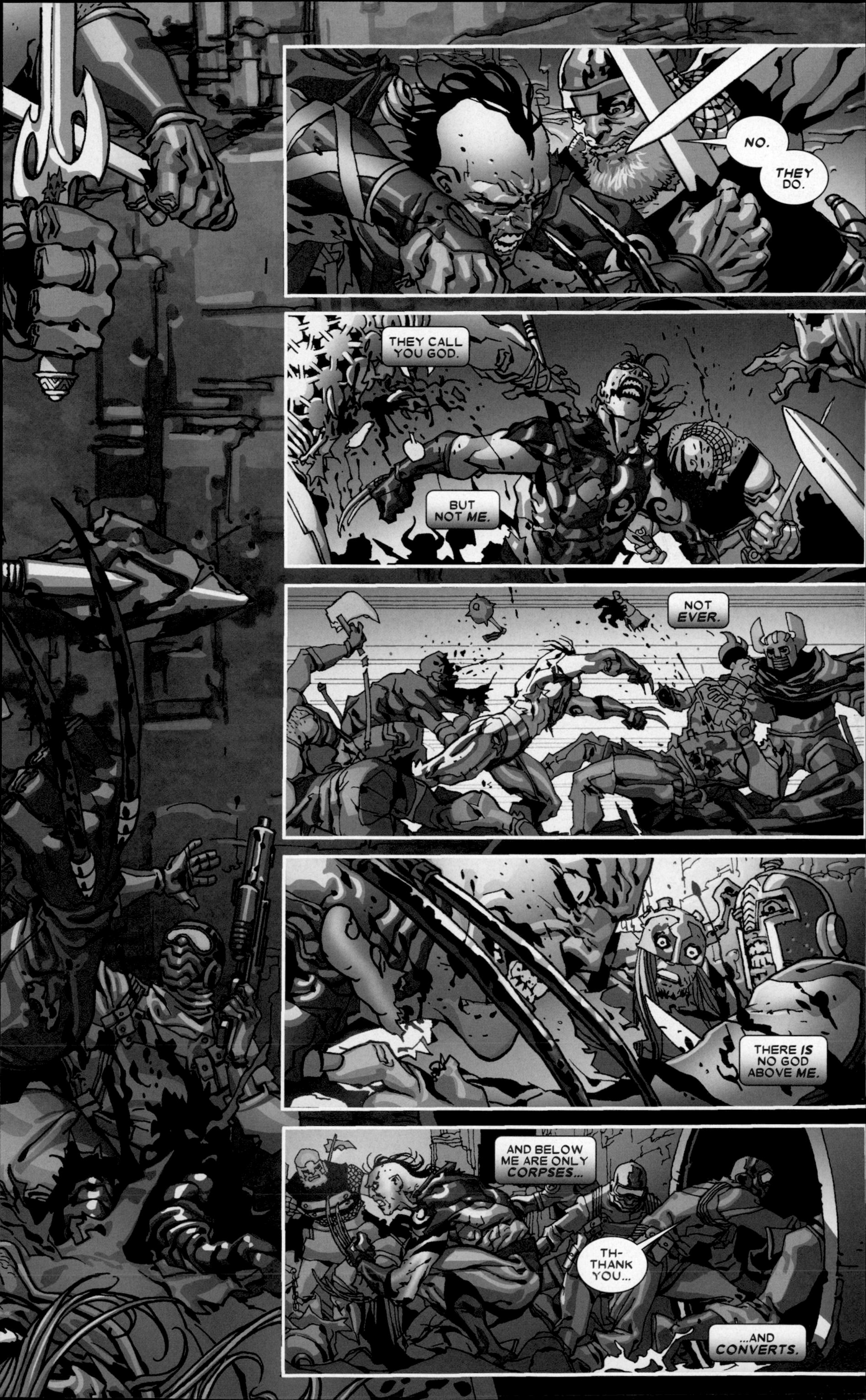
NO.
THEY DO.
THEY CALL YOU GOD.
BUT NOT ME.
NOT EVER.
THERE IS NO GOD ABOVE ME.
AND BELOW ME ARE ONLY CORPSES...
TH- THANK YOU...
...AND CONVERTS.

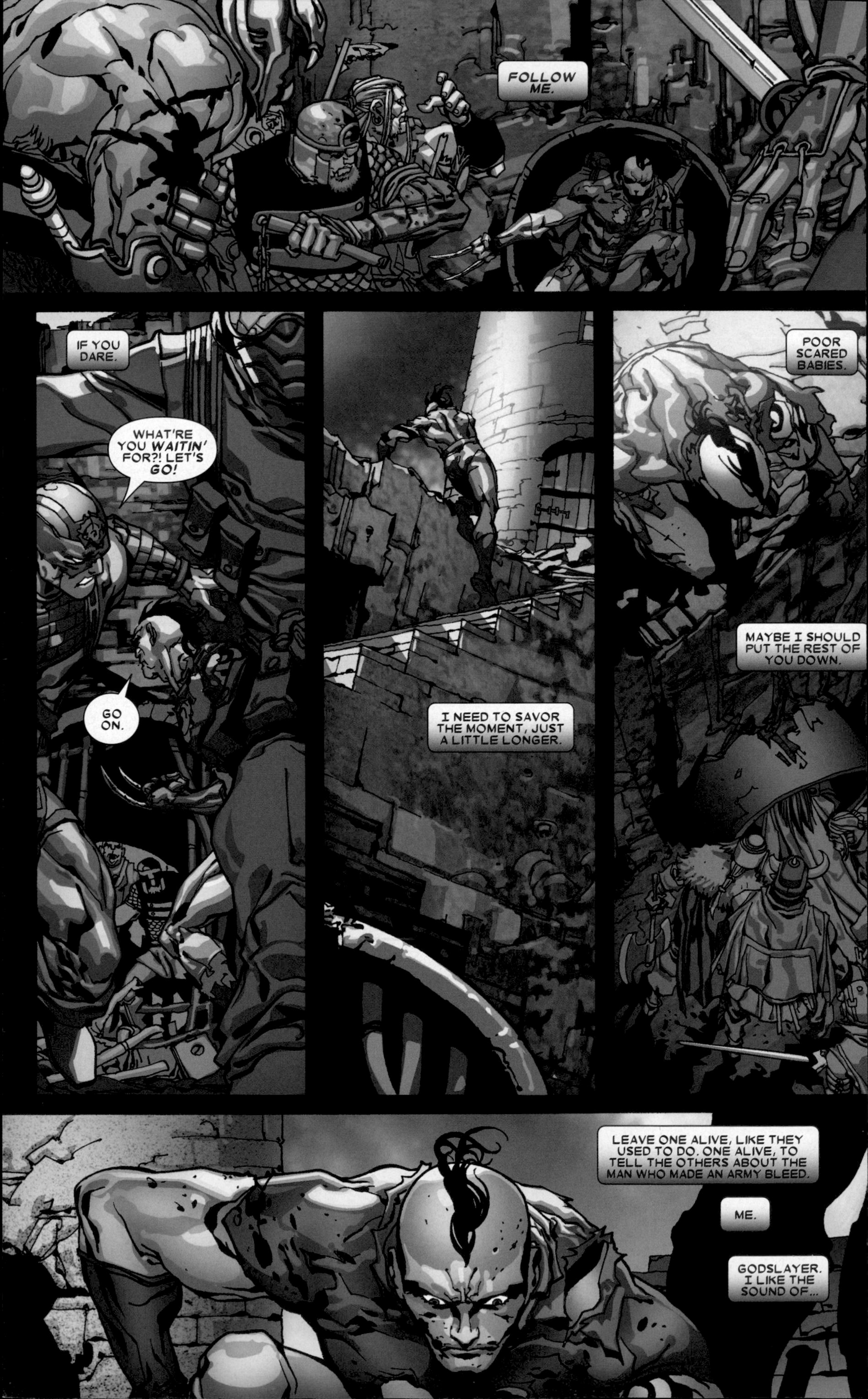
FOLLOW ME.
IF YOU DARE.
WHAT'RE YOU WAITIN' FOR?! LET'S GO!
GO ON.
I NEED TO SAVOR THE MOMENT, JUST A LITTLE LONGER.
POOR SCARED BABIES.
MAYBE I SHOULD PUT THE REST OF YOU DOWN.
LEAVE ONE ALIVE, LIKE THEY USED TO DO. ONE ALIVE, TO TELL THE OTHERS ABOUT THE MAN WHO MADE AN ARMY BLEED.
ME.
GODSLAYER. I LIKE THE SOUND OF...

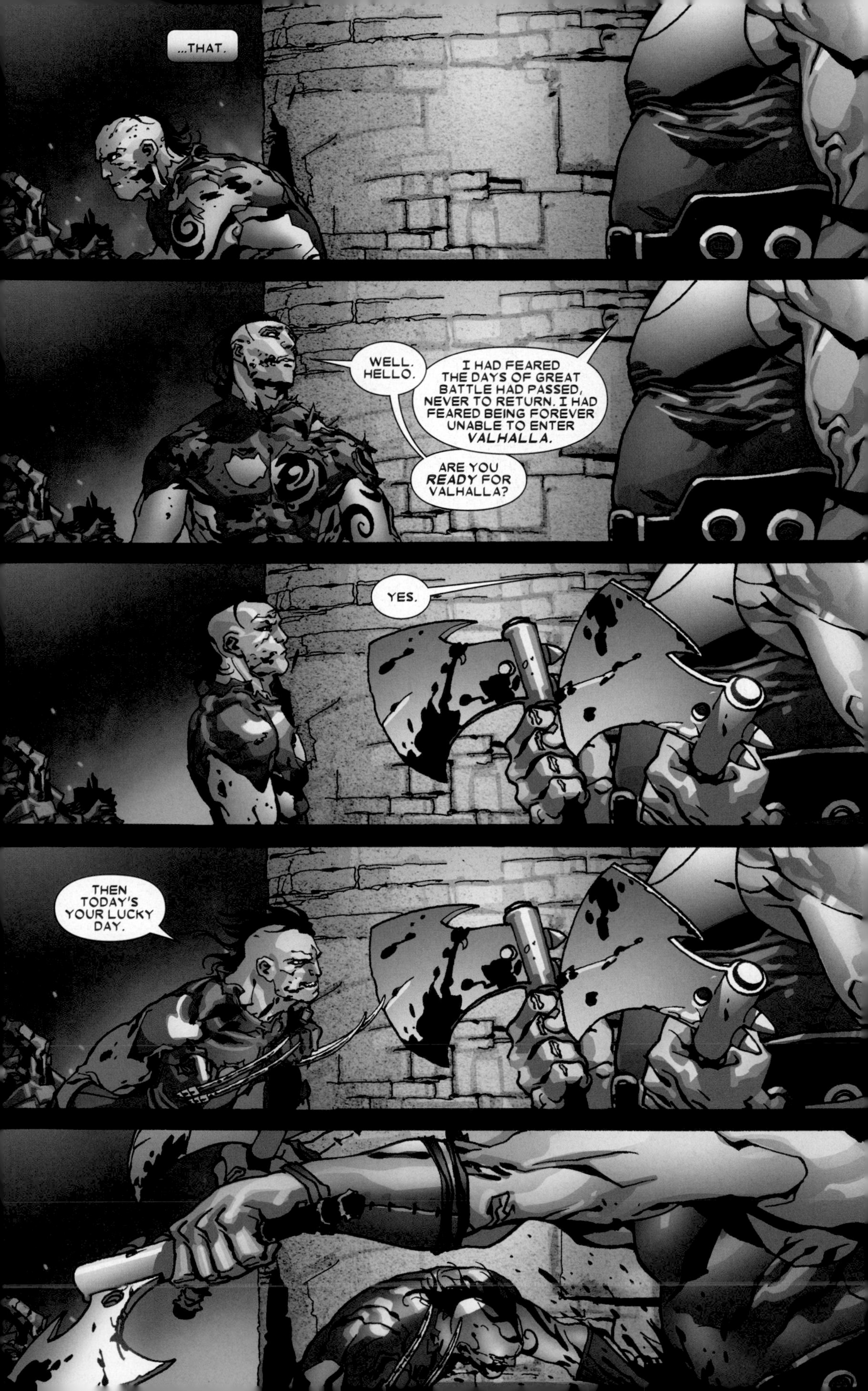
...THAT.
WELL. HELLO.
I HAD FEARED THE DAYS OF GREAT BATTLE HAD PASSED, NEVER TO RETURN. I HAD FEARED BEING FOREVER UNABLE TO ENTER VALHALLA.
ARE YOU READY FOR VALHALLA?
YES.
THEN TODAY'S YOUR LUCKY DAY.

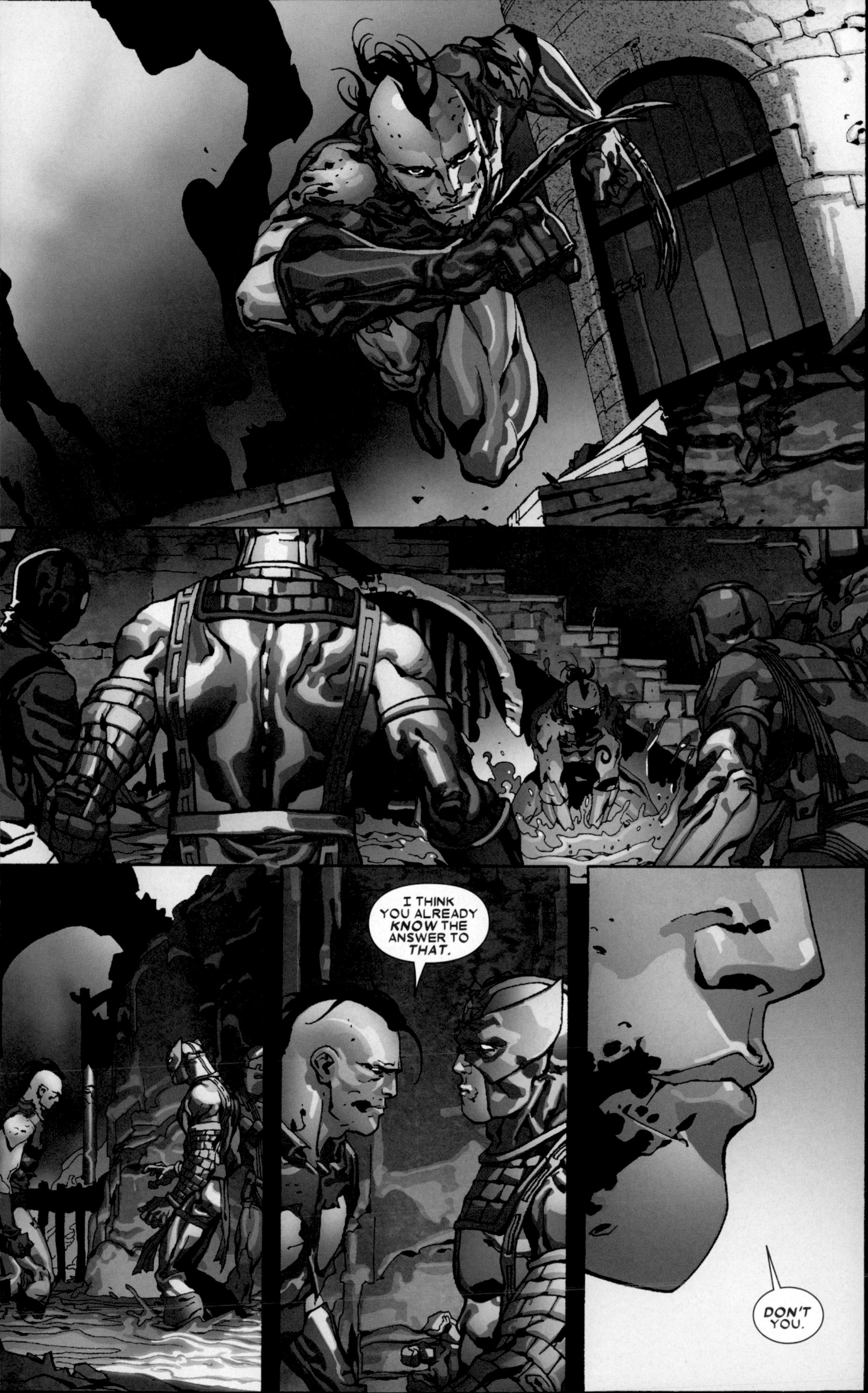
I THINK YOU ALREADY KNOW THE ANSWER TO THAT.
DON'T YOU.

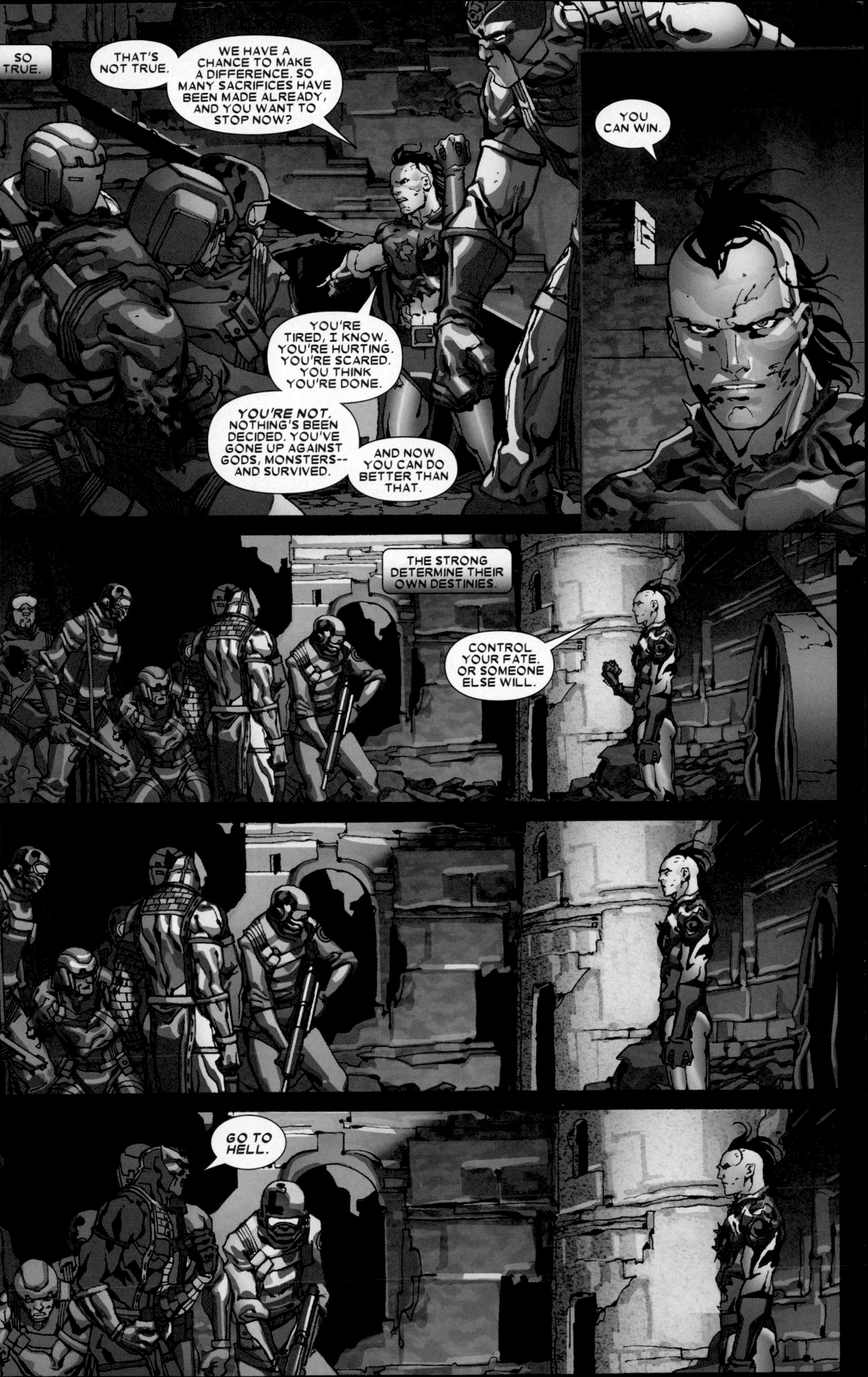
SO TRUE.
THAT'S NOT TRUE.
WE HAVE A CHANCE TO MAKE A DIFFERENCE. SO MANY SACRIFICES HAVE BEEN MADE ALREADY, AND YOU WANT TO STOP NOW?
YOU CAN WIN.
YOU'RE TIRED, I KNOW. YOU'RE HURTING. YOU'RE SCARED. YOU THINK YOU'RE DONE.
YOU'RE NOT. NOTHING'S BEEN DECIDED. YOU'VE GONE UP AGAINST GODS, MONSTERS-- AND SURVIVED.
AND NOW YOU CAN DO BETTER THAN THAT.
THE STRONG DETERMINE THEIR OWN DESTINIES.
CONTROL YOUR FATE. OR SOMEONE ELSE WILL.
GO TO HELL.

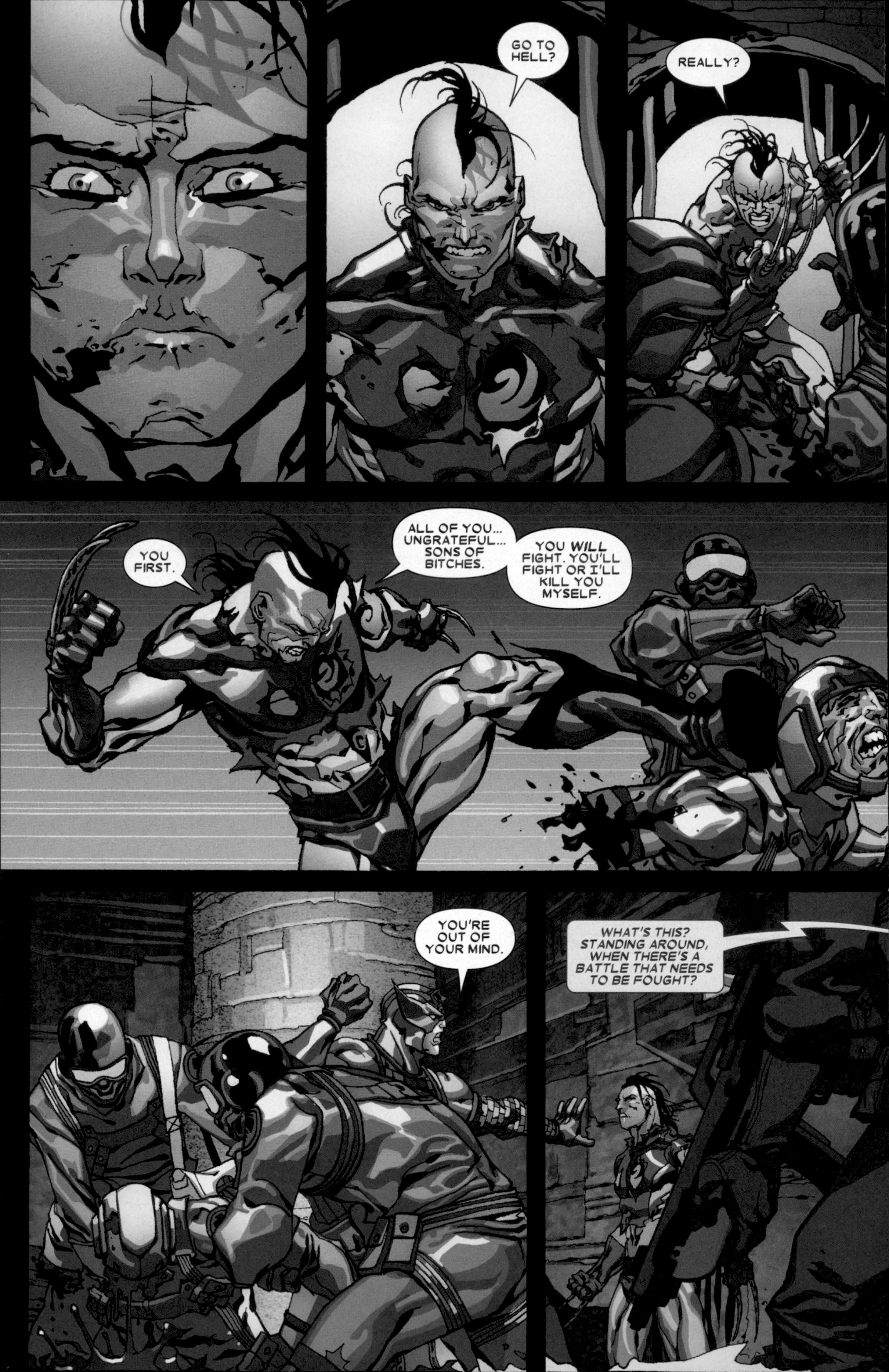
GO TO HELL?
REALLY?
YOU FIRST.
ALL OF YOU... UNGRATEFUL... SONS OF BITCHES.
YOU WILL FIGHT. YOU'LL FIGHT OR I'LL KILL YOU MYSELF.
YOU'RE OUT OF YOUR MIND.
WHAT'S THIS? STANDING AROUND, WHEN THERE'S A BATTLE THAT NEEDS TO BE FOUGHT?

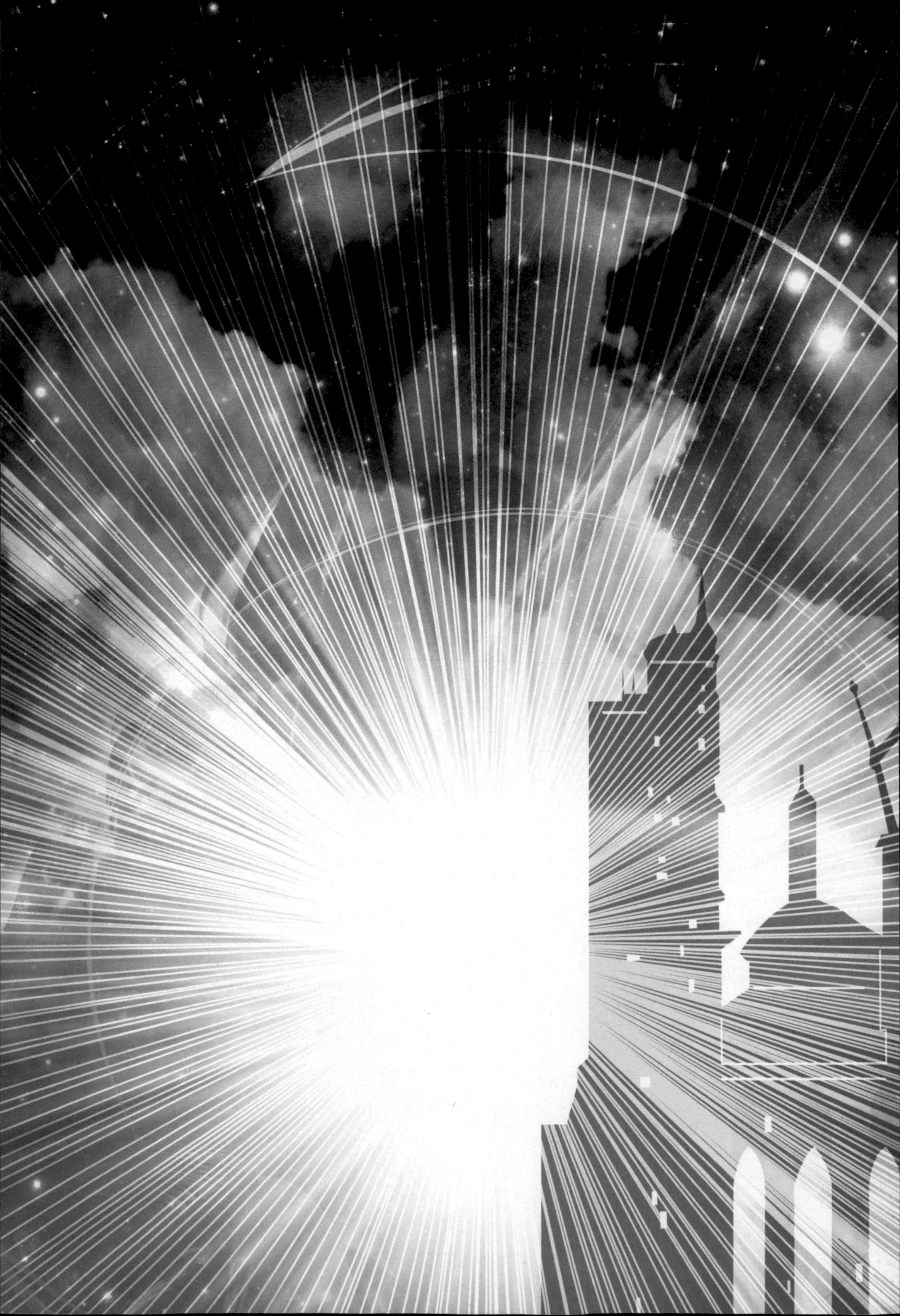

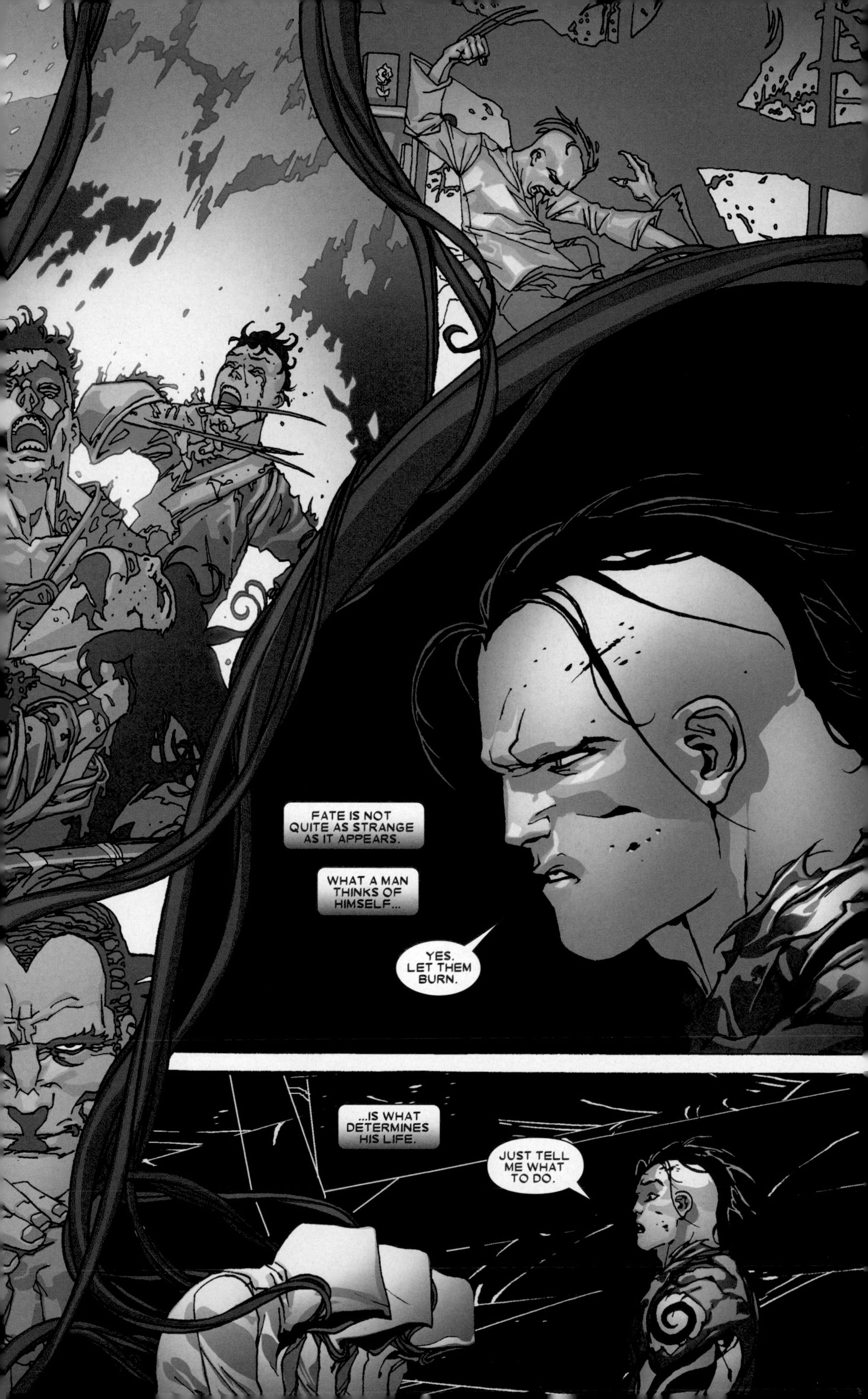
FATE IS NOT QUITE AS STRANGE AS IT APPEARS.
WHAT A MAN THINKS OF HIMSELF...
YES. LET THEM BURN.
...IS WHAT DETERMINES HIS LIFE.
JUST TELL ME WHAT TO DO.

DARK WOLVERINE #84 DEADPOOL VARIANT

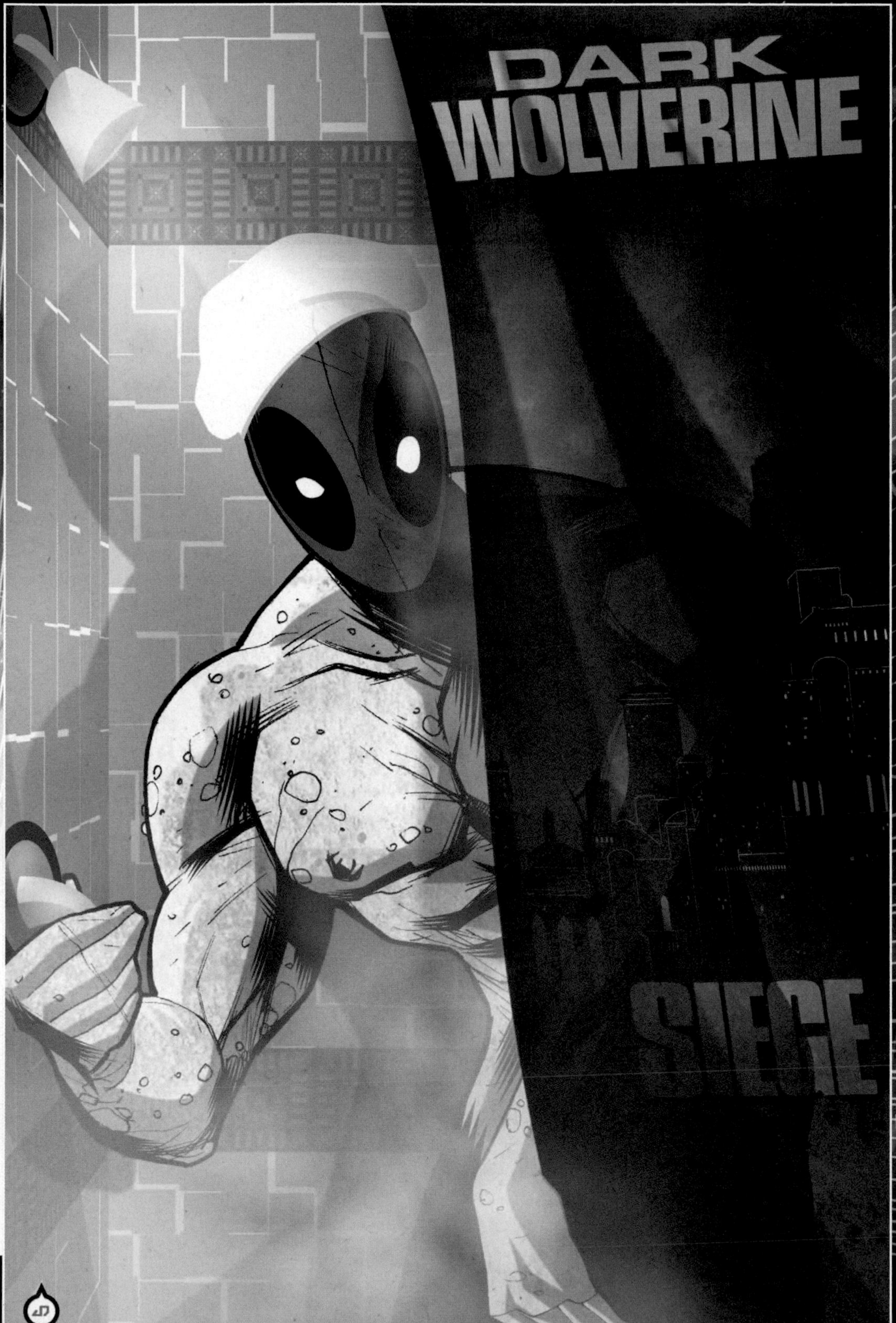
DARK
WOLVERINE
SIEGE

BY **JUAN DOE**

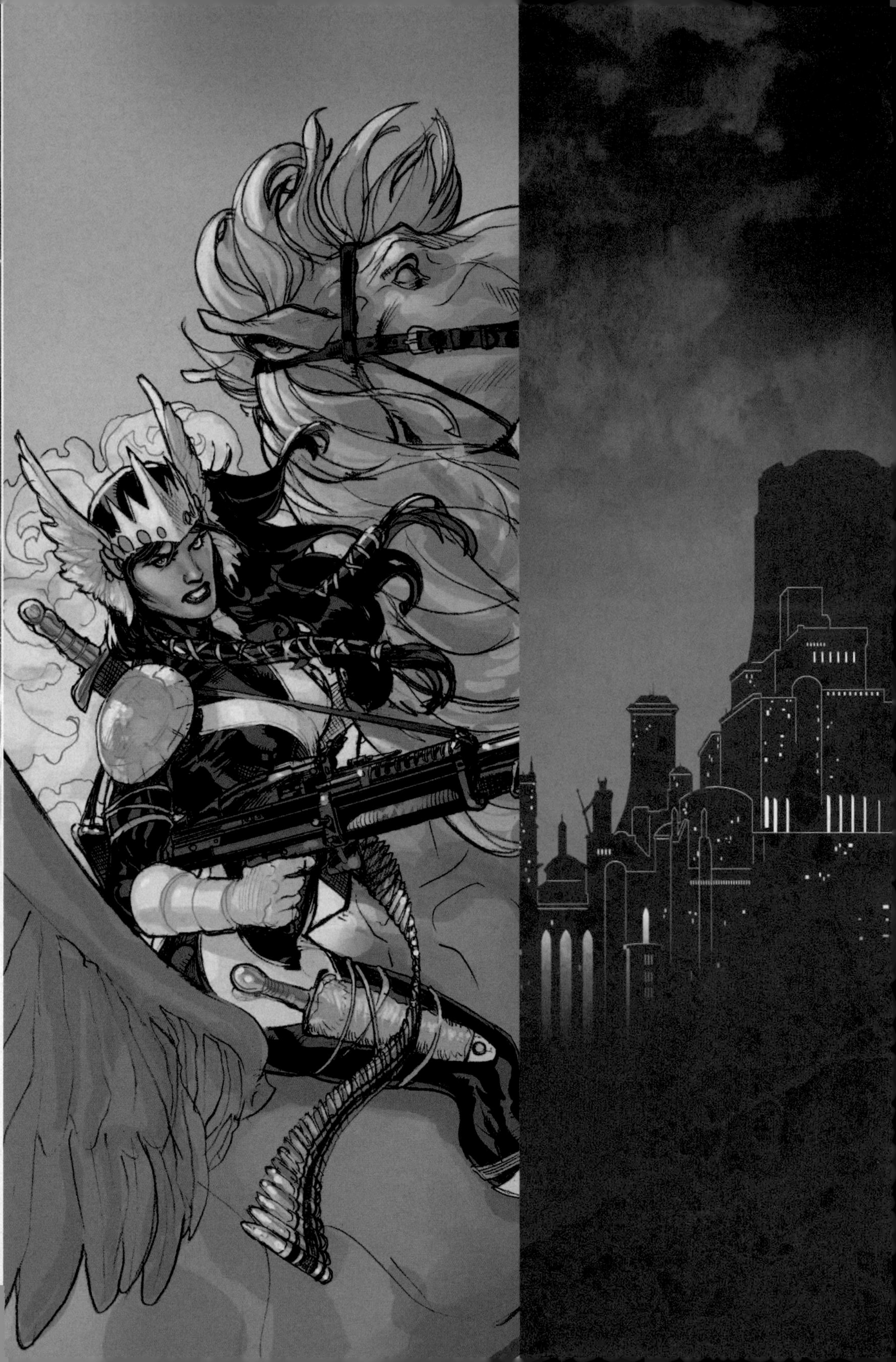

PREVIOUSLY IN

NEW MUTANTS

When Norman Obsorn, leader of the Dark Avengers, waged war on the X-Men, team leader Cyclops created a plan for fighting back. A key component of his strategy involved Dani Moonstar—depowered mutant and former Asgardian Valkyrie. Moonstar went to Hela, Asgardian goddess of death, and made a bargain with her: Hela would imbue Moonstar with the power of a Valkyrie once more so that she could repel the Dark Avengers' attack on the X-Men, but in turn, Moonstar would be indebted to the goddess.

"HEL'S VALKYRIE"

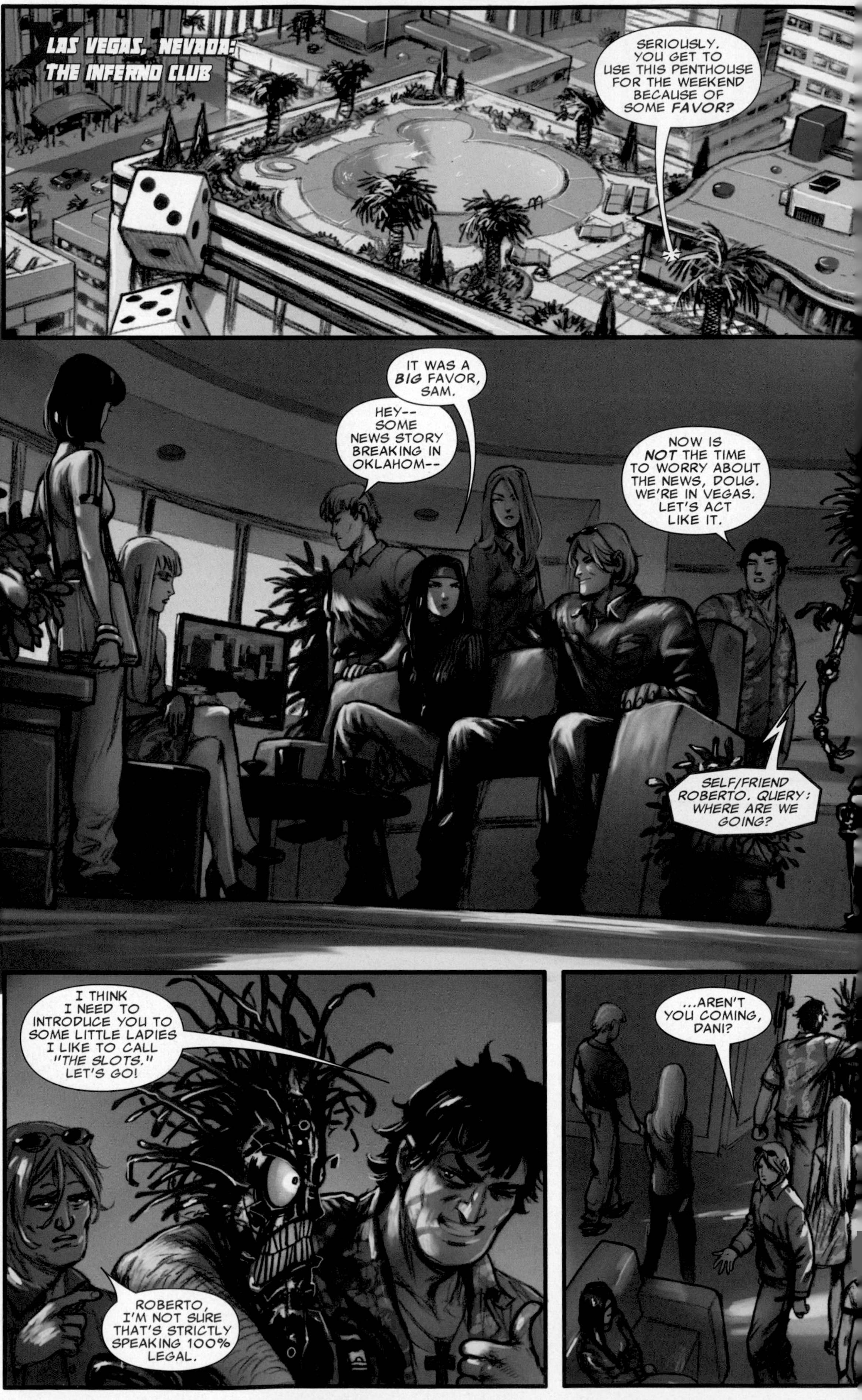
LAS VEGAS, NEVADA: THE INFERNO CLUB
SERIOUSLY. YOU GET TO USE THIS PENTHOUSE FOR THE WEEKEND BECAUSE OF SOME FAVOR?
IT WAS A BIG FAVOR, SAM.
HEY-- SOME NEWS STORY BREAKING IN OKLAHOM--
NOW IS NOT THE TIME TO WORRY ABOUT THE NEWS, DOUG. WE'RE IN VEGAS. LET'S ACT LIKE IT.
SELF/FRIEND ROBERTO. QUERY: WHERE ARE WE GOING?
I THINK I NEED TO INTRODUCE YOU TO SOME LITTLE LADIES I LIKE TO CALL "THE SLOTS." LET'S GO!
ROBERTO, I'M NOT SURE THAT'S STRICTLY SPEAKING 100% LEGAL.
...AREN'T YOU COMING, DANI?

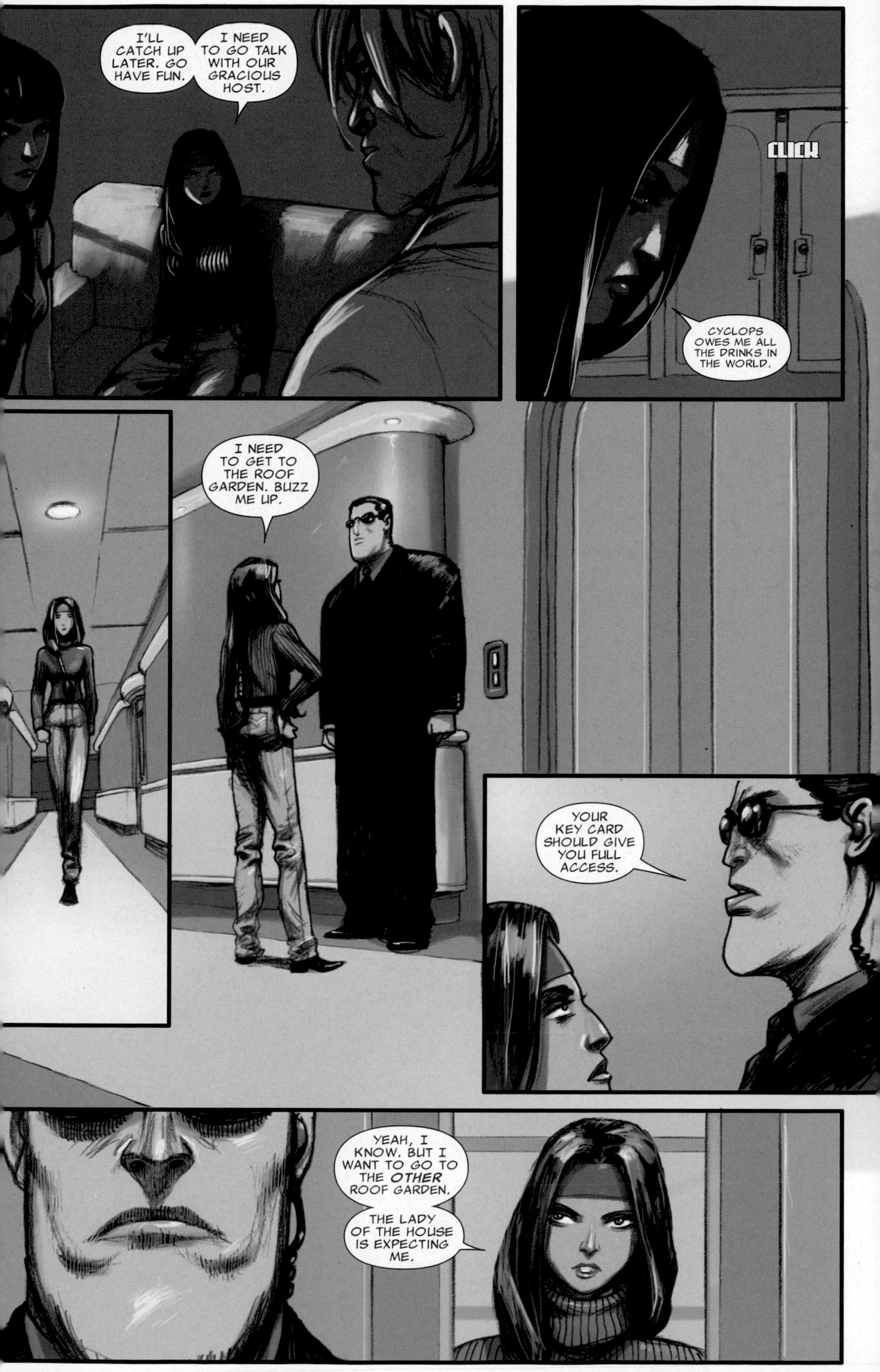
I'LL CATCH UP LATER. GO HAVE FUN.
I NEED TO GO TALK WITH OUR GRACIOUS HOST.
CLICK
CYCLOPS OWES ME ALL THE DRINKS IN THE WORLD.
I NEED TO GET TO THE ROOF GARDEN. BUZZ ME UP.
YOUR KEY CARD SHOULD GIVE YOU FULL ACCESS.
YEAH, I KNOW. BUT I WANT TO GO TO THE *OTHER* ROOF GARDEN.
THE LADY OF THE HOUSE IS EXPECTING ME.

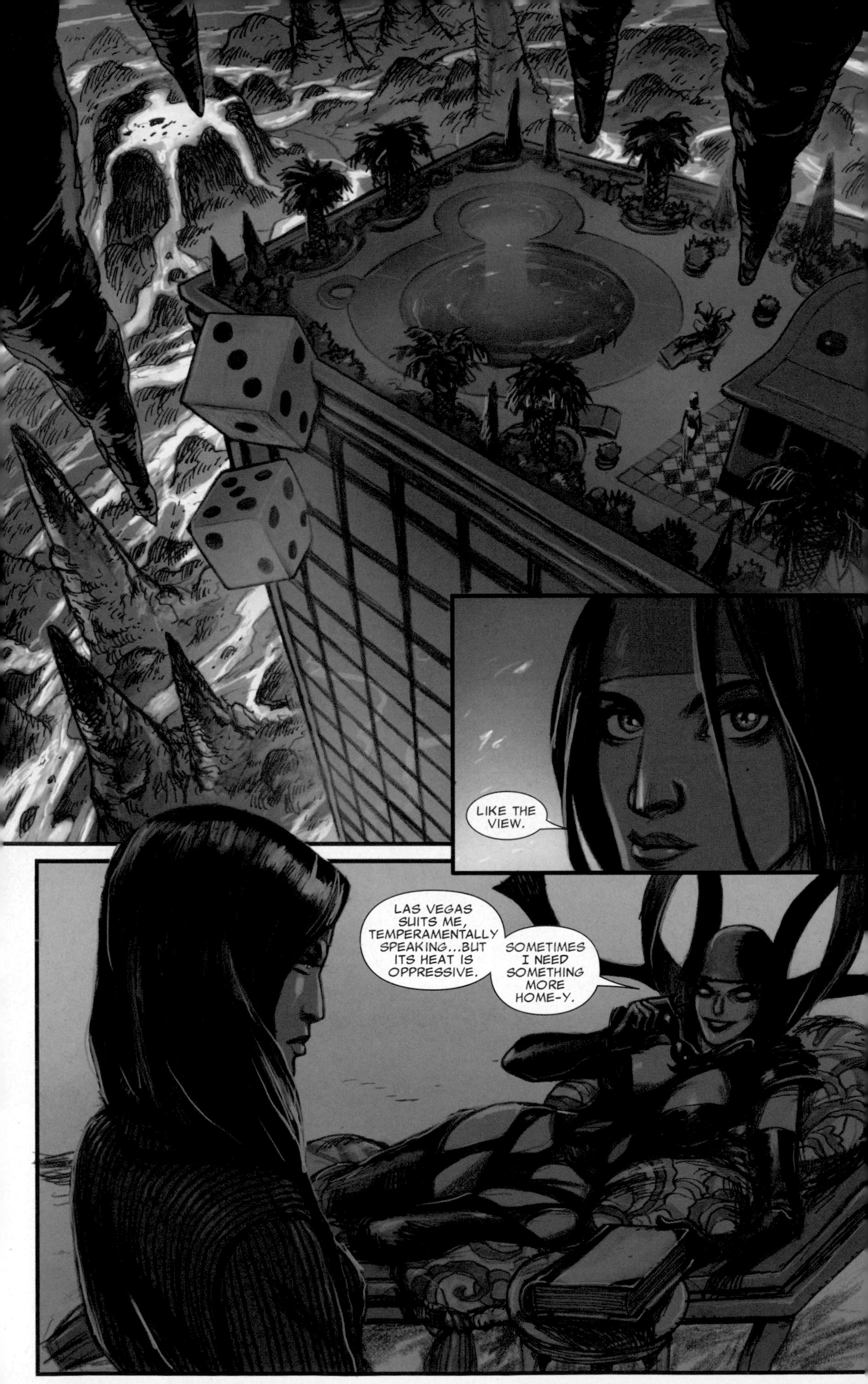
LIKE THE VIEW.
LAS VEGAS SUITS ME, TEMPERAMENTALLY SPEAKING...BUT ITS HEAT IS OPPRESSIVE.
SOMETIMES I NEED SOMETHING MORE HOME-Y.

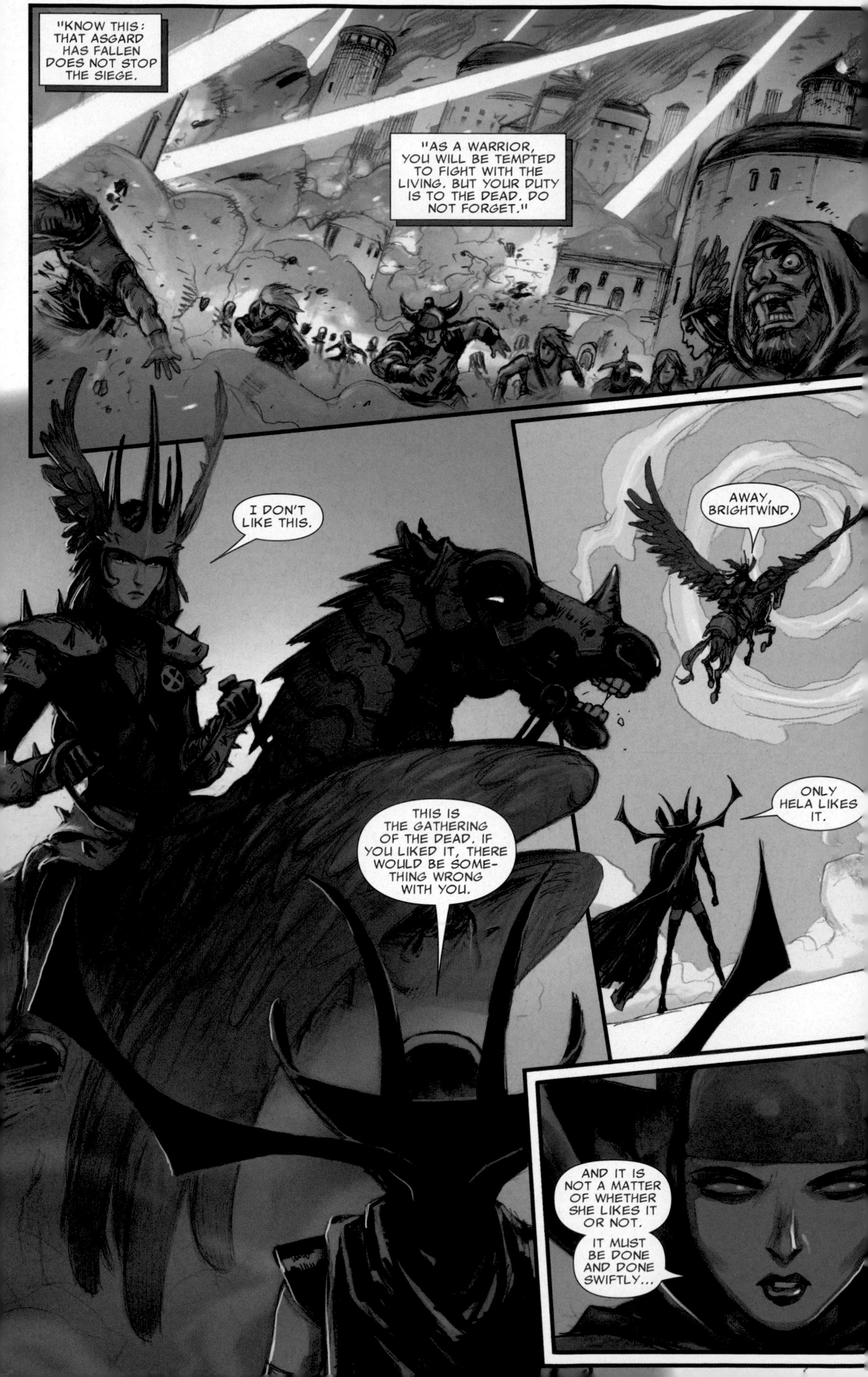
"KNOW THIS: THAT ASGARD HAS FALLEN DOES NOT STOP THE SIEGE.
"AS A WARRIOR, YOU WILL BE TEMPTED TO FIGHT WITH THE LIVING. BUT YOUR DUTY IS TO THE DEAD. DO NOT FORGET."
I DON'T LIKE THIS.
AWAY, BRIGHTWIND.
THIS IS THE GATHERING OF THE DEAD. IF YOU LIKED IT, THERE WOULD BE SOME-THING WRONG WITH YOU.
ONLY HELA LIKES IT.
AND IT IS NOT A MATTER OF WHETHER SHE LIKES IT OR NOT.
IT MUST BE DONE AND DONE SWIFTLY...

IS THIS... EVERYONE?

YES. WE GATHERED PRAYING FOR A GUIDE... ? ONE HAS COME.

OUR THAN TO YC HOUS

OKAY. WHO'S IN CHARGE HERE?

I AM TYR OF BATTLES. I WILL LEAD THE FALLEN ON THE HEL-MARCH.

NO, YOU'RE NOT IN CHARGE. WHO'S IN CHARGE HERE?

...YOU?

GLAD YOU UNDERSTAND. GATHER EVERYONE UP AND...

SISTER!

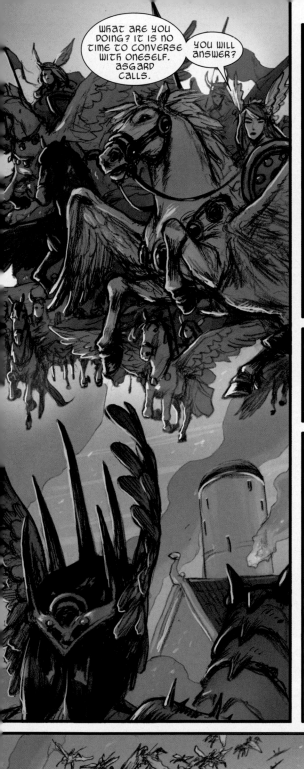

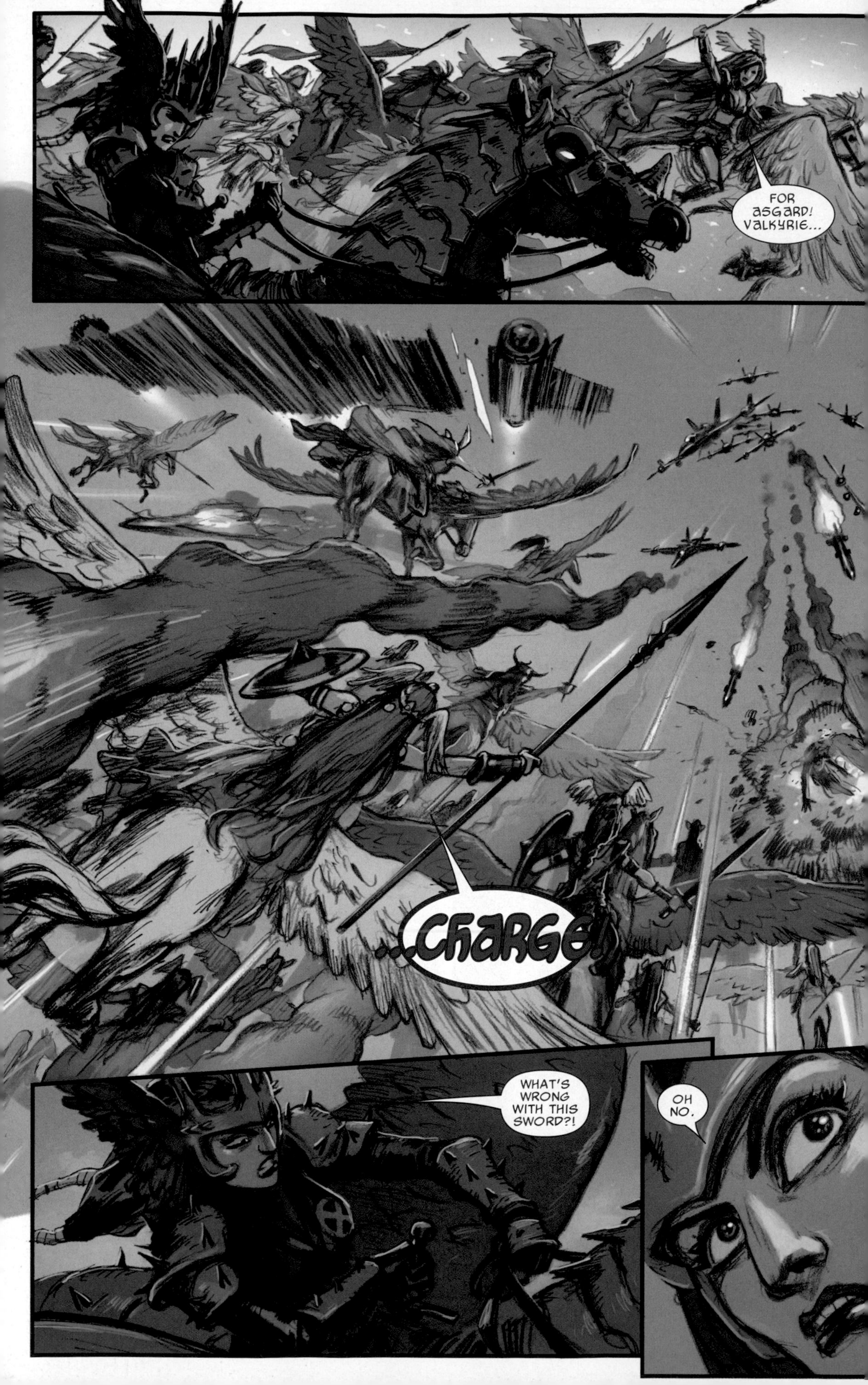
FOR ASGARD! VALKYRIE...
...CHARGE!
WHAT'S WRONG WITH THIS SWORD?!
OH NO.

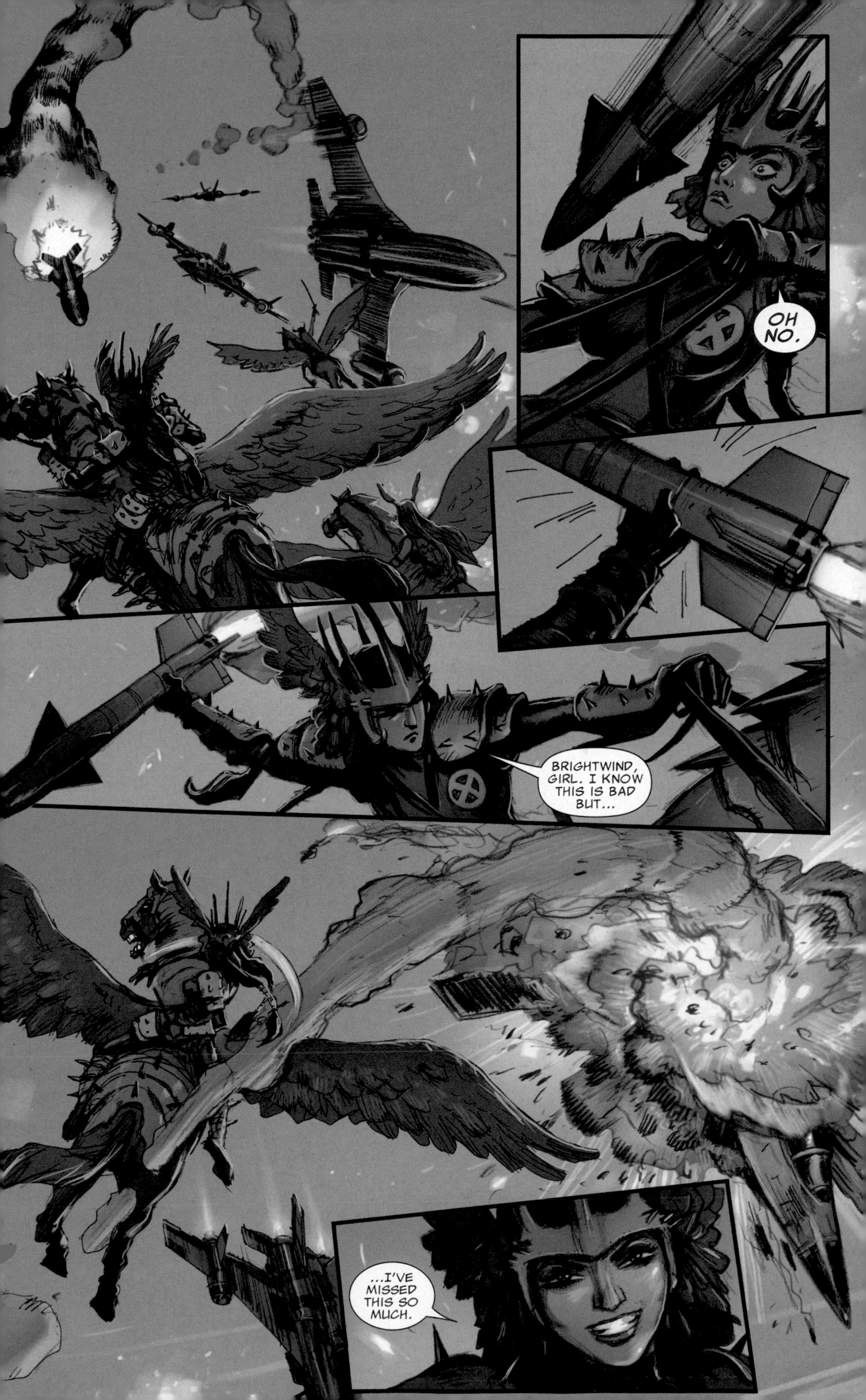
OH NO.
BRIGHTWIND, GIRL. I KNOW THIS IS BAD BUT...
...I'VE MISSED THIS SO MUCH.

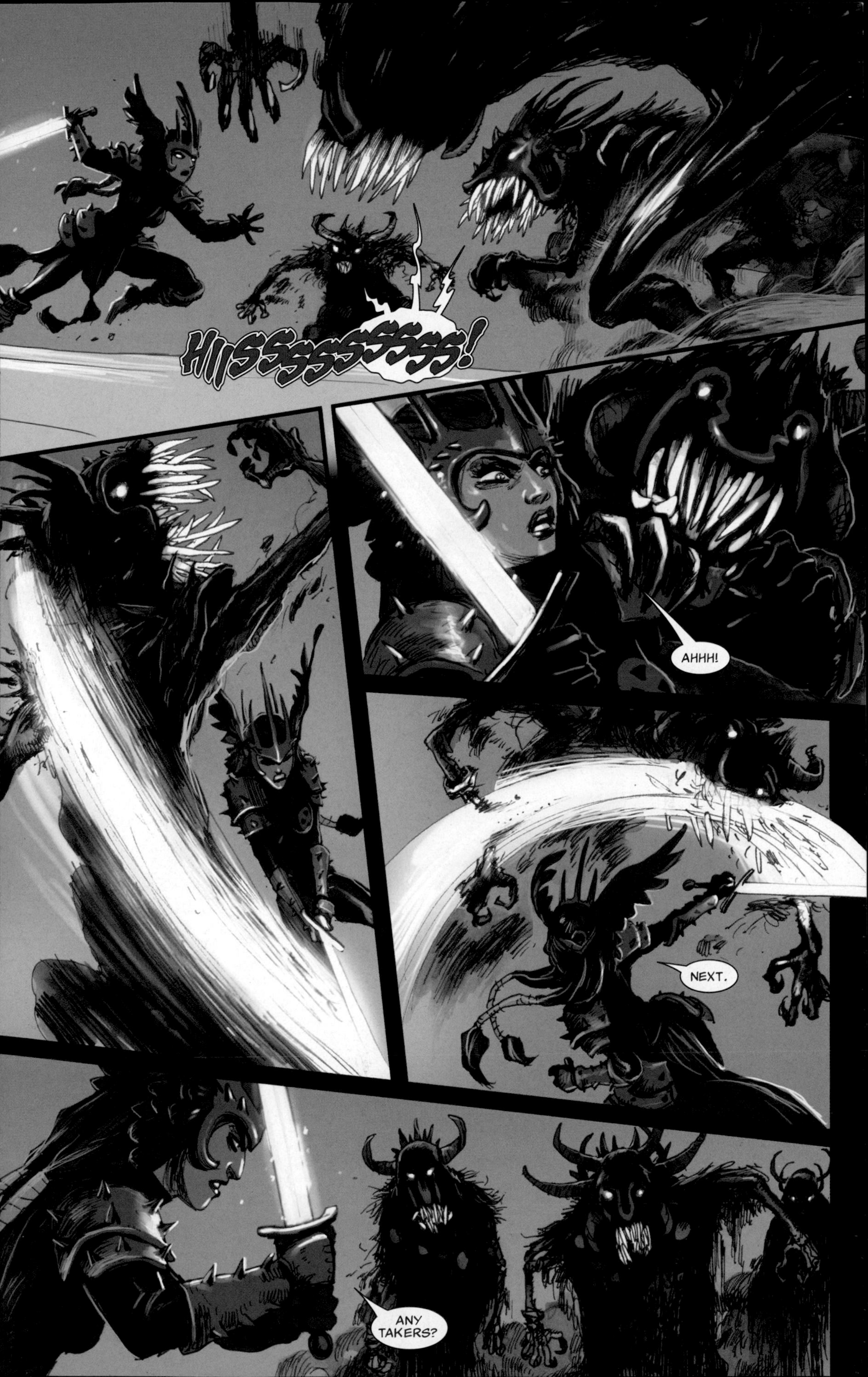
HIISSSSSSSSS!
AHHH!
NEXT.
ANY TAKERS?

WHY DIDN'T YOU TELL ME ABOUT THE DÍSIR?

I COULD HAVE SAVED THEM ALL. DAMN YOU, HELA, I...

THEY ARE CLOSE TO MYTH. THEY COULD HAVE NOT EXISTED...AND TO SPEAK THEIR NAMES IS TO RISK DRAWING THEIR GAZE.

BUT IF YOU WARNED ME, I'D HAVE--

DANI MOONSTAR, I TOLD YOU YOUR DUTY. YOU CHOSE TO IGNORE IT.

I ARMED YOU AGAINST THEM. I GAVE YOU GUIDANCE.

YOU CAME TO ME IN YOUR HOUR OF NEED. I SAVED YOU AND YOUR PEOPLE. I CAME TO YOU IN MINE...AND YOU ACT LIKE THIS.

WE DO NOT ALWAYS GET TO CHOOSE OUR DUTIES.

...IT WASN'T A SCHEME. YOU EMPOWERED ME TO *SAVE* THEM.

I EMPOWERED YOU TO MAKE SURE HEL GOT ITS DUE.

AND ITS TITHE IS NOW SADLY SHORT.

"*SADLY*"?

YES. *SADLY*. AND IF YOU REPEAT THAT, YOU WILL SUFFER. DREAD HELA HAS HER REPUTATION TO THINK OF.

LEAVE ME.

RING RING

YEAH?

HEY-- DANI. IT'S SAM. WHERE YOU BEEN? WE'RE ON THE ROULETTE. JOIN US?

NO...

...I DON'T THINK I'M LUCKY FOR ANYONE AROUND ME.

NEXT: SECOND COMING!

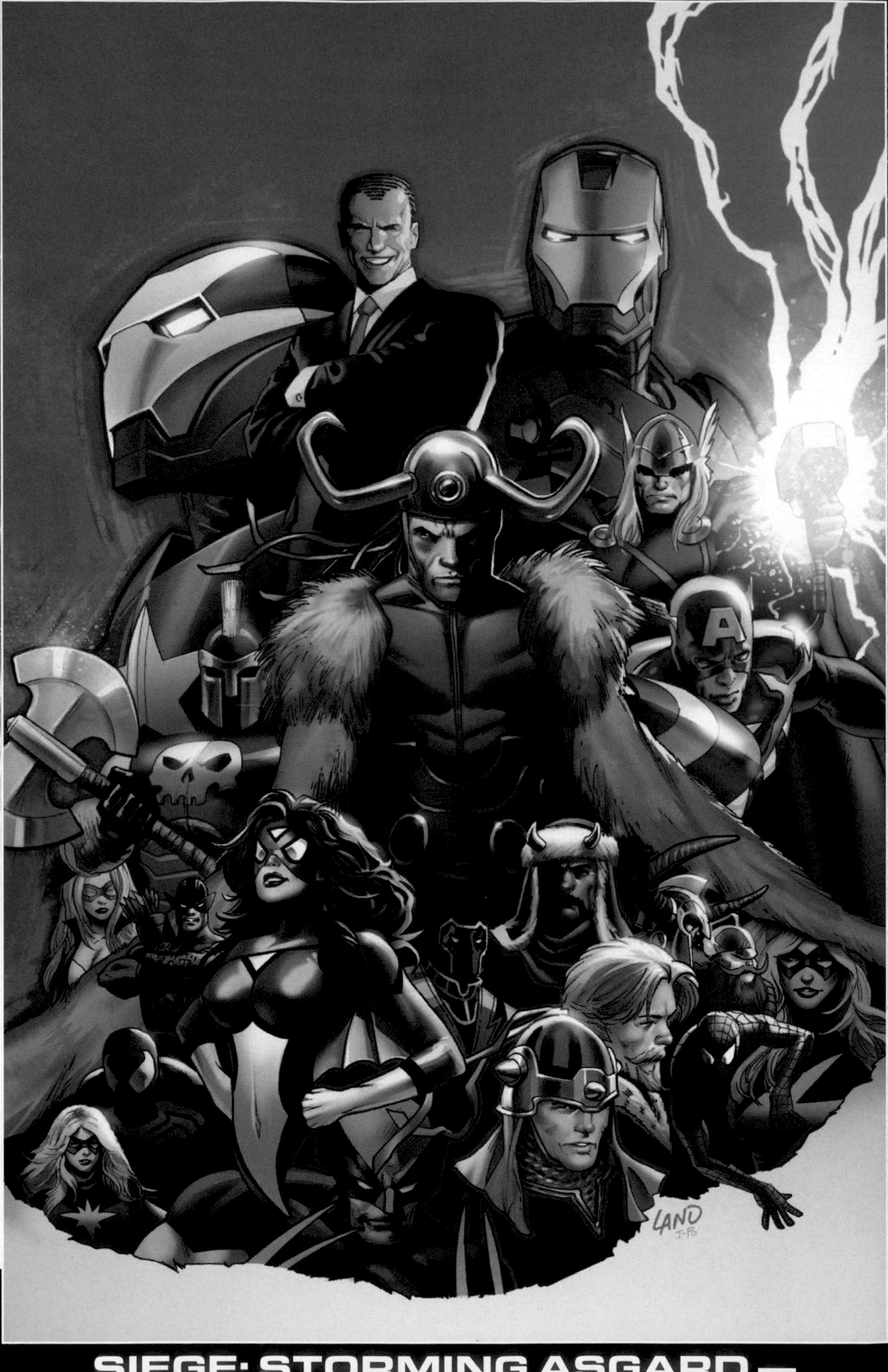
LAND

SIEGE: STORMING ASGARD — HEROES & VILLAINS

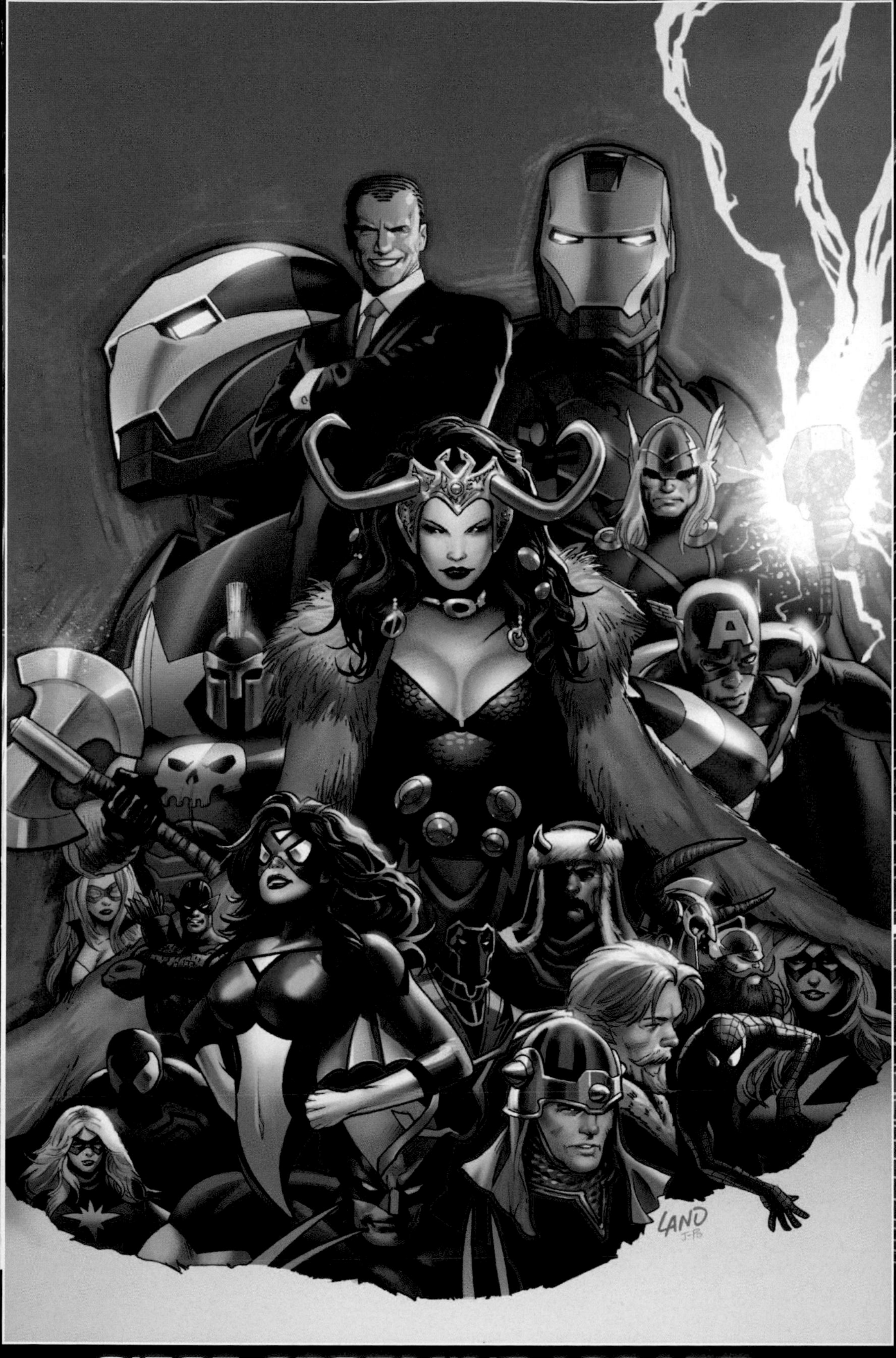
LAND
J-PB

SIEGE: STORMING ASGARD —
HEROES & VILLAINS VARIANT

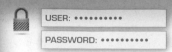

USER: •••••••••

PASSWORD: •••••••••

WATCHING OVER YOU

Norman,

This dossier represents one of our last preparations for the Siege. Storming Asgard is the final stage of a plan long in developement, and H.A.M.M.E.R. has done a thorough review of the threat we face from Asgard's protectors as well as our own assets we are bringing to bear. H.A.M.M.E.R. agents Jess Harrold and Dugan Trodglen have culled data from interviews done in the field with Loki, the Hood, and other Cabal associates, as well as fellow H.A.M.M.E.R. field agent Kieron Gillen, a psych evaluator assessing Ares.

DEFINING TERMS

For easy reference, we developed a shorthand when making mention of any of the myriad teams of Avengers now dotting the landscape. These are:

DARK AVENGERS: The officially sanctioned Avengers under the Iron Patriot's leadership; a roster of "under the radar" personalities.

NEW AVENGERS: The team of Avengers formed in the wake of the disassembly of the originals, currently underground and led by Ronin, Luke Cage, Spider-Man and others.

MIGHTY AVENGERS: The newest collection of classic Avengers, led by Hank Pym in his new guise as the Wasp.

AVENGERS RESISTANCE: A loose affiliation of classic Avengers, Initiative alumni and New Warriors, led by Tigra, Justice and Gauntlet.

THE INITIATIVE: Future Avengers from H.A.M.M.E.R. training. Led by Taskmaster.

And the epochal events that have altered superhuman history:

CIVIL WAR: The clash between superhumans on either side of the Registration issue.

SECRET INVASION: The stealth insurgency by Skrulls.

These encrypted files are for your eyes only. They deal directly with the Siege and its many contingencies, but their relevance may well extend beyond our successful Siege campaign and battle against Thor.

It's our H.A.M.M.E.R. against his. Let's go get him.

Victoria Hand
Siege Operations Manager

**STORMING ASGARD:
HEROES & VILLAINS**

CREDITS

Head Writer/Editor: John Rhett Thomas
Spotlight Bullpen Writers: Jess Harrold & Dugan Trodglen

Senior Editor, Special Projects: Jeff Youngquist
Editors, Special Projects: Mark D. Beazley
    & Jennifer Grünwald
Assistant Editors: John Denning & Alex Starbuck
Vice President of Sales, Publishing: David Gabriel
Book Design: BLAMMO! Content & Design,
    Rommel Alama, Mike Kronenberg
Editor in Chief: Joe Quesada
Publisher: Dan Buckley
Executive Producer: Alan Fine

Cover Artists: Greg Land &
Justin Ponsor

Special Thanks to Kieron Gillen,
Paul Cornell and Christos N. Gage

The views and opinions expressed in this issue are solely those of the writers, commentators or creative talent and do not express or imply the views or opinions of Marvel Entertainment, Inc.

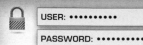

USER: •••••••••

PASSWORD: •••••••••

NAME:

LOKI

BACKGROUND:

From what we've been able to gather, Loki is Thor's half-brother and has been Thor's rival forever. Every plan Loki ever concocted has eventually been thwarted by Thor; in fact, according to old S.H.I.E.L.D. files it was a failed scheme of Loki's that brought the original Avengers together. This time may be different, however. He has thus far succeeded in running Thor out of Asgard, leaving a power vacuum filled by Balder, exactly as Loki had planned. .

Interestingly, when Loki first returned from the dead he was in the form of a female. We have no idea how this happened, but this female form seemed to serve Loki well. He/she was able to, if not exactly gain Thor's trust, at least not get beaten to a pulp or banished from the city. It was shortly after this that Loki once again became male, presumably because he had accomplished all he wanted in his female guise. Whether he can go back and forth is not known, nor does it seem relevant at this point.

ART BY AGENT MARKO DJURDJEVIC

ANALYSIS: AGENT TRODGLEN

It's pretty obvious that Loki is central to our plans to invade Asgard. Without his involvement, the Siege simply would not be happening. Let me start by saying I don't know if Loki, Thor, etc. are actually gods or that "Asgard" is the Asgard of Norse mythology. Ascertaining that as fact in no way changes either our goals or our methods. Whether or not these people are gods, they are immensely powerful and cannot be underestimated if this campaign is to work. I will be referring to these beings in my report as though they are the gods of myth rather than get bogged down in this detail. They look like gods, they have power like gods, and the Siege by its very conception treats them like gods; labels at this stage are beside the point. Now, as to Loki...

Loki can't be trusted. He simply cannot be trusted. He is the God of Mischief. He lies, therefore he is. Director Osborn has factored this into his strategic thinking from the beginning. Thus, our plan of attack must be Loki-proof. It must position Director Osborn in a way that will protect him from a sudden but inevitable betrayal on the part of Loki. But for now we must proceed as though he is our ally. This entire operation is doomed without Loki as an ally. With neither Thor nor Odin in power – and we have Loki to thank for this – Asgard has never been this vulnerable. He is the source of all of our intelligence, which amounts to quite a lot. We certainly have a common enemy, and H.A.M.M.E.R. and the Dark Avengers undoubtedly provide the resources to accomplish a siege of Asgard far beyond anything Loki can conjure on his own. So it's a good bet he wants us to succeed, and that he needs us.

EXECUTIVE ASSESSMENT:

Forge ahead. But never turn your back on him.

USER: •••••••••••

PASSWORD: •••••••••••

NAME:

THE HOOD

ART BY AGENT KYLE HOTZ

BACKGROUND:

Parker Robbins started out as a reliable ally for Director Osborn but recently has become anything but. His history has been hard to come by, but from what we can gather, he started out as a small-time hood. He was just another worthless street criminal until he came into possession a few years ago of an apparently **magical red cloak**, which granted him great power. If our sources are to be believed, these powers came from an other-dimensional demon, though that seems to no longer be a part of Robbins' makeup. Thanks to Loki he is now apparently in possession of something called **Norn Stones** and these are the source of his power now.

For a while he seemed content to go after his slice of the criminal pie, merely to support his girlfriend, small child, invalid mother, and personal indulgences, but sometime shortly before the Secret Invasion he was struck with inspiration. He assembled a virtual army of superpowered criminals and created his own super-crime syndicate. At first, while there were a few problems, things went much better than they usually do for groups like this, and Robbins, now calling himself The Hood, can claim much of the credit for his fresh approach. He didn't rely on the group's numbers, or even their power; instead, everything was carefully organized and everything they did had a specific, logical goal.

After the invasion, when Director Osborn came to power, he recognized The Hood as a valuable ally. They have worked together ever since. Among their agreements, the Hood was placed in charge of the **Initiative** program, and Director Osborn has agreed to overlook the activities of the Hood's group, with the understanding that the Director would occasionally call in favors. He was confronted by, if not a coup, at least a betrayal by most of his syndicate, who attempted to broker a deal with Director Osborn separate from the Hood's, who would have none of it. The Hood returned, and while their relationship was seemingly damaged, they remain allies.

ANALYSIS: AGENT TRODGLEN

If power corrupts, what happens when the already corrupt gain power? Parker Robbins seems to be a case study in this question. While he has shown excellent business acumen and a knack for self-preservation, over time he has grown increasingly unstable. The good news is that there is reason to believe even his new source of power is actually less dangerous to his mental faculties, but it is too early to know for sure.

But this potential stability comes at another cost. If indeed Loki is responsible for the Hood gaining new, even greater powers, where do you think the Hood's loyalty will ultimately lie? Yes, Loki is our ally, but he will remain an ally for only as long as it suits him. If and when the time comes when we find ourselves at odds with Loki, we need to be prepared for the fact that we will have lost the Hood as well, or take steps to ensure his loyalty to us before that happens.

EXECUTIVE ASSESSMENT: A loose cannon, now in Loki's pocket? How does that sound to you?

NAME:

TASKMASTER

BACKGROUND:

Taskmaster has "photographic reflexes," which is the ability to mimic any physical movement or activity he witnesses, and he has used this not so much to carve out a career in crime as a career in training criminals. With his ability, he has studied and learned the fighting and weapon-wielding techniques of just about everyone you can think of, but just as his only abilities come from taking cues from others, he similarly seems to have no ambition of his own, at least in the traditional sense. Hence, ever since Director Osborn has been in power, Taskmaster has eagerly followed orders and risen through the ranks. He took over the Initiative program to great success, including leading the mission that took back the Negative Zone prison. He apparently recently met with Director Osborn to discuss an increase in his responsibility and influence before becoming injured during an undisclosed skirmish, protecting Director Osborn.

ART BY AGENT HUMBERTO RAMOS

ANALYSIS: AGENT TRODGLEN

Taskmaster is quite content to follow the money and power without ever really seeming to seek that power for himself. Director Osborn loves this about him. I have, however, spoken with some fellow agents who have trained under Taskmaster and while they applaud his skill and his ability to train others, they are dubious about his ability to actually assume any sort of executive or administrative responsibility, and has been known to extract himself from any given situation when the heat starts to come down. He really doesn't like to get his own hands dirty.

ART BY AGENT JORGE MOLINA

Director Osborn obviously sees something in him, and a lot of what I am reporting comes from hearsay, but my impression is that he wants to get by while doing as little work as possible. Some agents have also reported that under his watch, the maintenance of Camp H.A.M.M.E.R. was a bit more freewheeling than he'd have Director Osborn believe. In short, I have formed a profile of Taskmaster as someone who is mentally lazy and am surprised to see him even want to move as far up the ladder as Director Osborn is leading him. Don't be too shocked to turn around one day to find him gone.

 EXECUTIVE ASSESSMENT: A good ally in the minor leagues. But are you sure he's fit for your Cabal?

USER: ••••••••••
PASSWORD: ••••••••••

NAME:

DOCTOR DOOM

ART BY AGENT OLIVIER COIPEL

BACKGROUND:

As one of his first acts as head of H.A.M.M.E.R., Director Osborn arranged for the release of Victor Von Doom from S.H.I.E.L.D. custody and his extradition back to Latveria, in return for Doom's allegiance. Shortly thereafter, the Dark Avengers stepped in to save Doom from the sorceress Morgan Le Fay amidst the wreckage of the tyrant's homeland. Doom's castle and nation were somehow rebuilt from scratch in time for him to offer Latveria as a new home for Asgard, in a pact with Loki. However, Doom's relationship with Asgard, and its ruler Balder, is now at an end following the revelation that he had been carrying out vivisection experiments on Asgardians. As yet, it is unknown to what extent Doom's personal relationship with Loki has been affected. Doom resigned somewhat dramatically from Director Osborn's Cabal in a devastating confrontation at Avengers Tower.

ANALYSIS: AGENT HARROLD

More so than any member of Director Osborn's inner circle, Doom was always going to be difficult to control. We gave him everything he wanted – freedom, his kingdom back, and saved him from Morgan Le Fay. But while he purports to be a man of honor, Doom was never likely to keep his side of the bargain for long. It is to be assumed that Doom was plotting against Director Osborn from the start, most likely together with his long-time associate Namor. Indeed, it was a dispute over Namor that led to the confrontation that ended Director Osborn's involvement with Doom. Only Director Osborn knows for sure what started the physical confrontation in his private office at Avengers Tower, but the retaliation of a Doombot, sent in Doom's place, almost killed the Taskmaster. The robotic insectoid attack that followed would have crippled the facility were it not for the Sentry, and Doom even had the audacity to threaten Director Osborn's son in the event of any retaliation. He is to be considered a top-level threat, one not to be engaged without very careful planning. As well as technological know-how that puts him among the most intelligent men on Earth, Doom has harnessed the power of time travel to research arcane and long-forgotten dark magicks. His powerful sorcery can be the only explanation for the rapid rise of Latveria from the ashes of destruction. It remains to be seen what new threats his experimentation on the Asgardians has added to his already considerable arsenal. However, this is a problem for another day. It is felt unlikely that he will involve himself in the Asgardian conflict in the light of his own dispute with Balder. In this respect, as his enemy's enemy, it may be that we are inadvertently Doom's friend. Once Asgard is conquered, however, Doom will find himself high on our list of subsequent issues to address.

EXECUTIVE ASSESSMENT:
Today Asgard. Tomorrow Latveria.

USER: •••••••••

PASSWORD: ••••••••••

NAME:
SUB-MARINER/ NAMOR

BACKGROUND:

At first an apparently obedient and willing member of Director Osborn's Cabal, Namor attempted to apprehend Iron Man on our behalf. However, when asked to denounce and exterminate Atlantean terrorists responsible for loss of lives in Los Angeles, Namor showed where his true allegiances lie and refused. Against his better judgment, Director Osborn was persuaded by Emma Frost to allow Namor onto the team of **Dark X-Men** sent in to resolve the mutant riots in San Francisco. With the Bay Area secured, and Director Osborn apparently victorious, the extent of Frost and Namor's treachery stood revealed: They had been working with Cyclops all along. Fending off the Dark Avengers, Namor, Frost, Cyclops and the X-Men evacuated the mutants and established a stronghold on the island of Utopia, the rocky surface of Magneto's Asteroid M newly raised by the mutants. In retaliation, Director Osborn obtained Namor's former wife Marrina in her mutated Plodex form. Genetically enhancing her to induce a voracious appetite for Atlantean flesh, he unleashed her into the oceans where she began the slaughter of thousands of the scattered sea-dwellers. Namor captured the monster, slew it, and hurled it through the windows of Oscorp's Atlantean offices before issuing a grave threat to Director Osborn: if he'd do something like that to his wife, imagine what he would do to an enemy.

ART BY AGENT ALAN DAVIS

ANALYSIS: AGENT HARROLD

Such is Namor's tremendous arrogance, self-importance and disdain for "surface-dwellers," his alliance with Director Osborn was always likely to be fragile. They can now be considered bitter enemies. The Atlantean monarch has found his way onto the growing list of targets for whom Director Osborn's well-earned enmity outstrips any strategic imperative. Having seemingly found a permanent home with the X-Men on Utopia, Namor should be considered highly unlikely to involve himself in the Siege on Asgard. He will be of greater significance in any future engagement with his frequent ally, Doctor Doom. Doom vehemently objected to Director Osborn's treatment of Namor, leading to the confrontation that saw him removed from the Cabal. Meanwhile, Atlantean troops are believed to have been given refuge in Latveria. Any attack on either man is likely to be considered a declaration of war upon the other. Namor is one of the few men alive to have held his own against the Sentry, and can command forces of unknown numbers currently scattered throughout the oceans. Further engagement with him or Doom is not recommended until detailed projections of acceptable losses can be prepared.

EXECUTIVE ASSESSMENT: Interference with Siege unlikely, but keep your nose open for that smell...

USER: ••••••••••

PASSWORD: ••••••••••

NAME:

WHITE QUEEN/ EMMA FROST

BACKGROUND:

When Emma Frost was recruited to Director Osborn's Cabal, the lure was an invitation to save her species. With the mutant population in seemingly terminal decline, Director Osborn offered her a way to stave off the prospect of those remaining mutants being rounded up and forced into concentration camps. He offered her the opportunity to become the face of mutantkind, with her own team of X-Men, albeit a line-up he himself would choose. She agreed, on the condition that **Namor** could take a place on the team. Her **Dark X-Men** helped quell mutant riots in San Francisco, and took the protestors into custody in H.A.M.M.E.R.'s remodeled Alcatraz facility. However, Frost discovered that the alternate reality Dark Beast was experimenting on the captured mutants and painfully siphoning their powers to augment Weapon Omega. She betrayed Director Osborn, aided the mutants in their escape, and returned to the side of her lover, **Cyclops,** on the newly raised island of **Utopia,** a haven for mutantkind outside of H.A.M.M.E.R.'s jurisdiction. During the ensuing battle with the Dark Avengers, Frost – who has served as an occasional therapist for the troubled Sentry – managed to unsettle him enough to make him flee. Sources confirm that whatever she did left her with a sliver of some sort of negative energy inside her head that requires her to remain in diamond form.

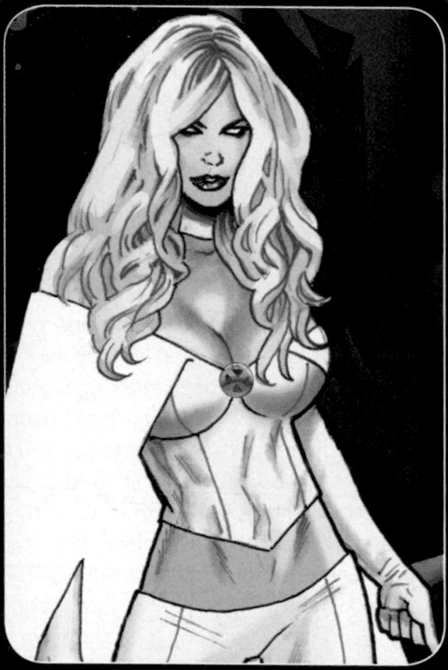

ART BY AGENT GREG LAND

ANALYSIS: AGENT HARROLD

Frost was a useful member of the Cabal, one whose psychic powers served to encourage honesty among its members. Had she remained in charge of the Dark X-Men, the resolution of the mutant problem in San Francisco would have been an excellent public relations boost. Nevertheless, Director Osborn was still able to claim victory when looking at the big picture. Frost and Cyclops' X-Men are confined to an island prison of their own making, and the mutant menace is under control. However, Frost's treachery could lead to further provocation if left unpunished. H.A.M.M.E.R. must be vigilant for probable cause that would justify a strike upon Utopia. In the meantime, Frost and the beleaguered X-Men are unlikely to be drawn into an involvement in the conflict in Asgard that could further reduce their dwindling numbers. Vigilance is nonetheless recommended, due to Frost's personal and professional history with the Sentry. She is one of the few people on Earth capable of taking Reynolds down. Reports of her current condition make interesting reading in the light of psych reports that evaluate "the Void," the dark half the Sentry claims to harbor deep inside. Further investigation is highly recommended. To that end, it should be noted that, while Frost's current permanent diamond form considerably increases her physical threat, it prevents her from using her far more deadly psychic powers.

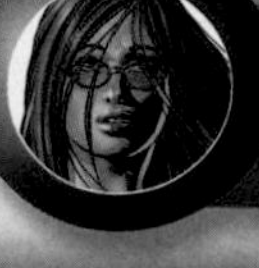

EXECUTIVE ASSESSMENT: Keep both eyes open and your mind closed around this witch.

USER: •••••••••••

PASSWORD: •••••••••••

NAME:

THOR

BACKGROUND:

Some time ago, Asgard suffered through Ragnarok, which saw the seeming death of Thor, Odin, and every other citizen. As is often the case with the superhuman community, this death was not permanent, and a few months ago Thor returned. He eventually brought back all of the citizens of Asgard save Odin, and even returned Asgard itself to existence, although now the majestic city found itself not in the heavens but floating above rural Broxton, Oklahoma. With Odin not among the returned, Thor was the new ruler of Asgard.

Soon after, Loki returned to the living Bor, Odin's father and Thor's grandfather, and placed him in the middle of New York City in a berserker rage. Thor could only halt Bor's rampage by killing him. This led to Thor's exile (Loki's ultimate goal), Thor having essentially slain the King of Asgard. Balder became the new ruler of Asgard and Thor was forced to go down and live on earth. Curiously, Thor seems not to be around that often, as though he leaves the planet, or perhaps our dimension itself, for significant periods of time. It is also not known if his major weapon asset, his hammer Mjolnir, is in working condition.

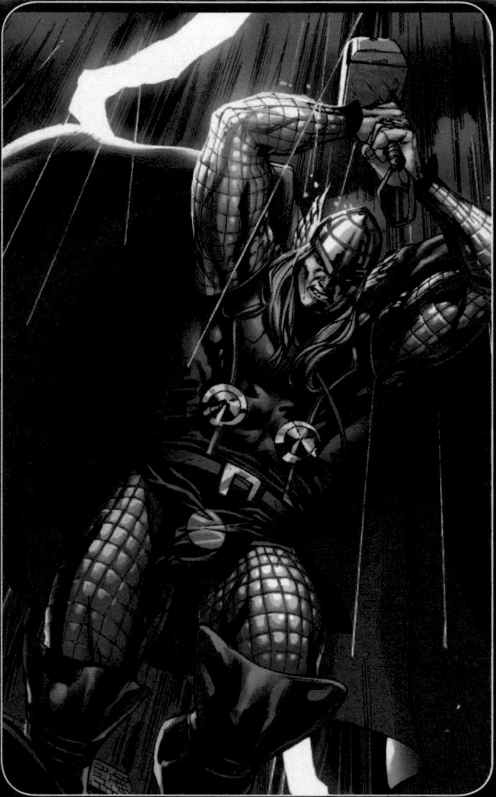

ART BY AGENT BILLY TAN

ANALYSIS: AGENT TRODGLEN

There is no question Thor represents the greatest threat to victory in Asgard. Even exiled, he will stop at nothing to defend his homeland, nor will the Asgardians hesitate to call on him to return home to do so. One wonders if even the Sentry is enough to deal with Thor. While comparable in terms of power, Thor would have the distinct advantage of fighting for the homeland that means everything to him. In short, it will take more than the Sentry to bring Thor down. It will take the combined efforts of all of our most powerful resources to take Thor down. The other possibility is that a proper threat to all of Asgard might be enough to persuade Thor to consider surrender.

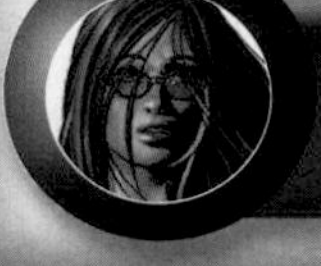

EXECUTIVE ASSESSMENT: Thor should keep us up at night. Dealing with him is beyond my pay grade.

USER: ●●●●●●●●●●
PASSWORD: ●●●●●●●●●●

BROXTON, OKLAHOMA

BACKGROUND: When Thor restored Asgard and positioned it on Earth, for some reason he chose Broxton, OK, 150 miles west of Oklahoma City, as its new locale. Broxton is fly-over country at its most insufferable. Everyone there is, by all accounts, the "salt of the earth." They have welcomed the Asgardians into their lives as only Mayberry-types could, and seem to have mostly gotten over the incredible nature of what they are dealing with. The bottom line is that a conflict with Asgard could turn into a conflict with Broxton, and from a PR standpoint, that could be trouble. Another threat the citizens of Broxton represent is the possibility of actually mixing with the Asgardians. The relationship between "Bill" (last name unknown) and the Asgardian Kelda proved to be dynamite that blew up in Loki's face.

ART BY AGENT OLIVIER COIPEL

ANALYSIS: AGENT TRODGLEN

Bill's discovery of Doom's vivisection lab illustrates how easily a simple hick can fly under the radar when dealing with larger-than-life adversaries. Real damage to our cause can come of this. We have got to avoid getting Broxton involved. In addition, we have to keep the media away from the citizens of Broxton. We cannot let Ma Kettle look into the camera and tell America that we're the bad guys here.

EXECUTIVE ASSESSMENT: Fifty square mile cordon, total population evac and standard issue media blackout.

FRONT LINE

BACKGROUND: Front Line is the left-wing rag run by **Ben Urich**, along with fellow executive **Robbie Robertson**, staff reporters **Sally Floyd** and **Norah Winters**, and longtime Spider-Man ally, photographer **Peter Parker**. Even before he started Front Line, Urich had been a thorn in Director Osborn's side for years as a reporter for the Daily Bugle. He and his paper are the only significant members of the media to have never backed Director Osborn in his position of power. It is not expected that he will in any way support the Siege with either fair and balanced reporting or objective editorializing.

ART BY AGENT MARCO CHECCHETTO

ANALYSIS: Ben Urich will undertake every effort to be at the scene in Broxton somehow. His tenacity is legendary. Count on it: His narrative will make villains out of us, and the way information travels these days, he will likely prove our greatest enemy in the war of public opinion. We need eyes on him. There ought to be multiple opportunities to lock him up, as he and his minions are sure to break the law in their attempts to gain access to our operation. As well, we need to be mindful of the Freedom of Information Act requests that are sure to come from Urich and other media outlets. Safeguard all paper trails and information exchanges so we can hide the design of Siege.

EXECUTIVE ASSESSMENT: I would drive to Broxton for the chance to put a bullet in him myself.

USER: •••••••••

PASSWORD: •••••••••

NAME: BALDER

ART BY AGENT OLIVIER COIPEL

BACKGROUND: Balder is currently the ruler of Asgard, son of **Odin** and half-brother of both **Loki** and **Thor,** taking the throne after Loki's machinations exiled Thor. Loki considered the idealistic Balder an easily manipulated figure whose presence on the throne was a key component in his/her plans. Balder agreed to move his people to Latveria where it wasn't long until the Asgardians found themselves at odds with Doom. Loki appeared caught in the middle and Balder's trust of Loki diminished.

ANALYSIS: AGENT TRODGLEN

While we can certainly expect Thor to take the lead at some point, as it stands, Balder rules Asgard. In battles like this, it's always desirable to break a people's will, but that would appear to be a near-impossible task when it comes to Asgard. Even before he was their leader, he was among their most inspiring warriors, second only to Thor. It is highly doubtful that we can look for surrender on the part of Balder, so a sound strategy must involve his swift removal. This won't be easy. It will take someone in the highest weight class to take out a warrior of Balder's strength and resolve.

EXECUTIVE ASSESSMENT: Eliminate quickly: Ares and/or Sentry.

NAME: SIF

BACKGROUND: Lady Sif has long been **Thor's** ally and lover. She was the final Asgardian returned to life by Thor after Ragnarok, and Loki recognizing her stature as both a warrior and stabilizer of Thor's emotional well-being — nearly succeeded in preventing her return. But he didn't, she's here, and we have to deal with that.

ANALYSIS: A significant adversary on her own, her greatest role and one we'd like to exploit is that of Thor's lover. Her presence helps bring focus and resolve to Thor. If we can eliminate her, it could damage Thor's morale, but it would also threaten to enrage him beyond our ability to contain. Somehow capturing her and using her as a bargaining tool is a high risk/high reward approach we may wish to consider.

ART BY AGENT MARKO DJURDJEVIC

EXECUTIVE ASSESSMENT: Disappear the $%#@& and we distract and potentially have leverage against Thor.

USER: ●●●●●●●●●●
PASSWORD: ●●●●●●●●●●

THE WARRIORS THREE

ART BY AGENT OLIVIER COIPEL

ART BY AGENT BILLY TAN

BACKGROUND:

Along with Balder, the so-called Warriors Three – **Fandral, Hogun** and **Volstagg** (the fat one) – are the foremost defenders of Asgard this side of Thor. They are as powerful as they are fiercely loyal, to Thor in particular. It is this loyalty – and a distrust of Loki – that led the trio to stay behind when Balder took the Asgardians from Broxton, Oklahoma to Latveria. They seem content, for now, to get to know their human neighbors and seemingly bide the time until what they assume will be Thor's eventual return to power. They currently run a diner in Broxton. That's not a typo. We saw it for ourselves. (Our stealth agents recommend the country fried steak.)

ANALYSIS:
AGENT TRODGLEN

Like Balder, there is no sound strategy that involves either capturing the Warriors Three or counting on their surrender. They must be eliminated. Again, it will take the most powerful beings at our disposal to accomplish this. Somehow separating them would probably be best.

One thing about their presence in the "outside world" is intriguing. With Asgard isolated, it's not easy to contrive any sort of aggression on their part. In discussing ways by which Asgard can be viewed publicly as aggressors, Loki mentioned the loyalty of these three as ripe for exploitation. He also thinks they are pretty dumb, particularly Volstagg ("oaf" was the term he used), and plans on discussing ways to take advantage of this with Director Osborn. If by this point the Director's strategy in this regard has gone beyond the talking stage, our analysis is perhaps moot.

EXECUTIVE ASSESSMENT: Sounds like Loki has this one.

USER: •••••••••
PASSWORD: •••••••••

NAME: **HEIMDALL**

ART BY AGENT OLIVIER COIPEL

BACKGROUND:

The brother of Sif, Heimdall is **Asgard's all-seeing sentry**. And as sentries go, our understanding is that he is pretty extraordinary. Through Asgardian magic he can see everything on earth.

ANALYSIS:

With Heimdall around, we cannot count on ever having the element of surprise. So we may as well forget about that. We want this guy out of the picture fast. What we'll need to do is remove Heimdall as a resource as soon as we can for the sake of any future strategy. We're working on ways to confound his magical senses, but so far we're stumped. Loki may ultimately be the best source for that.

EXECUTIVE ASSESSMENT: Suggest gouging this guy's eyeballs out be a priority for Loki. (And fast, please.)

NAME: **TYR**

ART BY AGENT BILLY TAN

BACKGROUND:

Tyr is the **Norse God of War**. He is their Ares. He had not made his presence known in Asgard until their battle with Doom, insisting that he is there only when needed.

ANALYSIS:

(Well, they'll be needing him now.) He represents a more headfirst battle mentality (the kind Ares encompasses) than the other Asgardians. This aggression could be trouble but it could also lead to injudicious movements on the battlefield that ultimately help the enemy – in this case, us. The right sort of emotional manipulation can lead him to make mistakes, Loki assures us.

EXECUTIVE ASSESSMENT: Wind Ares up and turn him loose. (How are we on our stocks of popcorn?)

USER: ••••••••••
PASSWORD: ••••••••••

NAME:

THE HOOD'S ARMY

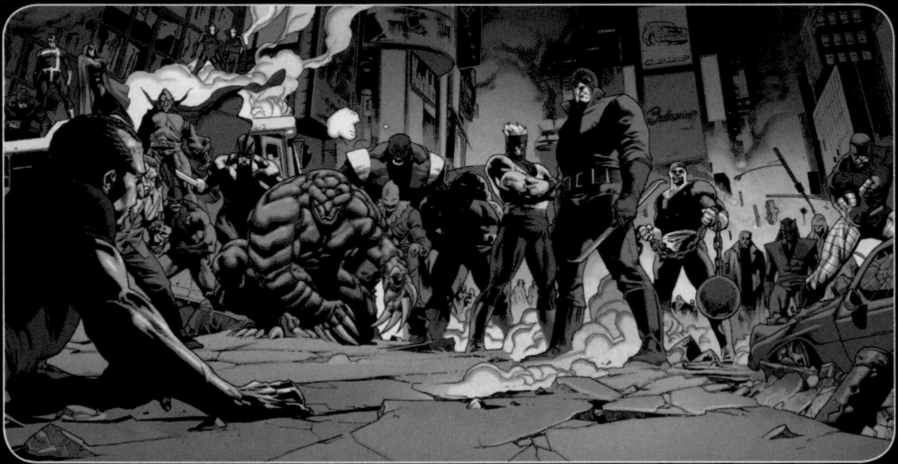

ART BY AGENT STUART IMMONEN

BACKGROUND: The Hood has gathered a very impressive group — the "Masters of Evil," if you will (he would never refer to them as that). Their goal is to pool resources, make each other aware of goals, and when necessary, go in together on certain activities and split the profits. Members of this group have included:

Madame Masque	Dr. Demonicus	Deathwatch	Living Laser
Dr. Jonas Harrow	Scarecrow	Blackout	Jigsaw
Wrecker	Bulldozer	Answer	Armadillo
Bulldozer	Mentallo	Centurius	Mr. Hyde
Piledriver	Mandrill	Controller	Mr. Fear
Thunderball	Razor Fist	Corruptor	The U-Foes
Griffin	Chemistro	Cutthroat	Graviton
Bushwacker	Piledriver	Purple Man	Grey Gargoyle
Crossfire	Brothers Grimm	Vermin	Shocker

ANALYSIS: AGENT TRODGLEN

The Hood's army screwed themselves and ended up in a position that is very beneficial to us. By assigning this powerful group to take down Cage's New Avengers, they will at the very least keep themselves occupied for the duration of the Siege of Asgard. At best, they'll permanently remove some serious thorns in Director Osborn's side.

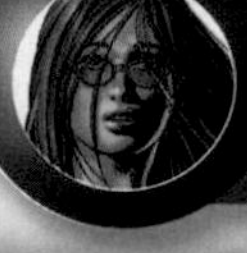

EXECUTIVE ASSESSMENT:
Cannon fodder. They have their mission.

USER: ••••••••••

PASSWORD: ••••••••••

NAME:

MADAME MASQUE

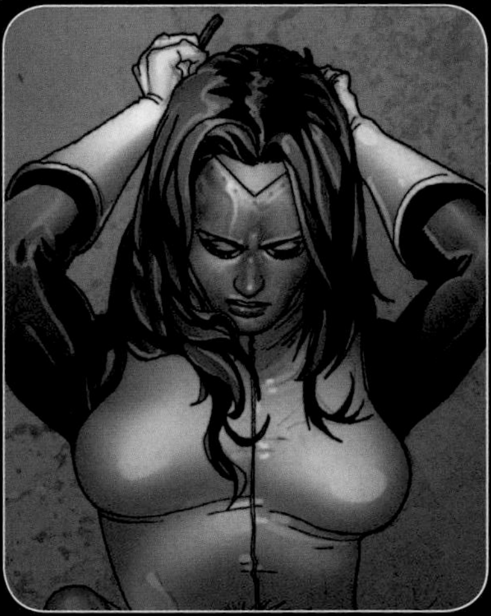

ART BY AGENT SALVADOR LARROCA

BACKGROUND: When the Hood gathered his army of costumed criminals, **Whitney Frost** quickly became part of his inner circle and soon their relationship grew beyond the professional. She was not among the group when it attempted its coup. Instead, she escorted Robbins as he journeyed with Loki to gain the Norn Stones.

Director Osborn did attempt to use her in his plan to assassinate Tony Stark, but instead she found herself trapped by Pepper Potts inside the Rescue armor and had to be cut out. This embarrassing incident was part of a successful strategy by Potts to spring Maria Hill and Black Widow from detention at Avengers Tower, which did not endear her to Director Osborn.

ANALYSIS: AGENT TRODGLEN

There are a number of ways to use Miss Frost going forward, but her greatest value has to come from Robbins' feelings for her, the pair having engaged in a persistent romantic affair. His army is a key component of this operation and if we need to use her to keep him focused on the matter at hand then let's do it. In other words, we need an agent ready at any moment to take her down so we can use her as a bargaining chip with Robbins.

EXECUTIVE ASSESSMENT: After the Iron Man fiasco, I want no part of her.

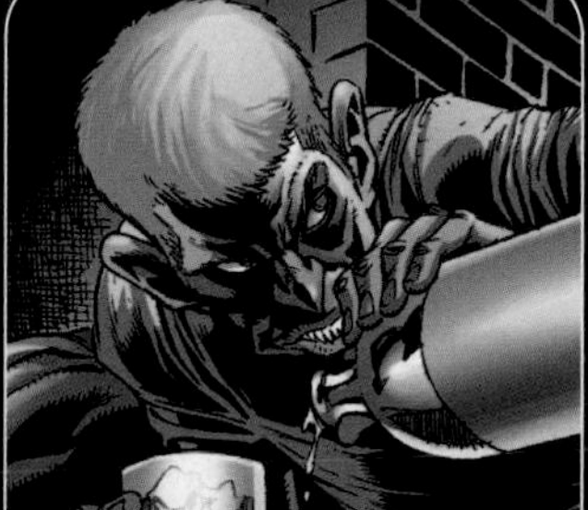

ART BY AGENT KYLE HOTZ

NAME: **JOHN KING**

BACKGROUND: John King is Parker Robbins' longtime right hand man. Robbins trusts him, probably more than anyone. Robbins and King are cousins and their business relationship goes back to their days as petty criminals. Whatever caper got the Hood his powers, King was there, and has been his confidant ever since his successful play for power.

ANALYSIS: AGENT TRODGLEN

Now that Director Osborn has pretty much seized control of the Hood's Army, there is less need to keep up with the comings and goings of someone like King. If Robbins goes off the reservation again, it's doubtful King would last very long in that group and Director Osborn would probably look to someone else as a liaison. Although looking at The List of names, he may prefer to assign someone from outside.

EXECUTIVE ASSESSMENT: Has chump written all over him.

USER: ••••••••••

PASSWORD: ••••••••••

NAME: U-FOES

BACKGROUND:
Director Osborn requested we specifically include the U-Foes in this dossier. The U-Foes – Iron Clad, Vapor, Vector, and X-Ray – have been loyal members of both the Hood's army and the Initiative (they currently serve as North Carolina's team in the Fifty State Initiative). They were recently used to go after the Heavy Hitters, after the Nevada team seceded from the Initiative, successfully capturing Prodigy.

ART BY AGENT OLIVIER COIPEL

ANALYSIS: AGENT TRODGLEN
Having apparently lost all ambition of their own, but still retaining quite a lot of firepower, the U-Foes have proven to be valuable assets and should continue to be so. They aren't able to lead normal lives and seem to genuinely appreciate being more or less taken care of in exchange for doing whatever is asked of them. If Director Osborn requested info on these guys because he's looking for someone for a specific mission, I can't think of a better group. They are much less trouble than the Wrecking Crew.

EXECUTIVE ASSESSMENT: Creepy, but effective group.

NAME: ZODIAC

BACKGROUND:
Zodiac is an anarchist. He is the thorn in the side of whoever is in power, so he is currently an enemy to Director Osborn. He is the antithesis of the Hood, as he favors dissension, disorganization and chaos. He apparently liked the name Zodiac so he killed the twelve leaders of the crime cartel known as Zodiac to clear up use of the name. He was also able to hack into H.A.M.M.E.R.'s planetary defense network, triggering false positives of the arrival of Galactus. He did this as a distraction while he unleashed the giant Japanese robot Red Ronin on New York City. He is currently at large.

ART BY AGENT NATHAN FOX

ANALYSIS: Zodiac is as psycho as anyone in our files. A perfect example of the kind of individual not even Norman Osborn or Parker Robbins has any hope of reasoning with, Zodiac is notable only as someone we should be wary of. He could unleash terror at any time and threatens to derail anything we attempt at any moment. He would do so not for any greater good, but for the love of sticking it to anyone in power. He tortured and killed 100 H.A.M.M.E.R. agents and would gladly do so again.

EXECUTIVE ASSESSMENT: Should have been on The List, Norman.

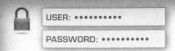

NAME:
ARES

BACKGROUND:

Ares claims to be the bona fide Greek god of war, who has turned his back on Olympus and chosen to raise his son, **Alexander**, on Earth in an effort to be a better father than he feels Zeus ever was to him. Ares has long been a thorn in the side of his half-brother, Hercules, and has been drawn into repeated conflict with the demigod's allies Thor and the Avengers. However, following the superhuman Civil War, Tony Stark hand-picked Ares for his Mighty Avengers, presumably seeking to combine the raw power of Thor and Hercules with the ruthlessness Wolverine brought to the team. Ares gladly remained with the Avengers after Director Osborn took charge. Of interest are numerous reports, including chaotic footage from the recent battle with the Skrulls, of a young boy matching Alexander's description currently serving with Nick Fury's band of Secret Warriors using the code name Phobos.

ART BY AGENT MIKE DEODATO

ANALYSIS: AGENT GILLEN

As an immortal Greek god, Ares brings great strength and resilience to the team, and a mastery of a wide array of weaponry from all eras. However, sheer power is not his most vital asset: it's how Ares thinks that sets him apart. He's a brilliant tactician and military strategist, the consummate soldier. It just happens that his idea of what that entails is at least a thousand years out of step with the rest of the world.

His experience is a great advantage: He led his exhaustively trained special forces team, the Shades, in a successful mission against overwhelming odds, instilling in them a camaraderie and desire for self-sacrifice. It can also, at times, be a disadvantage: The Shades all ended up dead. For the forthcoming siege of Asgard, Ares has promised a "Cannaean" victory, referring to the greatest of Hannibal's victories over the forces of Rome. Historians put Roman fatalities at about 50,000 in a single day – half of their men. Ares plans a similarly devastating, decapitating ambush that will ensure victory. But it must be remembered that one in eight of Hannibal's forces also lost their lives at Cannae, and Hannibal did not win the war. Ares may deliver the most striking victory imaginable, but there will be a price in blood. And Ares will savor every moment.

Fortunately, he has utmost respect for the chain of command. He shows fierce loyalty to Director Osborn, and disdain towards more reluctant teammates. His very nature means he is willing to lay down his life for his cause. But a word of caution: Ares has great nobility at his core. Woe betide anyone who manipulates him into fighting an unjust cause, especially one that pits him against a foe he respects. The rumors about Alexander and Fury raise a further concern: has he turned a blind eye to his son fraternizing with the enemy? Ares was notably absent during Fury's recent infiltration of Avengers Tower. What happens if Ares and Alexander find themselves on opposite sides? In Greek legend, when father is pitted against son, it almost always ends in tragedy.

EXECUTIVE ASSESSMENT: Ultimate Ballbuster.
We position him strategically, he takes it from there.

USER: ••••••••••
PASSWORD: ••••••••••

ART BY AGENT MIKE DEODATO

NAME:

SENTRY

BACKGROUND:

Everyone knows the **Sentry** has the power of a million exploding suns. What eludes our scientists, despite months of study, is exactly what that means. His power defies measure. Tests indicate that the man known as **Robert Reynolds** differs from regular humans on the molecular level, giving him limitless strength and speed, the power of flight and remarkably acute senses. He has survived more than one apparent "death," leading to a considerable body of opinion that he is effectively immortal. Files impounded during the S.H.I.E.L.D. handover suggest he may also have revived **his wife**, **Lindy**, after she was reportedly killed by Ultron. What little we know of his early history is derived from the medical records of psychiatrist Dr. Cornelius Lunt (accessed under H.A.M.M.E.R.'s Alpha Priority clearances).

Reynolds says he received his abilities from a formula far more potent than Captain America's super soldier serum. He claims to have removed the world's memories of him for years, after realizing that he and his archnemesis, the deadly **Void**, were one and the same. As will be seen, his belief that he harbors a murderous dark side has caused him troubling mental problems. Fuller documentation begins when Reynolds found himself in the middle of the jailbreak at the Raft, where he was being held as a prisoner. His heroic actions earned him a place on Captain America's New Avengers. However, he went on to side with Iron Man during the Civil War and served on Stark's Mighty Avengers, before remaining with the team after Director Osborn took control.

ANALYSIS: AGENT HARROLD

Reynolds' only ostensible weakness is his own mind. He has a proven vulnerability to mental attack, and his hyper-senses were once exploited by Iron Man: Stark overwhelmed him with details of simultaneous global disasters. On the battlefield, H.A.M.M.E.R. should be vigilant to keep Reynolds away from psychic or technological threats of this kind, and preventive measures should be thoroughly researched. Director Osborn has taken special interest in Reynolds, perhaps seeing in him a kindred spirit. Having overcome his own personal demons, Director Osborn has tried to convince Reynolds that there is no Void; that it is all in Reynolds' head. Though Reynolds has no need for food or sleep, Director Osborn has encouraged him to indulge in such everyday pleasures as a means of retaining his humanity. In return, the Sentry has shown unswerving loyalty, following orders without question. In strategic terms, he provides a vital role as the team's first – and often decisive – strike; he is "shock and awe" incarnate. As such, he has shown a surprisingly ruthless streak – annihilating an Atlantean terror cell, and ripping off sorceress Morgana Le Fay's head – though he has demonstrated almost childlike concern over whether such actions are good or bad. Clear concerns remain about Sentry's continuing fragile mental state after he abandoned the team during a confrontation with the X-Men. Our sources on the mutants' island nation Utopia report this had something to do with Emma Frost and the Void; the sliver of darkness now reported to be visible inside the diamond-form telepath's head suggest that perhaps there is more to this Void than Director Osborn believed. The Sentry's unpredictability and godlike power continue to cause considerable unease among his teammates and – according to S.H.I.E.L.D. files – even for his wife.

EXECUTIVE ASSESSMENT: Nutcase. Game-changing nutcase, but still... Proceed with caution.

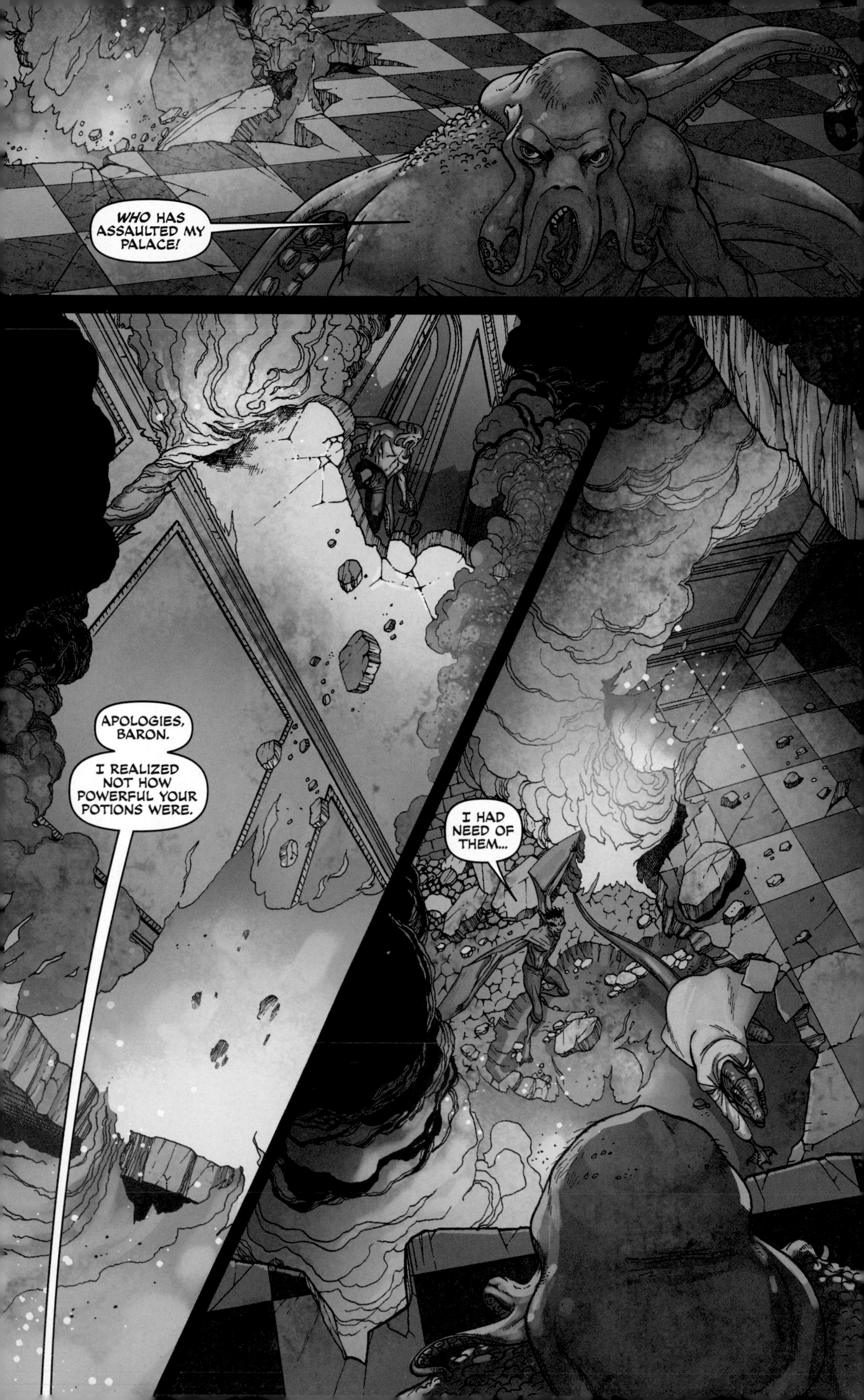
WHO HAS ASSAULTED MY PALACE!
APOLOGIES, BARON.
I REALIZED NOT HOW POWERFUL YOUR POTIONS WERE.
I HAD NEED OF THEM...

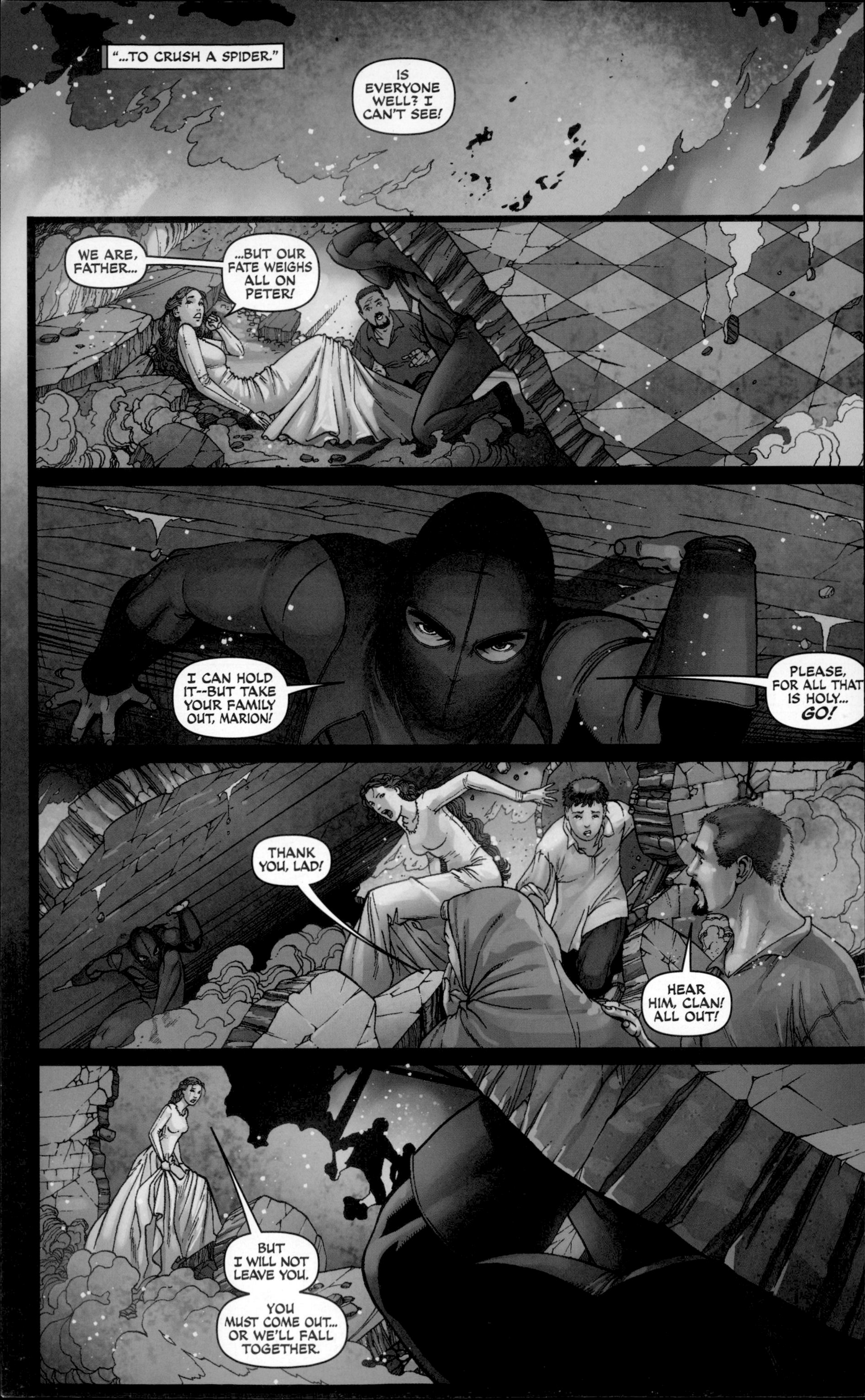

"...TO CRUSH A SPIDER."
IS EVERYONE WELL? I CAN'T SEE!
WE ARE, FATHER...
...BUT OUR FATE WEIGHS ALL ON PETER!
I CAN HOLD IT--BUT TAKE YOUR FAMILY OUT, MARION!
PLEASE, FOR ALL THAT IS HOLY... GO!
THANK YOU, LAD!
HEAR HIM, CLAN! ALL OUT!
BUT I WILL NOT LEAVE YOU.
YOU MUST COME OUT... OR WE'LL FALL TOGETHER.

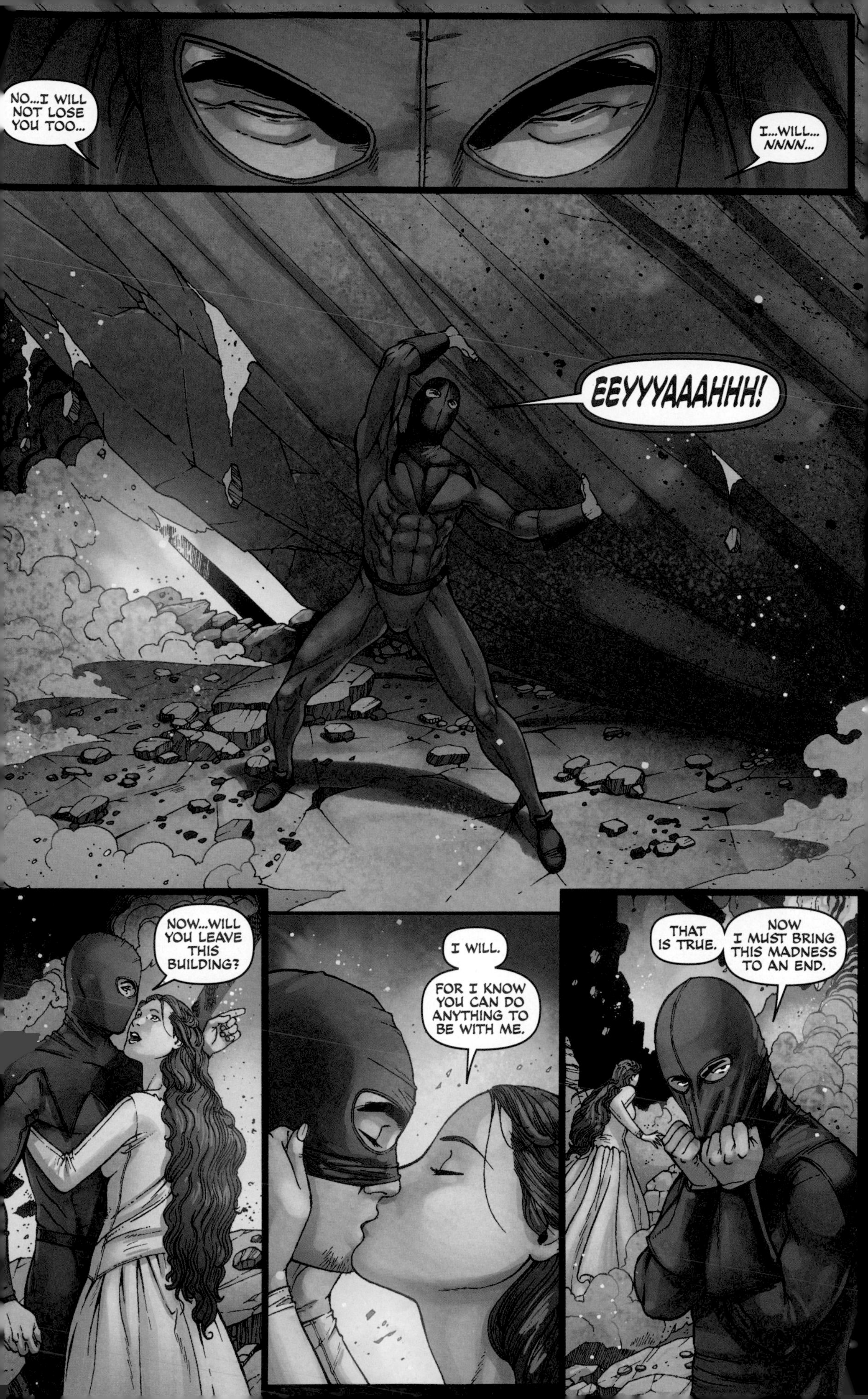
NO...I WILL NOT LOSE YOU TOO...
I...WILL... NNNN...
EEYYYAAAHHH!
NOW...WILL YOU LEAVE THIS BUILDING?
I WILL.
FOR I KNOW YOU CAN DO ANYTHING TO BE WITH ME.
THAT IS TRUE.
NOW I MUST BRING THIS MADNESS TO AN END.

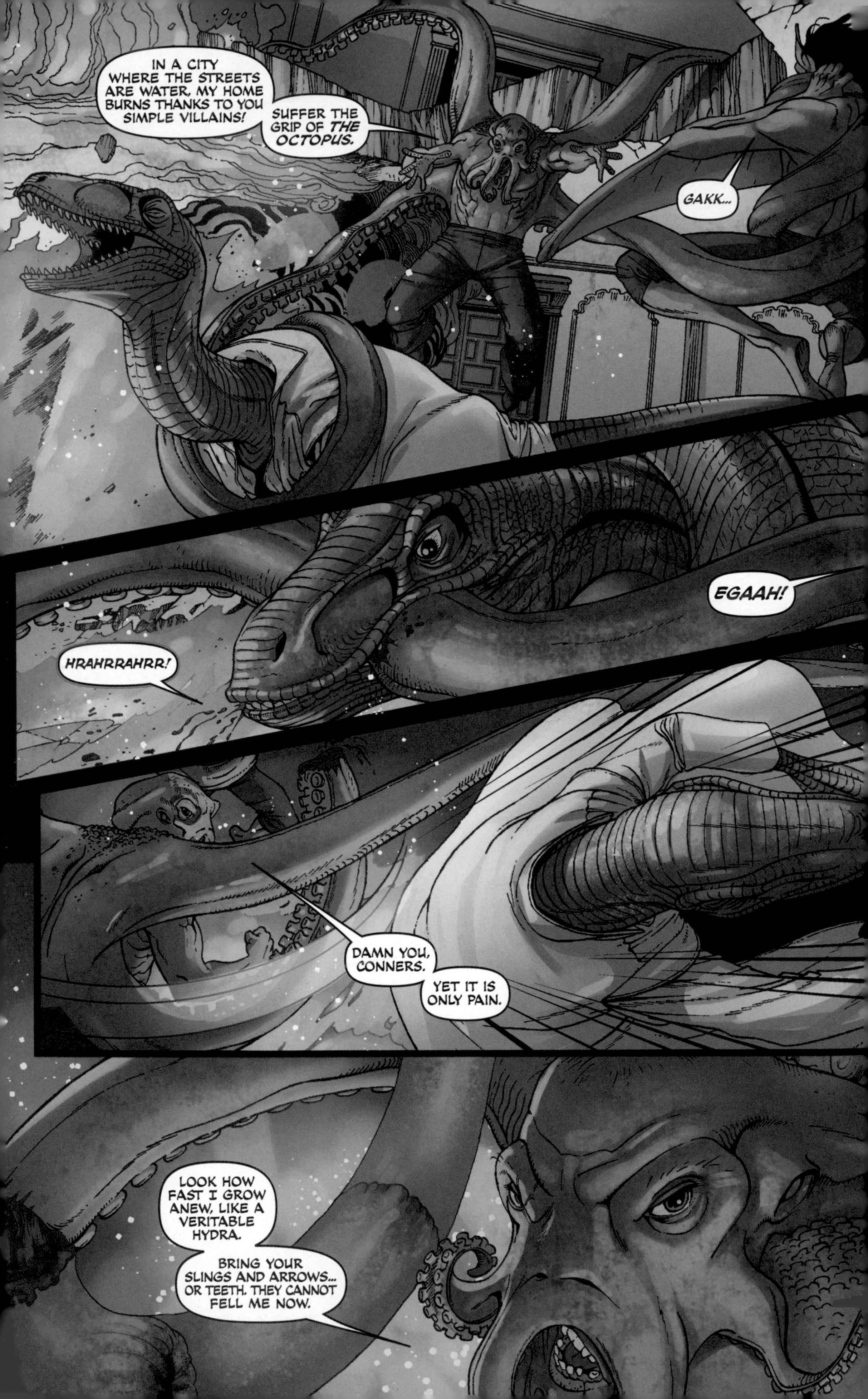
IN A CITY WHERE THE STREETS ARE WATER, MY HOME BURNS THANKS TO YOU SIMPLE VILLAINS!
SUFFER THE GRIP OF *THE OCTOPUS.*
GAKK...
EGAAH!
HRAHRRAHRR!
DAMN YOU, CONNERS.
YET IT IS ONLY PAIN.
LOOK HOW FAST I GROW ANEW, LIKE A VERITABLE HYDRA.
BRING YOUR SLINGS AND ARROWS... OR TEETH. THEY CANNOT FELL ME NOW.

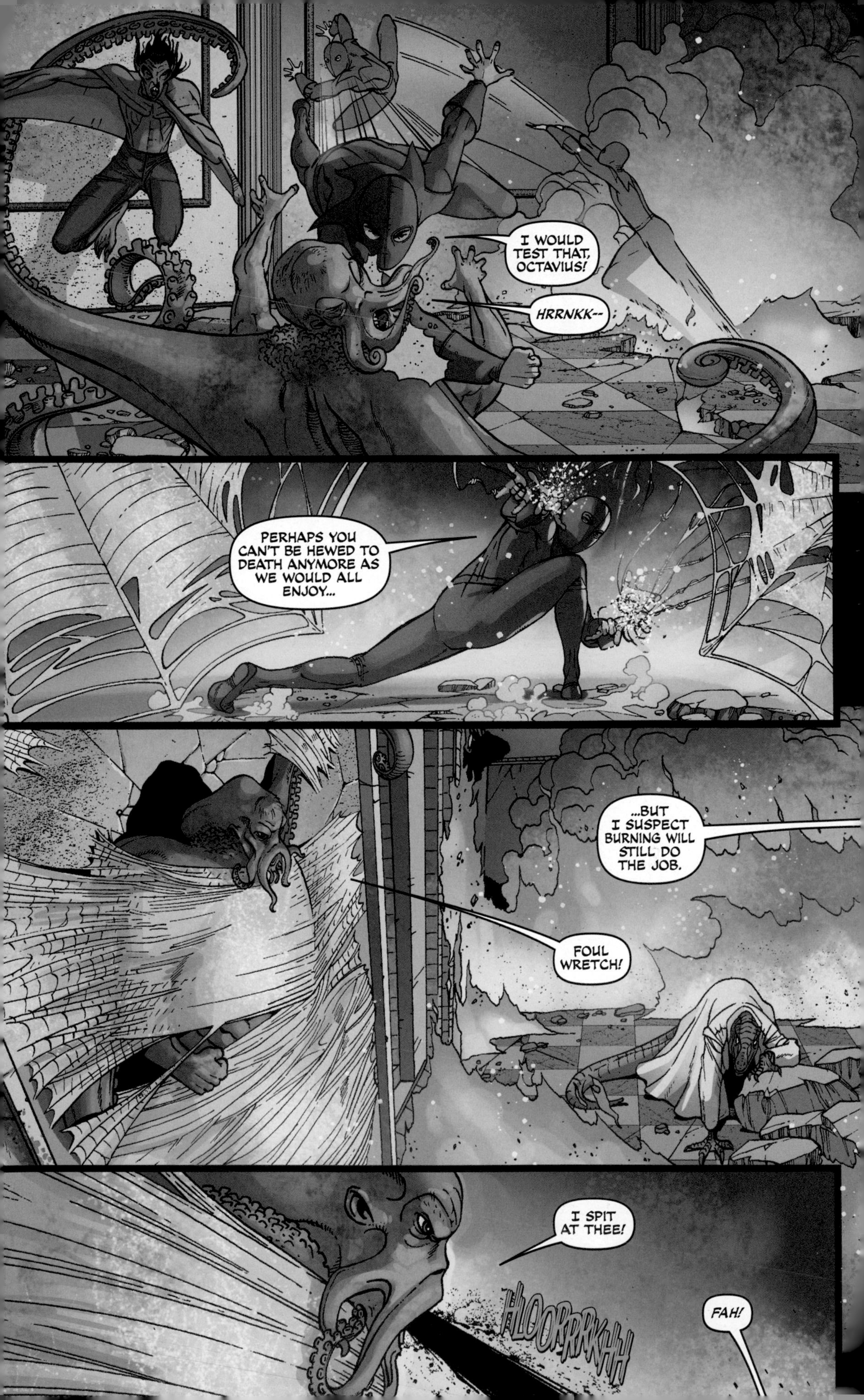
I WOULD TEST THAT, OCTAVIUS!
HRRNKK--
PERHAPS YOU CAN'T BE HEWED TO DEATH ANYMORE AS WE WOULD ALL ENJOY...
...BUT I SUSPECT BURNING WILL STILL DO THE JOB.
FOUL WRETCH!
I SPIT AT THEE!
HLOORRRKHH
FAH!

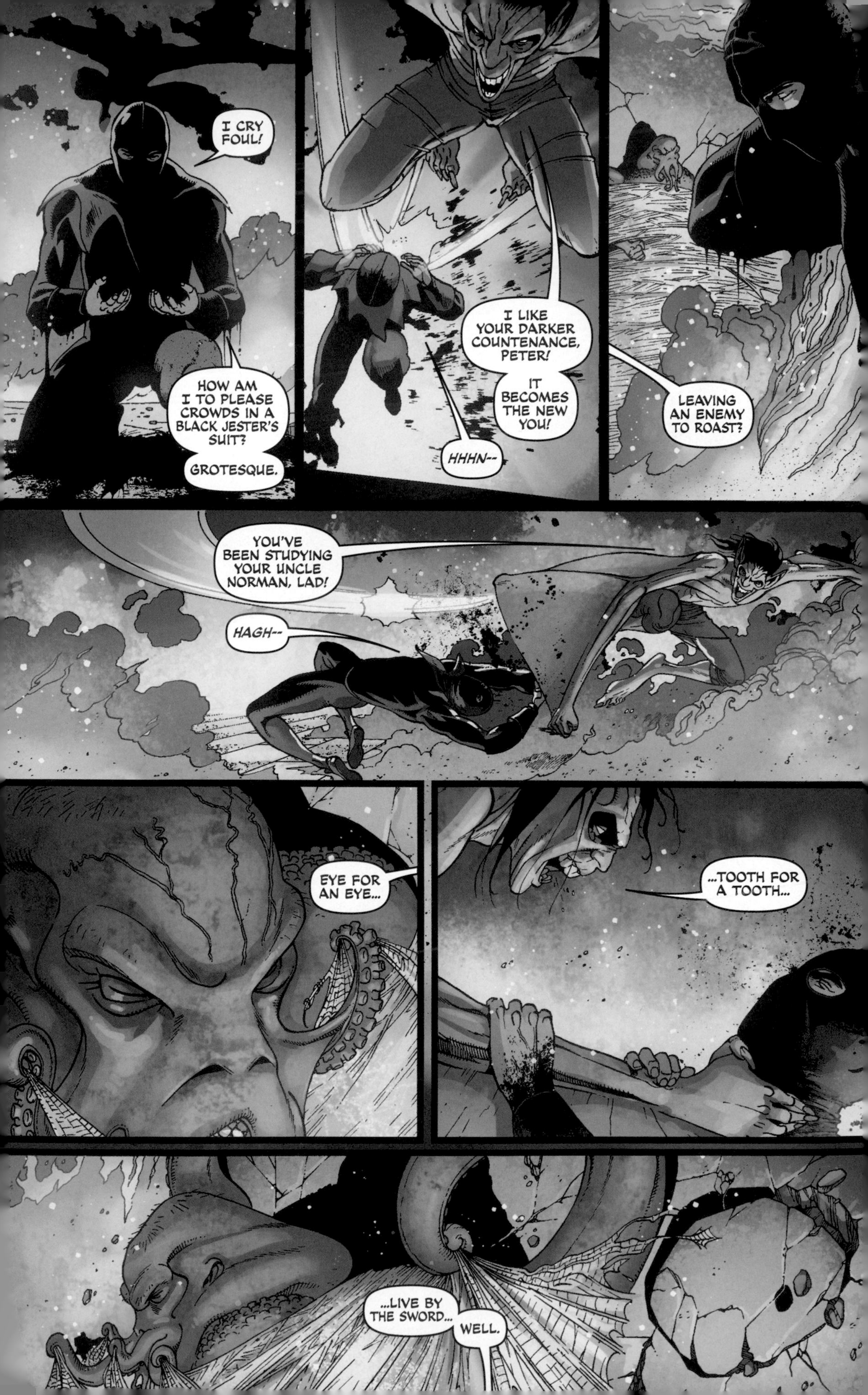
I CRY FOUL!
HOW AM I TO PLEASE CROWDS IN A BLACK JESTER'S SUIT?
GROTESQUE.
I LIKE YOUR DARKER COUNTENANCE, PETER!
IT BECOMES THE NEW YOU!
HHHN--
LEAVING AN ENEMY TO ROAST?
YOU'VE BEEN STUDYING YOUR UNCLE NORMAN, LAD!
HAGH--
EYE FOR AN EYE...
...TOOTH FOR A TOOTH...
...LIVE BY THE SWORD...
WELL.

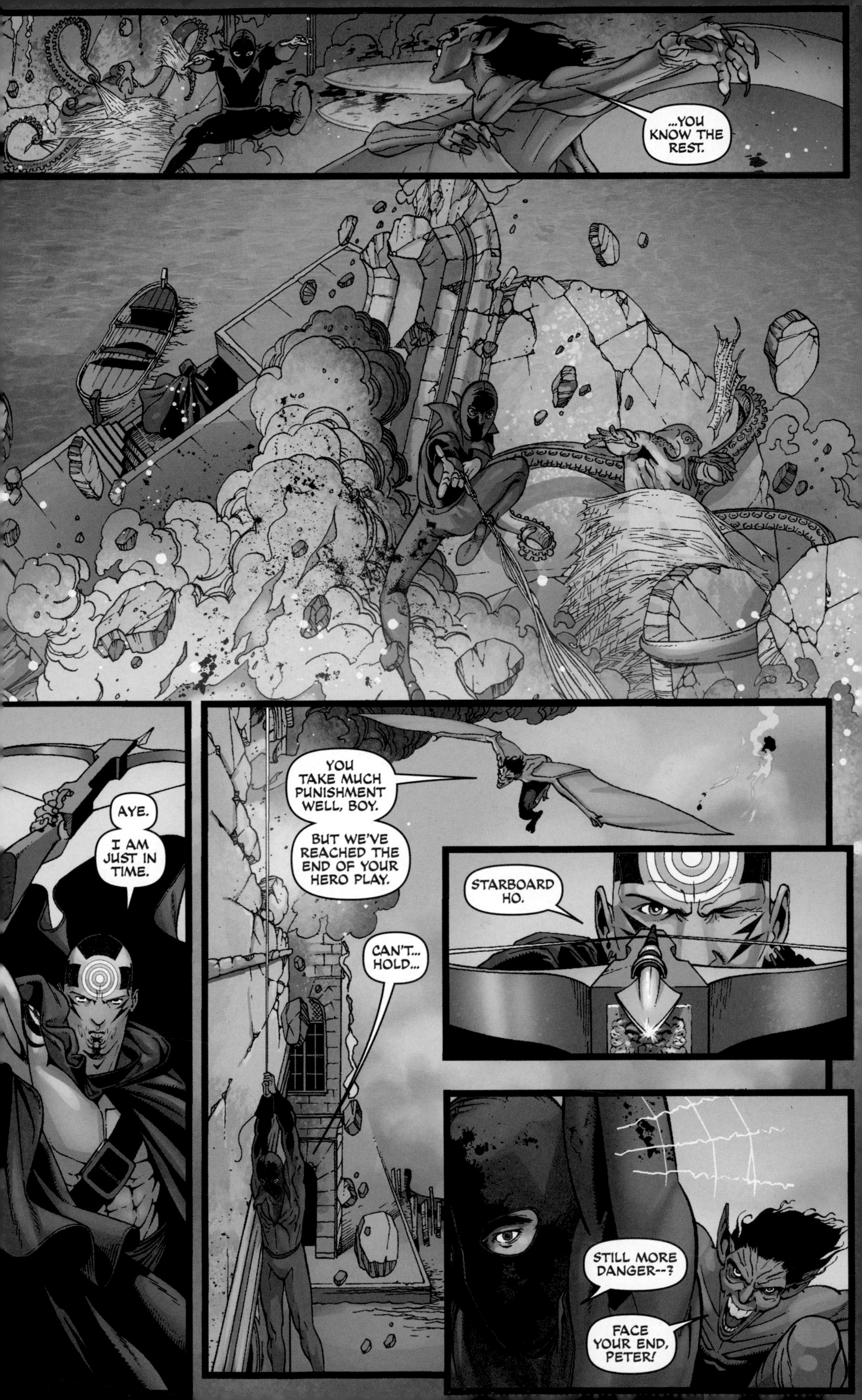

...YOU KNOW THE REST.
AYE.
I AM JUST IN TIME.
YOU TAKE MUCH PUNISHMENT WELL, BOY.
BUT WE'VE REACHED THE END OF YOUR HERO PLAY.
CAN'T... HOLD...
STARBOARD HO.
STILL MORE DANGER--?
FACE YOUR END, PETER!

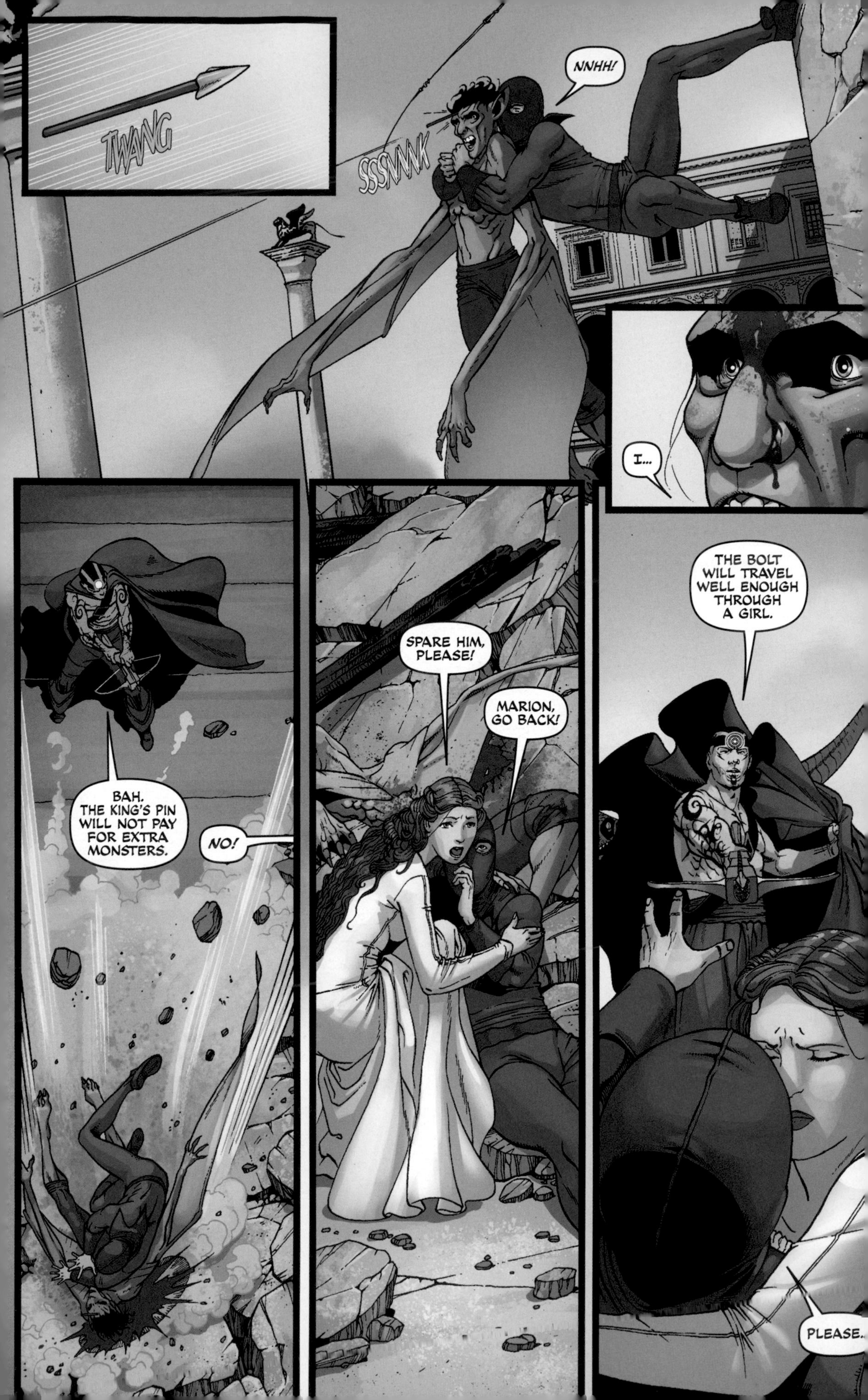
TWANG
SSSNNNK
NNHH!
I...
BAH. THE KING'S PIN WILL NOT PAY FOR EXTRA MONSTERS.
NO!
SPARE HIM, PLEASE!
MARION, GO BACK!
THE BOLT WILL TRAVEL WELL ENOUGH THROUGH A GIRL.
PLEASE.

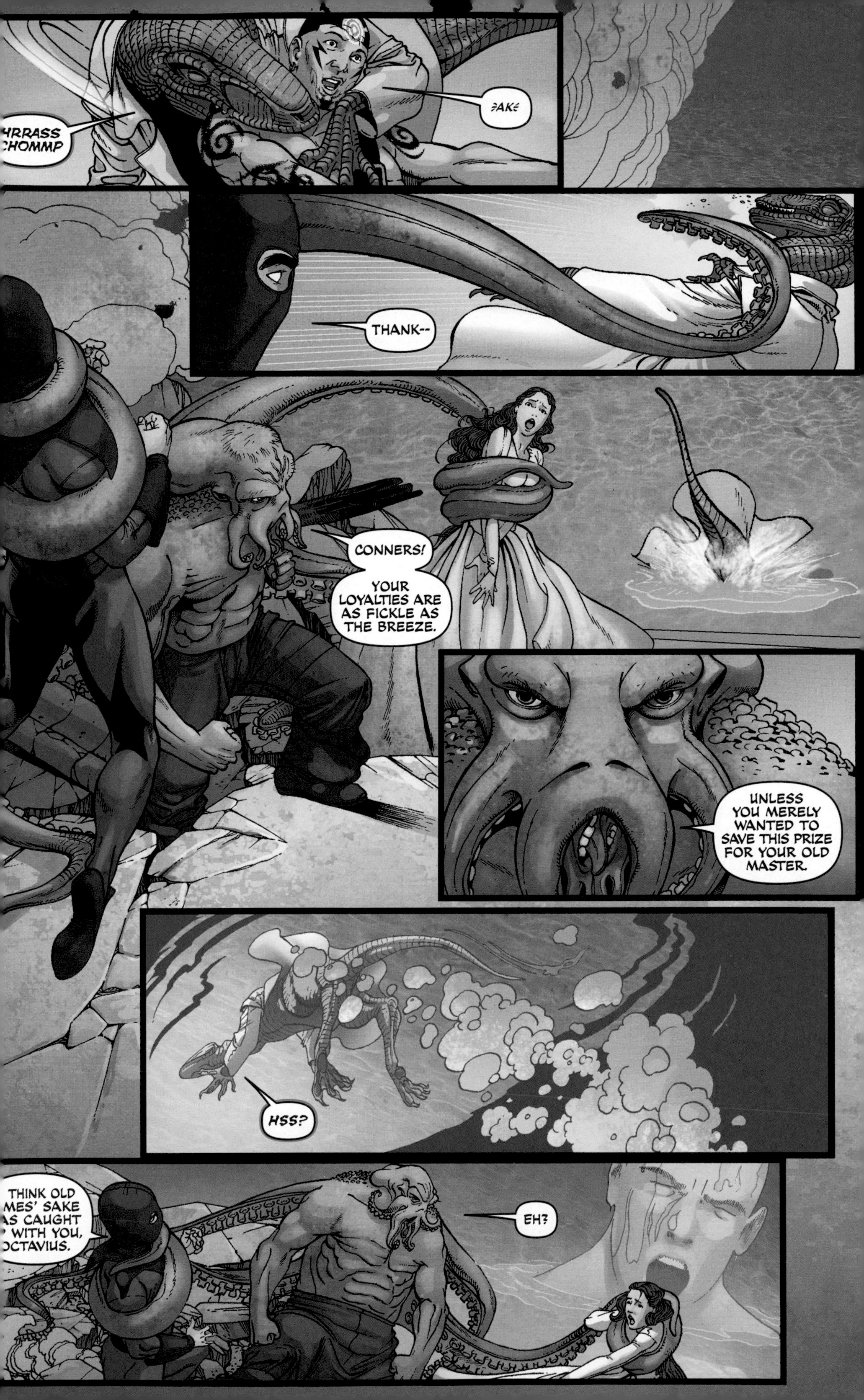
HRRASS
CHOMMP
≥AK≤
THANK--
CONNERS!
YOUR LOYALTIES ARE AS FICKLE AS THE BREEZE.
UNLESS YOU MERELY WANTED TO SAVE THIS PRIZE FOR YOUR OLD MASTER.
HSS?
THINK OLD
MES' SAKE
AS CAUGHT
WITH YOU,
OCTAVIUS.
EH?

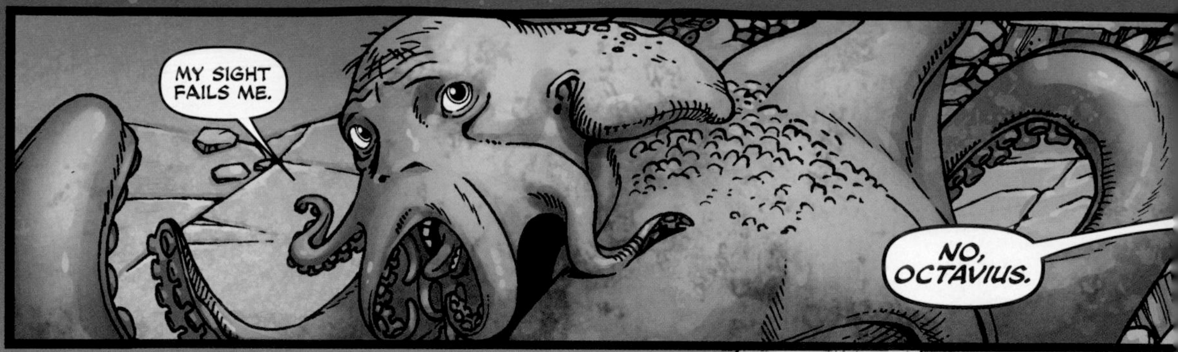
MY SIGHT FAILS ME.
NO, OCTAVIUS.

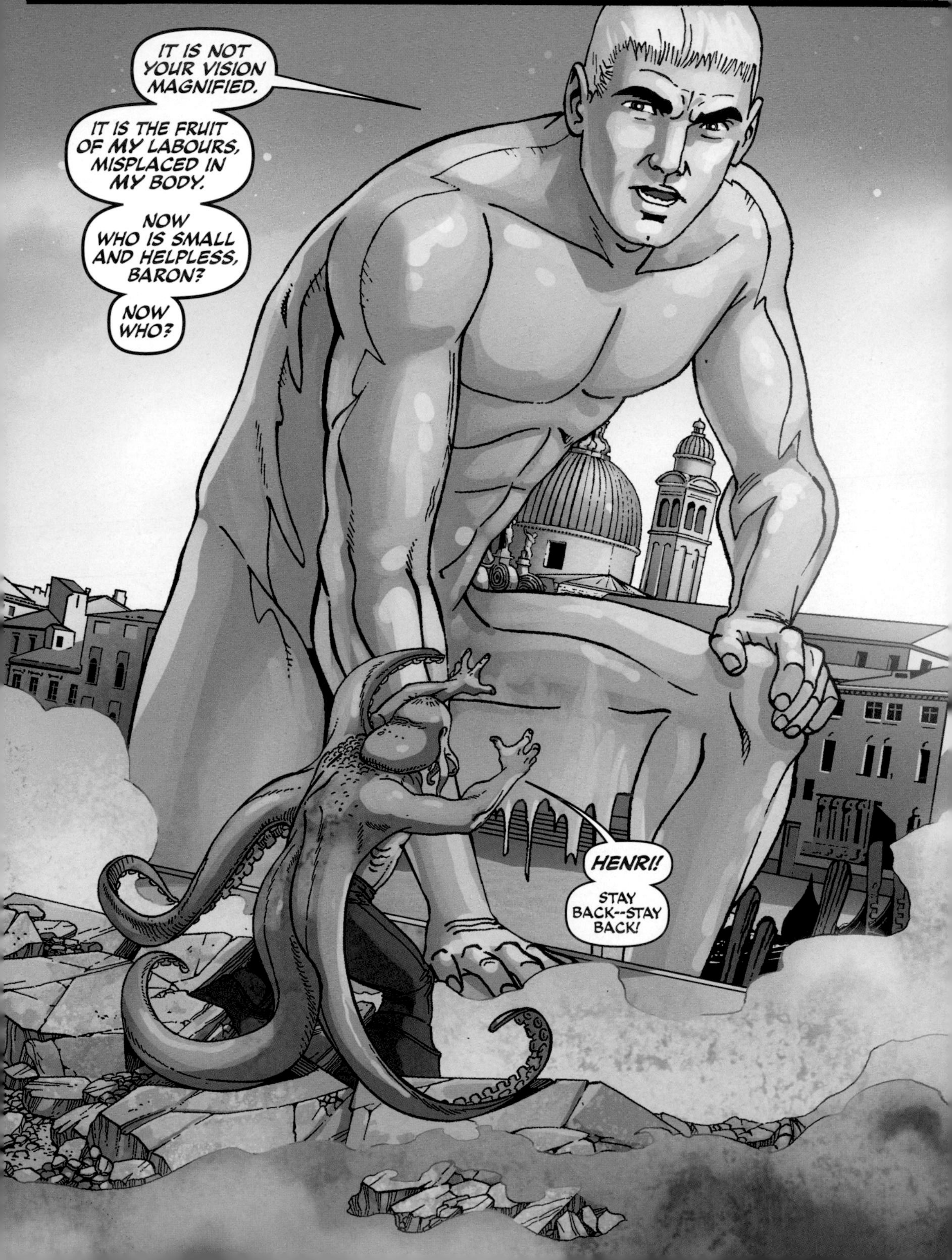
IT IS NOT YOUR VISION MAGNIFIED.
IT IS THE FRUIT OF MY LABOURS, MISPLACED IN MY BODY.
NOW WHO IS SMALL AND HELPLESS, BARON?
NOW WHO?
HENRI!
STAY BACK--STAY BACK!

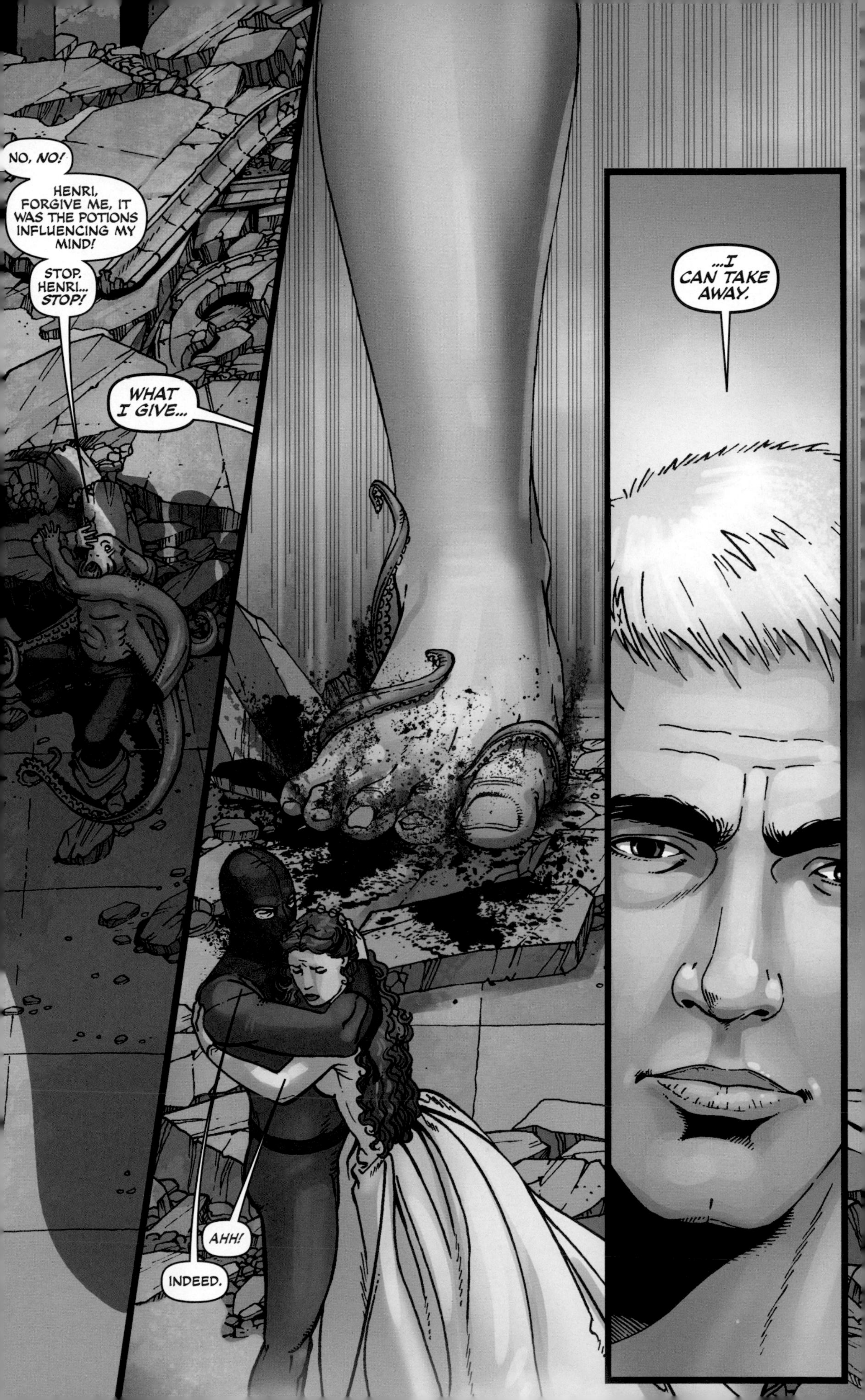
NO, NO!
HENRI, FORGIVE ME, IT WAS THE POTIONS INFLUENCING MY MIND!
STOP. HENRI... STOP!
WHAT I GIVE...
AHH!
INDEED.
...I CAN TAKE AWAY.

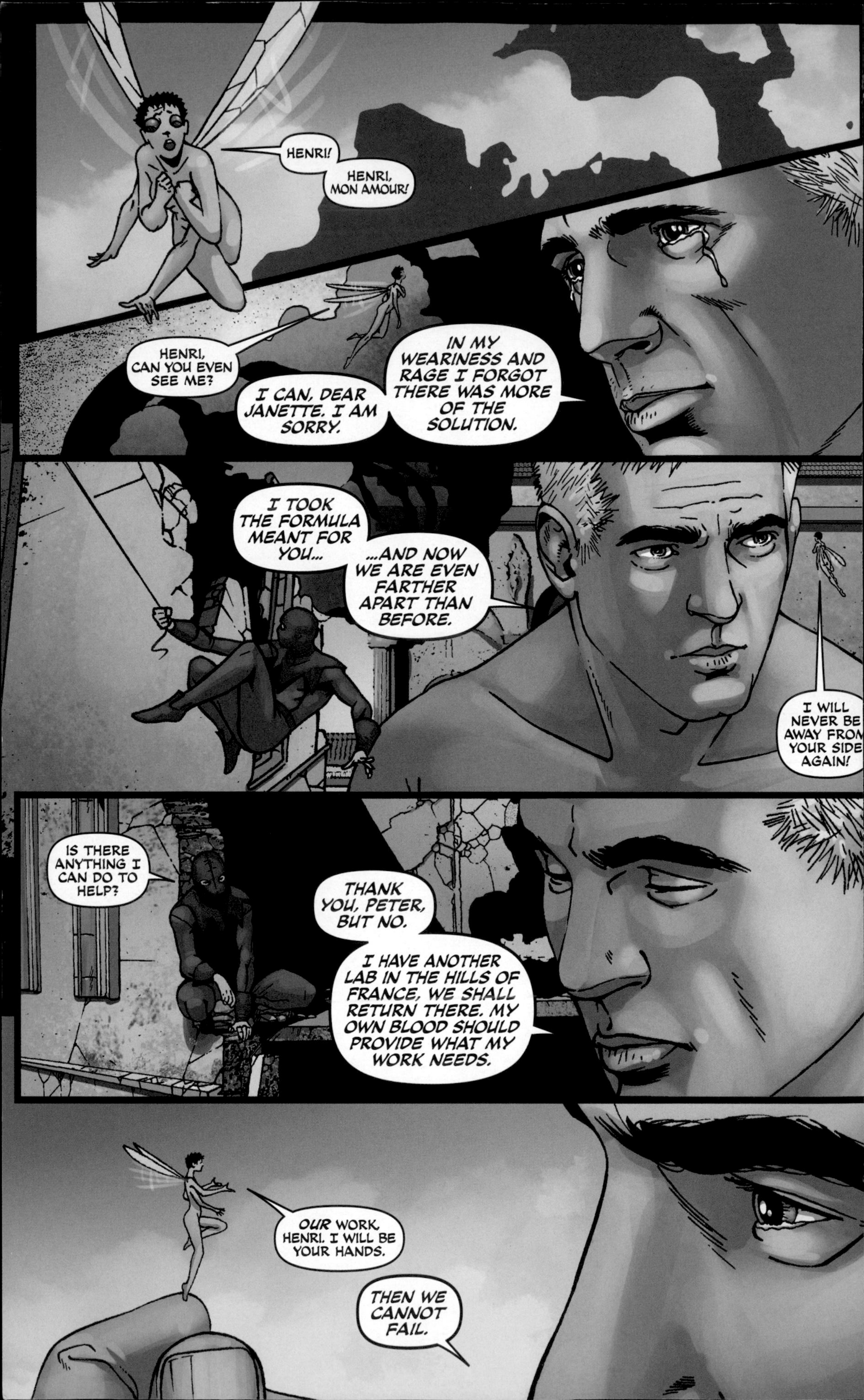
HENRI!
HENRI, MON AMOUR!
HENRI, CAN YOU EVEN SEE ME?
I CAN, DEAR JANETTE. I AM SORRY.
IN MY WEARINESS AND RAGE I FORGOT THERE WAS MORE OF THE SOLUTION.
I TOOK THE FORMULA MEANT FOR YOU...
...AND NOW WE ARE EVEN FARTHER APART THAN BEFORE.
I WILL NEVER BE AWAY FROM YOUR SIDE AGAIN!
IS THERE ANYTHING I CAN DO TO HELP?
THANK YOU, PETER, BUT NO.
I HAVE ANOTHER LAB IN THE HILLS OF FRANCE, WE SHALL RETURN THERE. MY OWN BLOOD SHOULD PROVIDE WHAT MY WORK NEEDS.
OUR WORK, HENRI. I WILL BE YOUR HANDS.
THEN WE CANNOT FAIL.

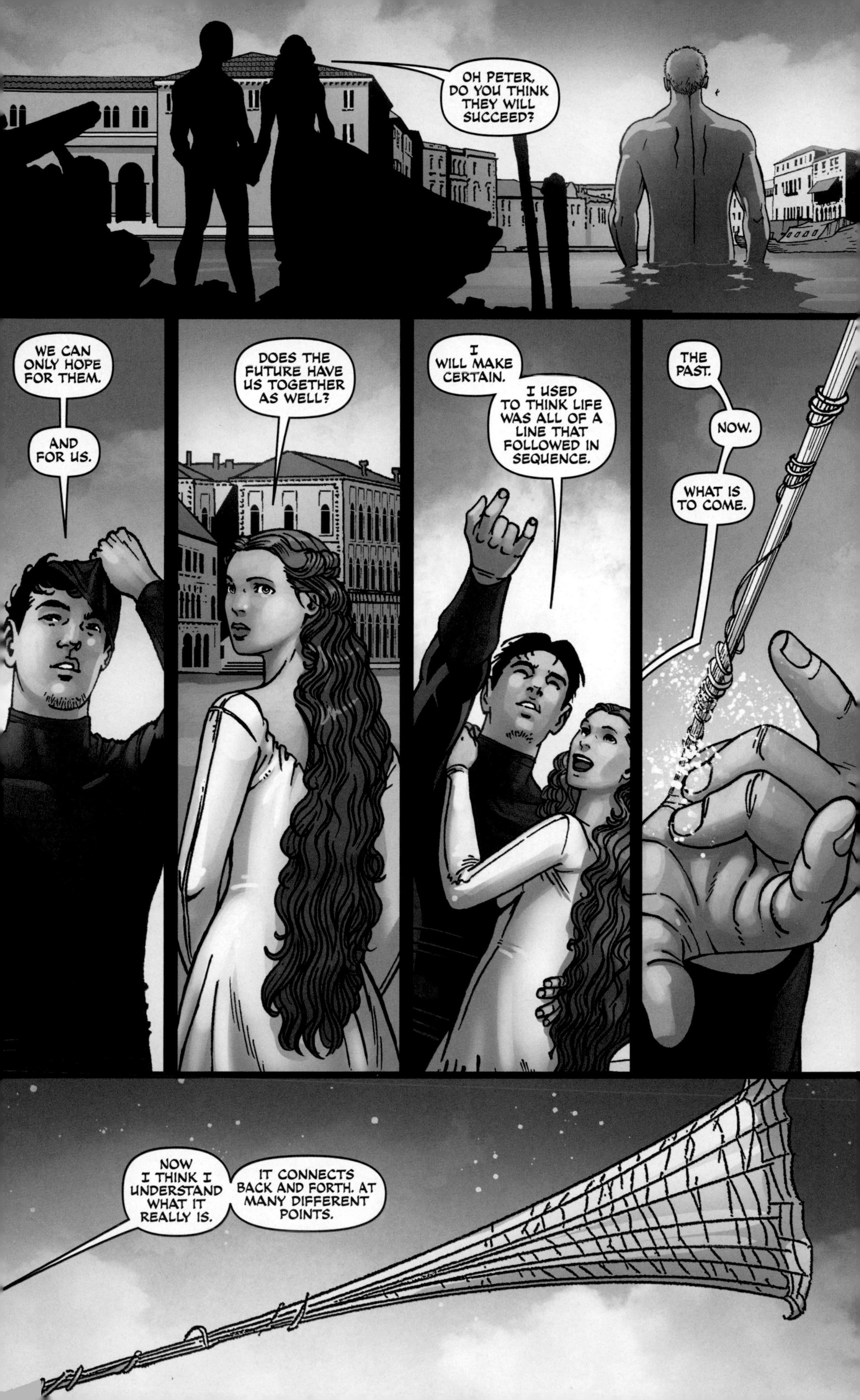
OH PETER, DO YOU THINK THEY WILL SUCCEED?
WE CAN ONLY HOPE FOR THEM.
AND FOR US.
DOES THE FUTURE HAVE US TOGETHER AS WELL?
I WILL MAKE CERTAIN.
I USED TO THINK LIFE WAS ALL OF A LINE THAT FOLLOWED IN SEQUENCE.
THE PAST.
NOW.
WHAT IS TO COME.
NOW I THINK I UNDERSTAND WHAT IT REALLY IS.
IT CONNECTS BACK AND FORTH. AT MANY DIFFERENT POINTS.

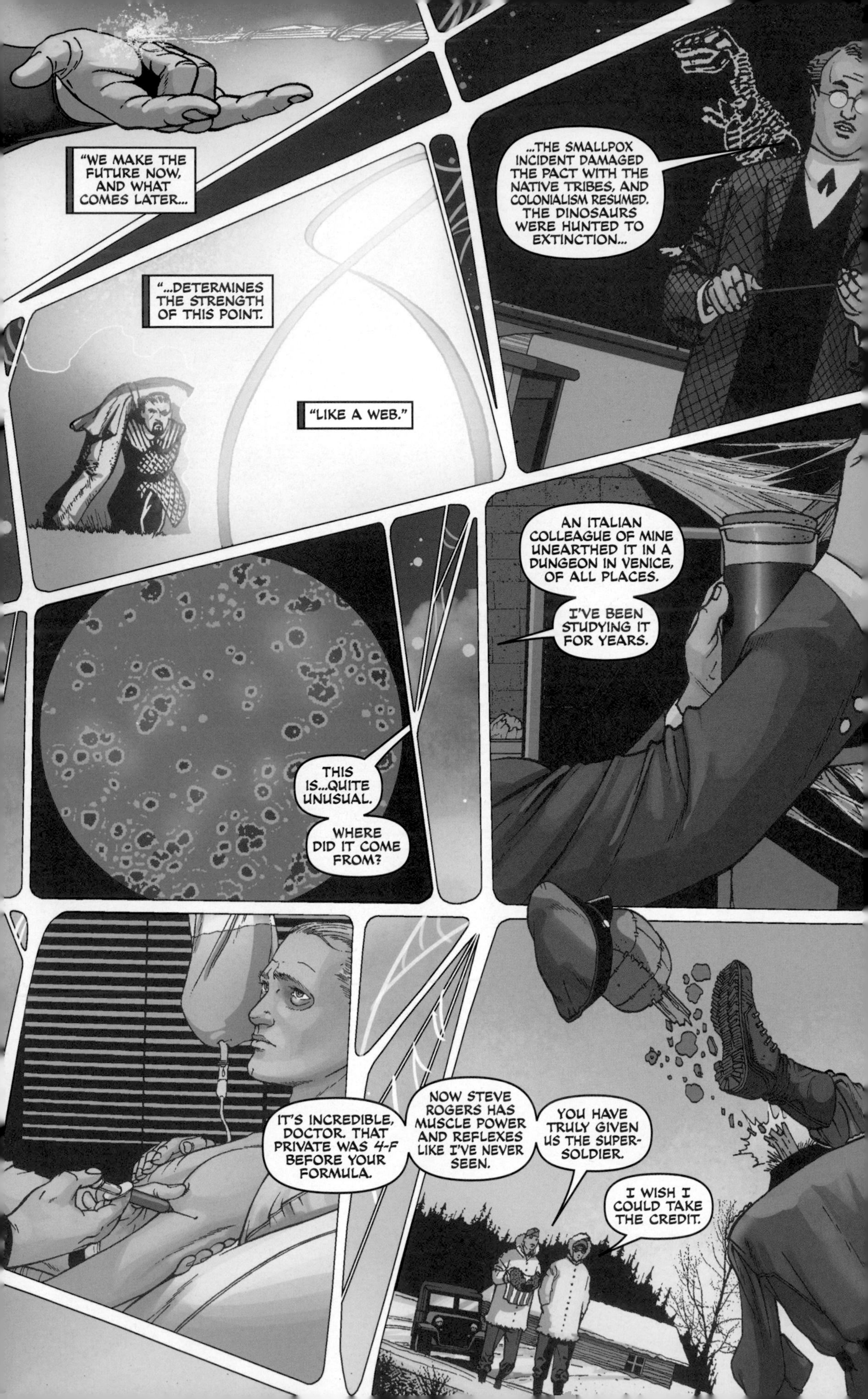
"WE MAKE THE FUTURE NOW, AND WHAT COMES LATER...
...THE SMALLPOX INCIDENT DAMAGED THE PACT WITH THE NATIVE TRIBES, AND COLONIALISM RESUMED. THE DINOSAURS WERE HUNTED TO EXTINCTION...
"...DETERMINES THE STRENGTH OF THIS POINT.
"LIKE A WEB."
AN ITALIAN COLLEAGUE OF MINE UNEARTHED IT IN A DUNGEON IN VENICE, OF ALL PLACES.
I'VE BEEN STUDYING IT FOR YEARS.
THIS IS...QUITE UNUSUAL.
WHERE DID IT COME FROM?
IT'S INCREDIBLE, DOCTOR. THAT PRIVATE WAS 4-F BEFORE YOUR FORMULA.
NOW STEVE ROGERS HAS MUSCLE POWER AND REFLEXES LIKE I'VE NEVER SEEN.
YOU HAVE TRULY GIVEN US THE SUPER-SOLDIER.
I WISH I COULD TAKE THE CREDIT.

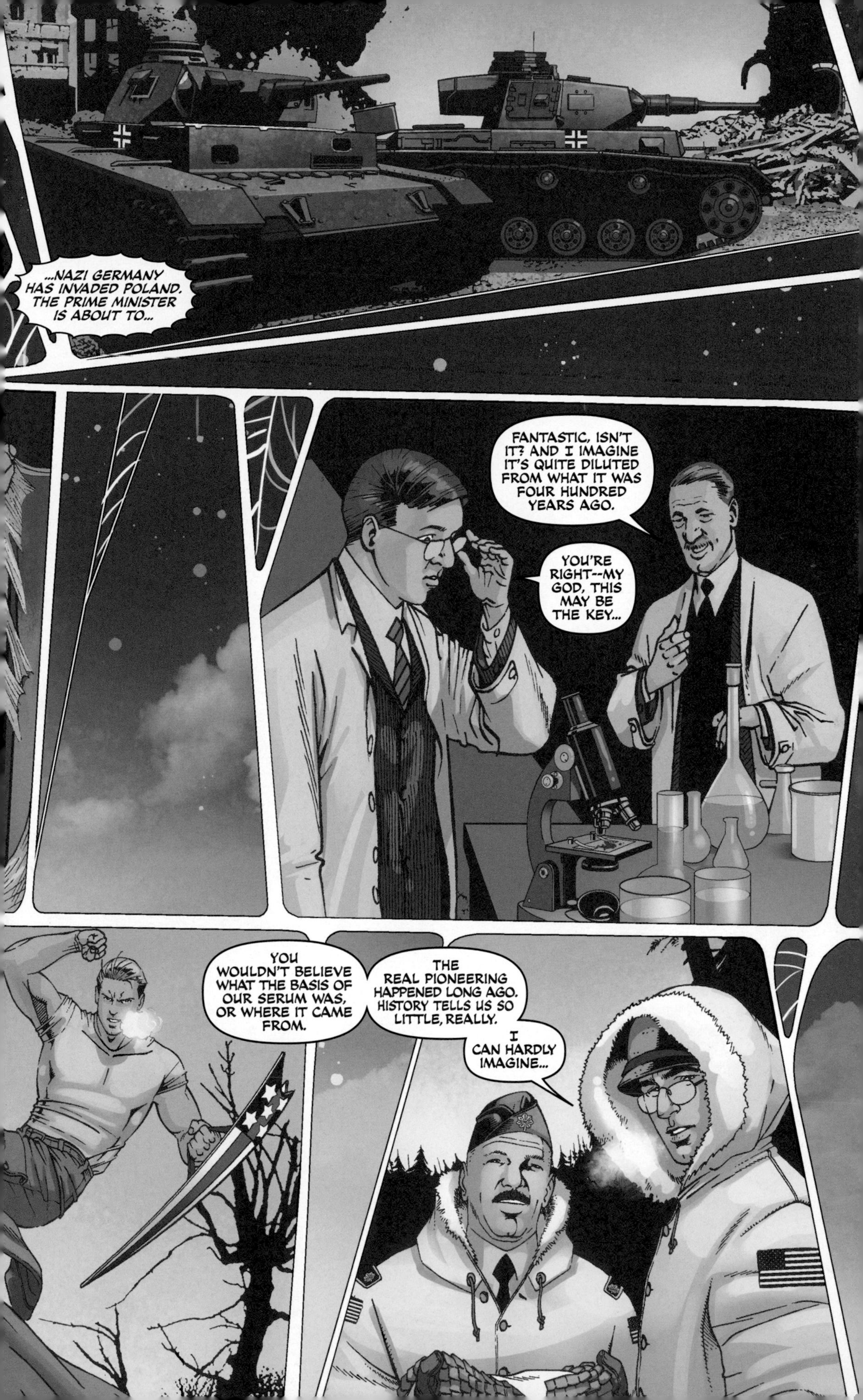
...NAZI GERMANY HAS INVADED POLAND. THE PRIME MINISTER IS ABOUT TO...
FANTASTIC, ISN'T IT? AND I IMAGINE IT'S QUITE DILUTED FROM WHAT IT WAS FOUR HUNDRED YEARS AGO.
YOU'RE RIGHT--MY GOD, THIS MAY BE THE KEY...
YOU WOULDN'T BELIEVE WHAT THE BASIS OF OUR SERUM WAS, OR WHERE IT CAME FROM.
THE REAL PIONEERING HAPPENED LONG AGO. HISTORY TELLS US SO LITTLE, REALLY.
I CAN HARDLY IMAGINE...

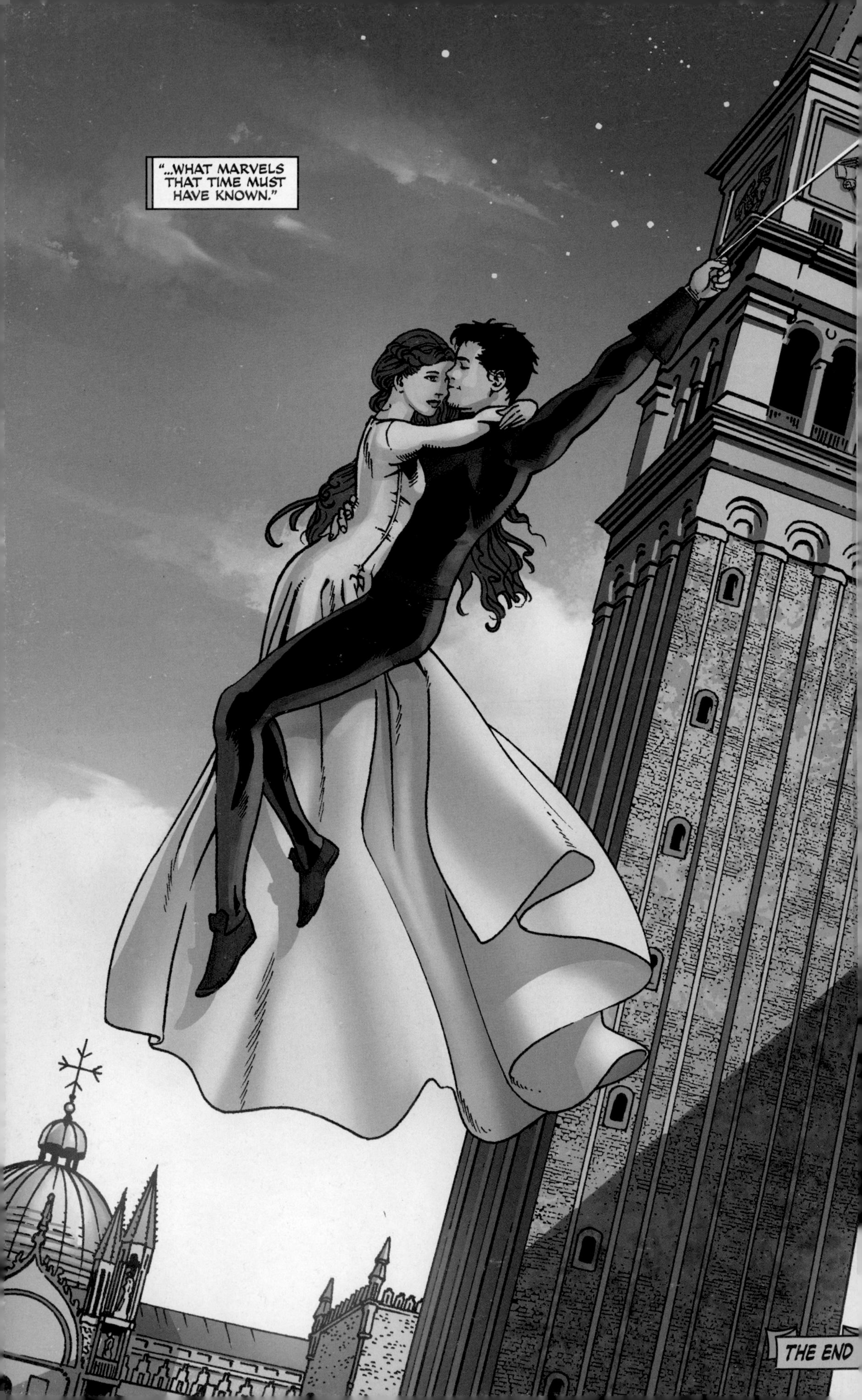
"...WHAT MARVELS THAT TIME MUST HAVE KNOWN."
THE END